Tragedy Walks the Streets

Tragedy Walks the Streets

The French Revolution in the Making of Modern Drama

MATTHEW S. BUCKLEY

The Johns Hopkins University Press

Baltimore

© 2006 The Johns Hopkins University Press
All rights reserved. Published 2006
Printed in the United States of America on acid-free paper

2   4   6   8   9   7   5   3   1

The Johns Hopkins University Press
2715 North Charles Street
Baltimore, Maryland 21218-4363
www.press.jhu.edu

Library of Congress Cataloging-in-Publication Data
Buckley, Matthew S., 1965–
Tragedy walks the streets : the French Revolution in the making
of modern drama / Matthew S. Buckley.
p.   cm.
Includes bibliographical references and index.
ISBN 0-8018-8434-9 (hardcover : alk. paper)
1. European drama—18th century—History and criticism. 2. European drama—
19th century—History and criticism. 3. France—History—
Revolution, 1789–1799—Literature and the revolution. I. Title.
PN1650.F74B83   2006
809.2'033094—dc22   2005033946

A catalog record for this book is available from the British Library.

CONTENTS

Acknowledgments

My intellectual debts are many. At Columbia, James Shapiro and David Kastan introduced me to literary history at the graduate level and fostered in me a clear sense of the value, the methods, and the stakes of critical inquiry. As professional mentors, as well, they have been invaluable and exemplary. Austin Quigley acted for many years as the patient critic, discerning reader, and encouraging guide of all my graduate projects and taught me in the process to think about language and thought not merely as formal structures but as cultural practices and immediate gestures. I could not have asked for a doctoral mentor and advisor better suited to my particular scholarly temperament. Julie Peters introduced me to the issues and materials that stand at the core of this project, and in her exceptional seminars on theatre and politics this book found both its inspiration and its initial form. Her generous advice and continued encouragement have proven invaluable at every stage and I am happy now to be indebted to her as a colleague and as a friend.

My gratitude is owed too to many other faculty members of Columbia University and Barnard College: to Franco Moretti, whose lively engagement honed much of my early thinking on the relation of the French Revolution to modern drama; to Martin Meisel, whose well-timed advice and discussion helped to give shape to the book's crucial arguments about Büchner and whose exceptional work enabled much of this study's attention to visual representation; to Michael Seidel, Jim Basker, Laura Engel, Siraj Ahmed, and David Liss, whose wonderful response to very early versions of this project in the Columbia English Department Eighteenth-Century Dissertation Group helped to form its initial shape and structure; to Steven Johnson, James Cain, and Emily Jenkins, fellow students whose reactions to this work informed many of its foundational ideas and arguments; and, finally, to Ehren Fordyce, whose thoughts and ideas, advice and encouragement have, for more than a decade now, informed my thinking about drama, theater, and modernity.

Equal thanks are due to the many friends and colleagues in the Department of English at Rutgers University who have contributed to the book's development and completion. To Elin Diamond, Michael McKeon, and Carolyn Williams, in particular, any thanks I could offer here would be inadequate. Their exceptionally generous readership, review, discussion, and encouragement were of vital importance during the project's most difficult phases, and their support as mentors, colleagues, and friends has meant more to this project—and to me—than I can express. My thanks are due also to the students of "Theater and Revolution" and "Spectacle, Spectatorship and the Urban Subject," two graduate seminars that I taught in conjunction with the final development of the book.

Portions of this work have been presented in several forums, and my gratitude is owed as well to the kind and useful responses of those various audiences. A section of the final chapter was presented at the Modern Language Association conference in December 1997; an early version of chapter four was offered at "Revolutions in Print," the Thirteenth Annual DeBartolo Conference on Eighteenth-Century Studies in 1999, and a portion of the final version of that chapter was presented at the North American Society for the Study of Romanticism conference (2005); a condensed discussion of chapter two and a brief summary of chapter three were offered at the British Society for Eighteenth-Century Studies conference (2001, 2003), and selections from those early chapters were presented at the American Society for Eighteenth-Century Studies conference in 2004. Among those audiences my particular thanks are due to John Greene, Reeve Parker, and Jeremy Popkin, each of whom offered valuable advice and encouragement. Finally, the 2001–2 seminar of Rutgers's Center for the Critical Analysis of Contemporary Culture generously and insightfully responded to an early draft of the book's introduction.

My thanks are due as well to the following individuals and institutions for assistance in the research and preparation of this work. In particular, I'd like to acknowledge the research staff of the Cabinet des Estampes of the Bibliothèque Nationale de France, and Pierre Blottière and Vinh N'Guyen of the Cabinet des Arts Graphiques of the Musée Carnavalet, whose enthusiasm, energy, and expert support were invaluable. Thanks are also due to the staff of the British Library's Newspaper Collection; to that of Columbia University Library's Rare Books Collection; to the research librarians of the New York Public Library's Map Collection, and to the staff of the New-York Historical Society Library. I would like also to thank Marina Rozenman, Sunny Stalter, Kristie Allen, and Megan Lau for having provided crucial research assistance. I owe a special debt of gratitude to the Johns Hopkins University Press for its ongoing support of this project. I'd like to thank in particular Carol Zimmerman, who has patiently guided the manuscript through production; Barbara Lamb, who gave me a joyous introduction to the art of copyediting; and especially Michael Lonegro, whose steady support and unhesitating assistance have been of inestimable value.

I am also indebted to several sources for financial and institutional support: at Columbia University, to the Whiting Foundation and the Presidential Scholars Fund; and at Rutgers University, to the Department of English, the Faculty of Arts and Sciences, and the Center for the Critical Analysis of Contemporary Culture. My particular thanks are due to Cheryl Wall, Richard Miller, and Barry Qualls, all of whom have offered timely encouragement, advice, and assistance, often at times of great personal need, and to Linda Kozusko and Clashaun Moyd, who provided administrative support.

Finally, I would like most to thank my wife, Stephanie Jones, whose love, support, indulgence, and patience made this work possible, and our daughter, Helen, whose birth graced—and impelled—its conclusion. I dedicate this work to them.

Tragedy Walks the Streets

Introduction

The aim of this book is to explore the role of the French Revolution in the history of drama. Specifically, it is an attempt to understand the Revolution's relationship to the formal development of modern drama between 1780 and 1840. Within literary history, that development has long appeared to be radically, even fundamentally discontinuous—less a coherent process of change than a clustered, disjointed, Janus-faced pattern of false starts, failed efforts to revive or recover traditional genres and apparently unprecedented innovations. On the one hand, the plays of Diderot, Mercier, and Beaumarchais, for example, appeared in the late eighteenth century at the forefront of innovation, but by the beginning of the nineteenth century they were already archaic. Romantic tragedy, similarly, began this period as a newly vital form, but by the turn of the century it was already a ghost.[1] On the other hand, melodrama seems to have burst onto the scene from out of nowhere, less the product of sustained dramatic innovation than the spontaneous conjunction of an ephemeral, "illiterate" form and a radically altered popular consciousness. "Modern" drama is understood to have begun in revolutionary fashion at the very end of this period with the apparently unprecedented, seemingly proleptic work of Georg Büchner.[2] Among all these changes one finds a proliferation of ephemeral subgenres, eccentric mixed modes, and a general destabilization of genre itself as a category and concept of dramatic form.

The French Revolution has long been understood to have played a crucial if indirect role in these developments, if only because about and around it cluster the period's various discontinuities. It is in the decade of the Revolution that the *drame* and the comedy of manners were made products of a bygone world, through it that tragedy was rendered troubling and then seemingly obsolete, and from it that melodrama took sudden shape and emerged to dominate the stage. And it was the Revolution, too, that marked Büchner's initial break with dramatic

tradition. If *Woyzeck* (1837) is the work that literary history most often nomi-
nates as modernist drama's starting point, behind it stands *Dantons Tod* (1835),
Büchner's first play, and a work that announced its radical originality not least in
its formal, explicit examination of the Revolution itself—a theme that had, since
shortly after the Revolution's end, been avoided and even banned.

In each of these histories, though in very different ways, the Revolution appears to mark a point of rupture, a moment of radical change in the conditions
and the form of the drama. However, a look at the decade itself reveals a curious picture—less a rupture than a hiatus, a long period of fairly static weakness
during which the formal evolution of the drama seems less to have undergone
a violent process of change than to have slowed or even stopped. Certainly, there
were moments and examples of striking innovation, but as much recent work
has revealed, the theater of the period, even in France, was distinctly conservative, clinging to standards, digging in its heels, and taking refuge in the past
more than pushing for change. The curiosity of this hiatus is all the more evident when placed in relation to the drama's intensively innovative formal development in the years leading up to the Revolution. The work of Diderot,
Mercier, Schiller, and Beaumarchais, for example, suggests not a slowing pace
of formal change but an accelerating one, in which the authority of traditional
genres rapidly weakened and the pressure for novel forms rose sharply.

Yet, in 1789, this intensive trajectory paused, seeming to await the outcome of
historical events before resuming. The gap is particularly marked in romantic
tragedy, where the empty decade of the Revolution is spanned almost too neatly
by Schiller's *Die Räuber* (1781) and Wordsworth's *The Borderers* (1797). Even
Goethe's work on *Faust* was suspended from 1790 to 1797, a period during which
his transformation of the Gretchen tragedy of *Urfaust* into Part One was tightly
gathered. Schiller sent off his *Letters on the Aesthetic Education of Man* in 1795,
but the fact that this most significant statement of drama took the form of an
epistolary series on aesthetic theory (and particularly on the relation of tragedy
to history) is just the point: during the Revolution, romantic tragedy appeared
to hesitate, or pause, to resume only with Wordsworth's anxious repetition *Die
Räuber,* an introspective return to the play that seemingly started the fall.[3] That
resumption, moreover, was marked by an evident reversal of perspective: while
pre-Revolutionary romantic dramatists pressed against the strictures of traditional genre, post-Revolutionary writers became concerned instead with the
opposite problem—that of maintaining the very possibility of such forms in
history.[4]

This curious pattern is evident in comic, domestic, and popular drama as well. In France, for example, one might expect the process of reform and innovation begun by Diderot, Mercier, and Beaumarchais to have continued in the ephemeral dramas of the liberated boulevard theater, but scholarship in recent years has shown this not to be so.[5] Rather than revealing a pattern of innovation, the repertoire of the popular stage during the Revolutionary era also suggests a distinct conservatism.[6] There were certainly radical plays in all genres and forms, including some that anticipated the radical drama of modernism, but these were more isolated than one might expect, and they appear to have exercised no discernible influence upon ensuing drama.[7] Instead, Revolutionary drama was soon dismissed, along with much of the period's cultural output, as an anomalous creation suited only to its time; within decades, its most significant works were viewed as failures and mere aberrations. As Hugo succinctly put it, "The society generated by the revolution had its literature, as ugly and inaccessible as itself. This literature and this society died together and are not going to come back to life."[8] Traditional literary history has tended, in consequence, to view the decade of the Revolution as a yawning gulf in the drama's development, a period defined only by the gap it described,[9] and so it is not surprising that the Revolution's impact on the drama first appeared in formal histories of the drama as an abstracted epistemological shift, the formally unspecified effect of a massive collapse of social order and religious belief. For George Steiner and Peter Brooks, for example, the Revolution marked "the final liquidation of the Sacred . . . , the shattering of the myth of Christendom, the dissolution of an organically and hierarchically cohesive society, and [hence] the invalidation of literary forms—tragedy, comedy of manners—that depended on such a society."[10]

More recent work, however, has begun to modify this view, not least by situating the drama's formal development within a broader and more continuous social history of the theater and in relation to attendant changes in the drama's status as both a literary and a theatrical mode. Studies of British romantic drama and popular theater, in particular, have subjected to closer scrutiny the traditional notion of the Revolutionary period as a point of rupture, suggesting that such impressions privilege the French context and overlook significant dramatic and theatrical innovation across the Channel.[11] Similarly, studies of romantic tragedy and melodrama have begun to draw a closer relation between the history of those dramas and the concrete experience of the Revolution, replacing the sense of the Revolution as an epistemological abstraction with a recognition of its spectacular impact on contemporaries.[12] In all these literary-critical studies, the changes in dramatic form that occurred during this period have come to seem more material, as the drama itself has come to be understood not only as a literary object but also as a social discourse responding to the rapidly changing cultural and political milieu of the Revolutionary era.

Indeed, recent scholarship by social and cultural historians of this period suggests a more reciprocal relationship between the drama and socio-political practice. Far from holding the drama in a state of dislocated suspension, the political cultures of Revolutionary Europe, and Revolutionary France in particular, turned to it as a uniquely powerful language of social and political expression within a radically theatrical context of public action. And this appropriative phenomenon should not surprise us. The political culture of the French Revolution faced an immediate need for some shared language in which to convey revolutionary political ideas, yet France was a nation lacking a widely shared language or tradition of political dissent.[13] In a situation that rendered the languages of religious revolution inappropriate from the start, dramatic narratives offered an expeditious armature, a lingua franca in which many leaders had been trained and in which the complexities of political idea and intent could be captured in a single gesture, an inflection, a word.

As is well known, a remarkable number of actors and dramatists rose to power during the Revolution, and their success bore more than a coincidental relation to their training.[14] Moreover, such appropriations of the languages and forms of drama were not limited to the most prominent actors, noblest genres, or most elevated stages of Revolutionary politics. The Revolution's political culture borrowed at many levels from dramatic and theatrical convention in its efforts to articulate and comprehend, and to shape, political change. In the July Days, and with the fall of the Bastille, in particular; in the October Days and in the March to Versailles; in the great Revolutionary festivals, the tribunals, and the scaffold— in all of these events and milieus we find performances that appealed not merely coincidentally or indirectly but quite explicitly and coherently to the languages and conventions of the theater and of the drama. Daniel Arasse, for example, has shown in rich detail the many ways in which theatrical practices and dramatic conventions informed and shaped the spectacular theatricality of the guillotine, and Marie-Hélène Huet has investigated the homologous theatrical logic that informed both the trial and execution of Louis XVI and theatrical re-enactments of the assassination of Marat.[15]

Moreover, while these political performances were extraordinarily varied, the work of Arasse, Huet, and others has revealed many fundamental modes, gestures, and actions, and Lynn Hunt suggested some time ago that a general trajectory can be discerned. Between 1789 and 1794, she observed, rather than figuring Revolutionary history in the negative terms of rupture and erasure, the Revolution's successive and competing governments and political cultures each attempted to stage its own fulfillment of Revolutionary history with something like an unconscious generic logic drawn from the drama: first as comedy (in the elimination of a blocking feudal figure and the reunion of people and king), then as romance, and later, more rigorously and explicitly, as tragedy. Such studies have had a powerful effect on contemporary understanding of the Revolution itself, prompting a radical re-evaluation of its nature and form. Most recently, Paul Friedland has taken such arguments much further, suggesting that there was in the French Revolution "a general merging of the theatrical and political stages" and that France's political revolution was not incidentally but "fundamentally related to a revolution in the theory and practice of theater."[16]

More than simply reshaping current understanding of the movement and structure of the Revolution, such historical scholarship has obvious consequences for our understanding of what happened to the drama during the decade of the Revolution, for it reveals within the blank space of that epistemological shift registered by literary history a full, finely articulated history of formal change— a tumultuous history, which involves a violent disruption of theatrical and dramatic consciousness and takes place in many different contexts of performance and various representational modes but which exhibits a fairly clear larger structure, with strong patterns of local continuity and stability.

Taken seriously, such work thus suggests a rather different account of the transition from traditional to modern drama than those "stories of rupture" that have been developed by either traditional literary or theater history. It also implies, however, a revised understanding of the relationship between the history of modern drama and that of political and social revolutions. Michael McKeon, reflecting upon an "apparent discontinuity" in the development of the English novel during the first half of the seventeenth century, asks these pertinent questions:

> If the English novel began to rise toward the end of the sixteenth century, why was this literary revolution abruptly curtailed after 1600 and postponed for the better part of a century? As the foregoing chapters make abundantly clear, the first half of the seventeenth century was a comprehensively "revolutionary" period, witnessing not only successful political revolt and unprecedented social mobility but also the establishment of the Baconian revolution, the climax of Puritan radicalism, and the flowering of pamphlet and periodical publications. Is it plausible to regard these striking developments as relatively "materialized" alternatives to

the nascent literary revolution in prose fiction, alternatives that did the "work" of revolution "by other means" and with an efficiency and immediacy that temporarily diverted the energies that had begun to be expended on the comparatively mediated activity of specifically literary revolution?[17]

My contention here is not that the French Revolution "did the work" of literary change "by other means"—that politics for a time replaced literature as the determining context of the drama's formal development—but that during the decade of the Revolution these two realms of activity could not be disentangled, and that the French Revolution should be recognized not as a background to the history of the drama but as a primary event within that history. As I hope to suggest, it was in and through the dramatic politics of the Revolution and not "around" them—or in merely reflective response to an abstracted epistemological shift that they forced or signified—that tragedy was transformed as a genre, that traditional conceptions of genre were rendered obsolete, and that the genre of melodrama was formed. And it is in and through Büchner's reflection upon the political history of the French Revolution at the distance of four decades—and through his recognition of that history *as* drama—that he developed what would become the radical dramaturgy of modernism.

That event in the history of the drama, I argue, was not only or even primarily a process of conceptual change. The French Revolution, by quite literally *enacting* the historical failure of traditional drama—not in the theater or in literary form but in political performance and as embodied historical action—became a nightmarish, originary drama of modernism, a material, historical experience of drama's failure that could be neither reversed nor banished from cultural awareness. The Revolution must, I think, be recognized in this sense as an event that also became a latent structure in the drama's subsequent history, a "ghost" narrative that continued to hold enormous if largely implicit authority. It was, however, an event that forced a decisive conceptual change, for the particular epistemological separation that it catalyzed—the rupture of a viable formal correspondence between drama and history—not only marks a definitive renegotiation of boundary conditions in both the history of the drama and that of historical consciousness but also defines the epistemological and formal quandary of both modern drama and modern revolution.

This argument also implies, as part of its thesis, that the drama was not simply one aspect of French Revolutionary history but one of its primary "scripts," not merely the outer trappings of its players but a shaping force in

their conduct and course of action. Although much of the work of recent Revolutionary historiography supports such a theory in general terms, historians
have to date shied away from extending the broad recognition of a theatrical
metaphorics in the politics of the Revolution to the notion that political action
was shaped in specific terms by the narrative forms of the drama. Marx, of
course, pointed this out explicitly when he discussed the Revolutionaries' adoption of the "stern classical traditions of the Roman republic," though readers
continue to assume that he was speaking metaphorically, of "mere" rhetoric.
The French Revolutionaries may have adopted these traditions as rhetorical de-
vices, we tell ourselves, but their actions were shaped by Enlightenment ideals,
by the demands of history and not drama. I am not arguing for anything like an
inversion of this view. As Marx is careful to note, the Revolutionaries' use of
classical traditions was not a masquerade but a self-deception, and to suggest
otherwise *would* be to confuse history and drama. However, I do want to suggest
that the connection between the two was precisely what the performance of
Revolutionary politics challenged, tested, and found wanting. What I hope to
show is that such confusion was a central problem of the Revolution—a problem that continually informed political action and representation, both as an
opportunity for accusation and as a self-doubting threat, and a problem that
shaped not only the performance and the reception of the Revolution but also
the period's violent reconceptions of the status, meaning, and potential of both
drama and history.

The aim of this book's first chapter is to describe what might be understood
conceptually as the formation of Revolutionary theatricality. Specifically, it traces
the emergence of a distinct form of radical political performance in response to an
extended crisis of social and political representation in pre-Revolutionary and
early Revolutionary Paris and its transformation of the theatrical conditions in
which representational authority was asserted, evaluated, and contested. That
transformation, I suggest, culminated in the formation of the "politics of publicity," a set of theatrical practices and spectatorial conventions that would fundamentally inform the Revolution and virtually define the profoundly *anti*theatrical
attitudes and mechanisms to which such performance would be subjected. The
Manichean dynamic of these politics, which found its most extreme expression
in the Revolution's continual obsession with plots, conspiracy, and vigilance,
would serve as a driving force of the Revolution's appropriation and evacuation
of traditional languages of authority, for it presented the Revolution's actors
with a constant problem of locating "authentic" modes of representation within

an environment defined by a continual, accelerating process of disillusionment and unveiling.

Chapter 2 summarizes the way the political performance of the French Revolution appropriated and transformed dramatic form. Specifically, my goal is to outline the manner in which the performance of Revolutionary politics—the continual effort to gain, hold, and undermine authority within that theater— enlisted the drama as a language of political and historical action and to explore the ways in which this process of appropriation transformed the drama's form, status, and meaning. This goal is quite limited in comparison to the work of the Revolutionary historians noted above, much of which concerns itself with the complex structure of Revolutionary theatrical and political representation. My aim is to bring such work to bear on the history of drama and to use it, specifically, to understand how the Revolution's political performances shaped and participated in the historical shift from traditional to modern drama. However, this chapter adapts in consequence a longer view, for that shift was not limited to the Revolution, nor was it determined only by the Revolutionary era's crisis of social and political theatricality. It was instead, as I hope to show, born of a long series of transformations in the construction of dramatic narrative and of the convergence, in the Revolutionary era, of this development and a coincident crisis in the authority of historical narrative. However, this historical shift culminated in the Revolutionary decade, when the dramatic performance of the French Revolution tested the historical potential of the drama and in so doing brought the traditional languages of dramatic form to their grinding exhaustion. In that intensified process of disenchantment, I suggest, a definitive moment of modernity—the failure of classical dramatic poetics—can be discerned.

And yet in the genealogy of that failure one finds only half of its meaning and only one aspect of its significance to the drama's history. To capture some idea of its full meaning it is necessary also to understand the subsequent and reverberating effects of that failure, and the second half of this book, therefore, turns from the Revolutionary collapse of the drama to its reception and external impact. In consequence, it is rather different from the first half, for responses to the political drama of the Revolution were shaped not merely by the logic of that drama but also by the complex processes of mediation through which those events became known to the world and through which they were shaped, inflected, experienced, and remembered. In Chapter 3, to provide some comparative perspective, I explore in brief the manner in which this dramatic revolution in France was reshaped by its encounter with Britain's very different culture of theatrical politics. Focusing on Burke's and Sheridan's diverse activities and influence, this chapter shows how Britain's political culture combined theatrical, journalistic, and political authority to shape and contain the Revolution's representational threat. Much of that effort consisted in questioning the legitimacy and sensibility of the dramatic politics taking place in France while asserting, as forcefully as possible, the order and authenticity of Britain's own political stage. However, these oppositional strategies were also reinforced and inflected by a complex process of absorption and imitation, largely but not wholly conservative, through which the theatrical events, dramatic rhetoric, and spectacular languages of the Revolution were transformed to suit British representations of history and appropriated to the construction of a rival stage of British power. The chapter closes with a closer look at Sheridan's triumphant *Pizarro* (1797), in which these dual tactics find theatrical realization in the sensational birth of British spectacular drama.

In Chapters 4 and 5 I adopt a localized focus to examine what seem to me to be two instances in which the political drama of the Revolution had an especially significant impact on the history of drama. In an effort to understand something of the specific relationship between the tragic disillusionment of Thermidor and romantic tragedy, Chapter 4 takes a close look at the manner in which Britain's mediated experience of Robespierre's fall from power shaped the development of Coleridge's tragic imagination. In an examination that focuses on British press coverage of events in France in the summer of 1794, I show how an extraordinary series of disruptions in news transmission led the British—and Coleridge, in particular—to indulge for a brief moment a sympathetic but illusory view of the Jacobin leader's deposition and death as tragic. In that wrenching process of imaginative investment and disenchantment, a process articulated in stark clarity by *The Fall of Robespierre* (1795), Coleridge's abortive attempt to render that fall in dramatic form, I find a specific and strikingly contingent account of the Revolution's impact on romantic drama.

In the fifth and final chapter I turn my attention to Georg Büchner's *Dantons Tod* (1835) to explore the more distant but no less direct impact of Revolutionary history on the formation of radical modernist drama. In contrast to traditional accounts of Büchner's work, which treat his influential aesthetic as an unprecedented, proleptic intervention in dramatic form, I show how Büchner derives that aesthetic specifically from his belated dramatic examination of the Revolution's radical theatricality and its political appropriation of the drama. By repudiating romantic drama's turn away from the Revolution's violent history, Büchner is able, I argue, to confront the formal implications of that history's dramatic politics and to reappropriate to the drama its radical dramaturgy.

In a certain sense, these last two chapters are efforts to interrogate, respectively, the leading and trailing edges of the drama's prolonged displacement of the French Revolutionary experience—the waking margins to a period of haunted aversion. However, the final chapter on Büchner is also intended to explore the Revolution's impact on a larger and longer history than that of romantic drama. In its resuscitation of the Revolution's political theatricality, Büchner's work also reveals modernist drama's link to Revolutionary history.

CHAPTER ONE

The Theater of the Revolution

Spectacular Tensions and Political Theatricality

The political performances of the French Revolution did not take place only in Paris, but Paris was their central stage. The French capital was also the primary locale in which the language and conventions of Revolutionary theatricality—those practices of performance and of spectatorship that would drive much of the Revolution's action—were developed. That development did not begin in 1789, however, nor was it at first political in the strict sense of the term. Revolutionary theatricality seems, rather, to have been the product of a longer history of increasingly contestatory and finally radical practices of social and political performance in the pre-Revolutionary city. These practices, which may be seen as responses to a gradual weakening of surveillant authority over public space and a widening crisis of traditional codes of social representation, contributed to the emergence of what I call "spectacular tensions" within the city's culture: increasingly pressurized and oppositional relations between contesting cultures of appearance and action, between public order and popular license. By 1789, such relations had become unstable, and popular acts of political theatricality began not only to articulate and negotiate spectacular tensions but also to stage spectacles of violence, revealing an effective absence of authority over the city and offering both a model and a prompt for revolutionary action.

Paris remained, throughout the eighteenth century, a city ordered by absolutism's spectacular organization of political authority.[1] The most emphatic reminder of that authority was the great extension, far out over the Champs-Elysées, of le Nôtre's grand avenue. The chief mechanism of that authority was a powerful apparatus of royal surveillance and control, for Paris, unlike London, was a royal city, governed directly by the monarchy's centralized administration. This apparatus took institutional form in the absolutist structure of licensing, law enforcement, and policing, including the monarchy's long-established network of paid informants, which extended into and throughout Parisian society the gaze of that "Prince whose eyes," as Molière had put it a century before, "can see into our inmost hearts" (Un prince dont les yeux se font jour dans les coeurs).[2] However, absolutist power over Paris also took more concrete form, for Louis, like Haussmann after him, reshaped the city itself to facilitate both surveillance and the imposition of authority. Perhaps most significantly, the king demolished the city's defensive walls, creating its first great boulevards, widening its entry points to enable the rapid entry of troops and installing there the great, later notorious gates of royal taxation. These changes gave rise to the culture of the boulevard, which by the second half of the eighteenth century had joined and even eclipsed the fairgrounds as the privileged locale of popular leisure and entertainment.[3] At the same time, they created a deep sense of vulnerability that would drive the Revolutionary city's extreme responses to rumors of attack.

Louis's changes within the city were no less significant. He literally opened the streets to the gaze, sweeping away the ubiquitous street-furniture of the medieval city, removing its hundreds of hanging signs and symbols, and installing, in a move that marks the birth of Paris as the city of light, an enormous system of street lighting.[4] Certainly the candlelit lanterns put in place by Louis XIV produced nothing like the gaslit extravaganza of the nineteenth-century capital. Yet they changed in significant ways the atmosphere and the social activity of the city, for they established a new, scopic mechanism of order and control. Situated along main thoroughfares and at important junctions and squares, the new lighting enabled the regime to replace wandering security forces with surveillance posts. In addition to enabling and imposing a higher degree of social order, this new apparatus was also intended, and understood, as a gesture and reminder of absolutism's exercise of surveillant power.[5] As the most ubiquitous signs of the king's royal authority over the city, the lanterns of Paris were understood immediately as objects invested with unusual symbolic weight, and acts of violence against them were treated, Wolfgang Schivelbusch notes, "not as disorderly conduct (*contravention aux ordonnances*) but as a criminal offense not far short of lese-majesty."[6]

However, the reorganization of surveillant power in absolutist Paris, if it imposed a much closer sense of royal authority, also increased personal security and allowed safer movement after dark through the city streets. In consequence, it initiated a transformation of urban social life, opening the evening hours to collective leisure activity and expanding the potential for commercial entertainment. This transformation was slow in the early decades of the century, but with the Regency and the return of court life to the city the pace of change accelerated. By Diderot's time, the city's royal lighting, rather than serving only to increase order, enabled the emergence of a recognizably modern culture of popular as well as elite leisure, not only spurring a profusion of cafés, salons, shops, and theaters but also contributing to the rise of boulevard culture.

By the 1760s, if the image and symbolic presence of the Sun King still dominated the city, the symbolic power of the absolute monarchy had diminished. Louis XV had no desire to impose his authority upon the urban space of Paris in such a forceful manner, and the royal architectural projects of his reign reflect both a weakening of absolutism's assertion of surveillant authority and a distantiation of its symbolic presence in and over the city itself. The most telling public manifestation of this shift in the construction and assertion of royal power was the Place Louis XV, now the Place de la Concorde, the most prominent public work of the Louis XV's reign and later a central stage of Revolutionary politics.

The design of the new plaza, which constituted a significant addition to the city's public space, seemed to announce the continuity of the new regime with that of the Sun King. Jacques Ange Gabriel's project superimposed Louis XV's memorial to himself directly upon the monumental landscape laid out by his predecessor, situating the Place Louis XV at the nexus of the Louvre with the great axis of the Tuileries and the Champs-Elysées. Gabriel adopted as well (as one can see on the left in L'Espinasse's perspective view) the elevated colossal order that Claude Perrault had conceived for Louis XIV's reconstruction of the Louvre's east façade.[7] This homage was in part pragmatic; like Perrault, Gabriel was building upon a site that looked out over an enormous open space, and the colossal order, by lifting and enlarging the classical vocabulary, gave, at a distance, the effect of classical balance, the impression of "one huge story standing on a podium sufficiently high to prevent an effect of sinking into the ground."[8]

However, Gabriel's design departed from Perrault's in one crucial respect: rather than opening the huge space of the plaza itself to an unimpeded extension of the gaze, Gabriel cut down the sense of the site's scale, introducing "intermediary members" (large moats, retaining walls, and small pavilions) to define a smaller, more intimate central plaza, and one more detached from the monumental architecture around it. By this strategy, the design "succeeded—not in giving the feeling of triumphant architectural strength . . . but in giving one the satisfaction of finding oneself in a pleasantly framed landscape. As a prominent contemporary of Gabriel, M. A. Laugier, expressed it: 'Surrounded by gardens and groves, the plaza gives one only the feeling of a beautiful promenade in the midst of a smiling countryside, whence one observes several distant palaces.'"[9] Rather than memorializing Louis XV as a monarch who maintained or extended

Louis Nicolas de l'Espinasse, *Vue perspective de la place Louis XV*, c. 1778 (detail). © Photothèque des musées de la ville de Paris / Photo: Jean-Yves Trocaz.

absolutism's spectacular regime, Gabriel's project thus presented him as a ruler who mitigated the severity of his predecessor, withdrew to a position of distant pleasure, and limited the extension and force of his gaze.

This architectural distantiation of royal power was paralleled and reinforced by changes to the city's apparatus of surveillant control. By 1770, Louis XIV's six thousand royal lanterns had been replaced by twelve hundred new, more powerful oil lamps, known, by virtue of their highly effective system of reflectors, as *réverbères*. As Schivelbusch observes, the greater intensity of the *réverbères* was more than offset by increases in the distances between them, so that what had been a fairly uniform level of illumination now became a series of "islands of light in the darkness."[10] Like Gabriel's architectural innovations, the *réverbères* marked, in a symbolic as well as a material sense, the recession of royal power to a less imposing position; the lanterns still stood out as signs of the gaze of royal authority, but that gaze was now attenuated, softened, and localized.

Such reductions in the force and presence of royal authority were accompanied by and contributed to a sudden, sustained intensification of public social life in the city. Both bourgeois and libertine cultures, no longer forced to the shadows and the margins of absolutism's gaze, began to assert their presence and power within the city, creating new social spaces within it rather than at its margins, and asserting there new practices of social performance, spectatorial pleasure, and spectacular display.[11] By the 1760s, the pleasure garden of the Palais-Royal, that first and most important of these new spaces, had been joined by a host of additional gardens, tearooms, cafés, and private theaters; by the 1770s, the Palais was only the central, most extensive of an entire network of such venues.

One interesting element of that shift—a shift that marks the birth, in Paris, of something like mass culture—was a notable expansion of socially mixed commercial entertainment within the public space of the city, and with it an increasing level of interaction between isolated individuals of different classes and social types, many of whom were dressed in such a manner as to blur identity and status and to challenge the normative conventions of both social appearance and social behavior. Louis-Sébastien Mercier, the most influential observer of late-eighteenth-century Paris, pointed out in his *Tableau de Paris* that by the 1780s even middle-class individuals began to take on an "entirely different appearance" (*un tout autre extérieur*) than that imposed by their profession, adopting different manners and styles of dress as a means of concealing personal, professional, and class identity.[12] Social encounters in these contexts possessed an ambiguous theatricality, drawing much of their frisson from the mixed pleasure and threat of their uncertainty. However, they also had political implications, for

they suggested—and implicitly demonstrated—the contingency of social identity
and the arbitrariness of class and privilege.

By this decade, too, the city's move toward a mass culture of public leisure
was experienced, as Mercier noted, not merely as a quantitative increase in the
density and multiplicity of social life but also, and almost definitively, as a quali-
tative change in its intensity and pace.[13] We find for the first time in those years
accounts that reflect that peculiarly modern experience of the city not as the mi-
crocosm of the world but as the emblem of its incessant flow, its streets filled not
with multiplicity but with masses, their actions signifying not quotidian variety
but ephemeral variation and continual flux.[14] This new sense of urban tempo-
rality found privileged articulation and embodiment in the rise of fashion, particularly in late-eighteenth-century French fashion's remarkable, frenetic acceleration of changes in style and appearance—an acceleration that responded to,
contributed to, and commented upon the increasingly disorienting pace and texture of daily experience.[15] More than merely signifying an increase in the rate
of social change, such acceleration also highlighted the wastefulness of fashionable society, pointing out all the more clearly a growing gap between the life of
the privileged and that of the poor. In consequence, fashion itself became, by the
1780s, a focal point for social critique, signifying both the careless extravagance
and inequities of French society and the obvious erosion and weakness of established codes of social representation and authority.

One contemporary print delineates this sense of erosion and captures the hostility it produced with exceptional clarity. Most obviously, the scene is a mockery
of the sort of short-lived establishments that characterized the Palais-Royal
and a satirical critique of the vain society that patronized such an economy. However, its satire is rather more grotesque and pointed than a mere caricature of the
fashion trade, for this shop deals not in clothing or wigs but in bodies and mostly
in heads—new looks to be set in place of those aged, unappealing visages that
the shop's patrons carry in upon their shoulders. In the cabinet that surmounts
the scene, we are shown a dazzling array of contemporary coiffures; around and
beneath it, we find not merely a collection but an obviously theatrical parade of
customers (a divine, a magistrate, a fashionable woman, an aging man, and an
ancient woman), each a recognizable social type, each in a different stage of the
grisly transaction of changing an old head for a new.

The key to this grim procession is provided in the underlying caption, a bitter
lyric to be sung, the verses imply, to the familiar tune of "Malbrouk s'en va-t-en
guerre" (or "For he's a jolly good fellow"), but with the more chilling refrain of
"Changez-moi cette tête." Starting with a caustic indictment of the malicious

Anonymous, "Têtes à Changer: Vaudeville du Temps" (1783). Bibliothèque nationale de France.

old foxes (*Vieux Renards en malice*) who use black arts to plunder the poor, the lyric condemns the character of each of the customers in turn, exposing intriguers as sexual predators, protectors as despots requiring base subservience, aging coquettes as monsters of vanity, cuckolded husbands as self-abasing fools, and ancient dowagers as souls lost to artifice—all of whom, the anonymous poet observes, find in fashion the instrument of their dishonest and self-deluding behavior. In the final two verses—the second of which offers a caption to the lyric itself—the critique becomes both more general and more particular, offering first a murderously suggestive rant against women who vainly pursue the latest look and then, finally, a cautionary paean to the author's mistress, the "Divine Elmonde," who is reminded that if she too changes her lovely head, she must also bid adieu to the pleasures of her love.[16]

However, such intimacy is here set within a larger implicatory context, for if we can read in its lyric caption the reflections of a bitter lover, we can see in its dramatic scene reflections of a more potent social critique. On the left, catalyzing that entry into the self-regarding delusion that drives the patrons' transformative choices, are Harlequin and Hermes, a pair suggestive not merely of the theatrical vanity of courtly pretense but also of the destabilization, within such an ephemeralized world, of clear categories of sexual identity and order. Accordingly, the magistrate who contemplates a new head is shown yielding to the flatteries of a female companion and an insinuating clerk, while the woman standing at the center of the shop is depicted in a posture of placid complacency that contrasts sharply with the bloody sword and decapitated head that has been hewn from her torso. On the right, appropriately enough, we find not an everyday shop clerk but Pierrot himself, that rococo amalgam of Harlequin and Hermes, assisting an enraged customer, the cuckold of the song, whose frantic effort to secure a suitable new head (a head, that is, with an appropriate set of horns) is figured as a groping, hungry stab at Pierrot's androgynous groin. Certainly, one might read in this scene a condemnation of the stage, as its theatrical figures function allegorically as emblems of the various stages and metamorphoses of this baleful social transformation. However, to do so is to forget that these figures appear here less as emblems of fashion's pursuit than as theatrical impresarios, intervening gods whose machinations render visible the self-deluding, hypocritical endeavors of the patrons who stand below. Rather than standing as indicators of a coincident indictment of the theater, these figures imply that one finds in that theater's farcical dynamic the true image of a society that has lost—and, the author suggests, should lose—its head.

The intensification of such an unstable social environment, the growing ubiquity of the sense that novelty was not new but merely different, the transition from a social theater in which fashion constituted a departure from static, hieratic modes of interaction to one in which such superficiality constituted an inescapable condition of all interaction, gave rise in turn to new modes of social behavior and apprehension and new ways of staging, seeing, and making sense of urban experience. By the mid-1780s, the theatricality of the mid-century city had given rise to a more popular, more commodified, more subversive culture of passing and disguise. Transvestism became a remarked-upon phenomenon of contemporary life, along with similar behaviors that played upon momentary effects of misrecognition, upon the glancing pleasures of ironic duplicity, and upon the fleeting engagement of transgressive desire.[17]

This culture of change had gained much of its momentum from the redevelopment at this time of the Palais-Royal. What distinguished the new Palais, reopened as a commercial venture by the Louis-Philippe d'Orléans—the most notorious libertine of his day, cousin of the king, and the property's owner—was the addition of a whole host of interior spaces. Shops, printing houses and booksellers, coffeehouses and cafes, brothels, and theaters were opened, all reached through the grand, illuminated galleries constructed along either side of the refurbished *allées*. More than merely altering the milieu and atmosphere of the Palais, the creation of these spaces changed its character and use, freeing activity there from the passage of the day and producing within its bounds the unmitigating sensational rhythms and the sense of temporal anomie that are more often associated with the modernist metropolis. Here, as in Walter Benjamin's capital of the nineteenth century, the stage of that shift, its concrete mechanism and mise-en-scène, is the interior, artificial arcade, its illumination constant, its scenes a continual progression of interaction, both public and sheltered, open to circulation but sheltered from the surveillance and the rhythms of the city without. As Mercier noted, in the Palais the whirl of fashionable pleasure had become unceasing, its transformation of style a daily occurrence and its commodified social and sexual interactions reduced to a flow of brief, anonymous encounters.[18]

Among the prosperous bourgeoisie in particular, the Palais and its associated spaces of idleness had by this time come to seem a dangerous source of both moral contagion and social disorder, particularly in a city increasingly influenced by that rising culture's ideas of propriety, privacy, and honesty. The Palais-Royal was, in many ways, not just a destination but a space of illicit circulation, one through which the world of the court and the aristocracy was itself made visible to the rest of Paris, both in person—in the mixed intercourse of the coffeehouses and cafés, theaters, gambling dens, and brothels—and in print. In the protected booksellers' shops of the Palais one could find radical pamphlets, scurrilous prints, satirical verses, and all manner of pornographic and scandal-mongering novels and *faux* memoirs: works that, like the immensely successful *Anecdotes sur Mme La Comtesse du Barry* (1775), claimed to reveal the corrupt inner workings of the court and suggested (as did the figure of du Barry herself) a basic continuity between the lowliest brothel and the bedchamber of the king.[19] In short, the Palais was not only a dangerous space of saturnalia, opaque to the external, ordering gaze of the city's authority, but also a spectacular theater of sexual circulation and social flux, revealing the falsehood, the arbitrariness, and the brutal inequity of late-ancien-régime society.[20]

The social tensions raised by this economy of pleasure had been anticipated by Mercier, but their privileged observer and finest journalist was Rétif de la Bretonne, who extended Mercier's tableau of the city's new social life with his own immensely popular stories of the city's nocturnal culture. Posing as the "Night-Owl of Paris," a sort of latter-day Quixote, Rétif's narrative persona recounts both real and fictive meanderings about Paris after dark, seeking out interesting scenes and intervening, from time to time, on behalf of those whom he perceives (correctly or incorrectly) to be in distress.[21] Typically, he remains an anonymous, cloaked voyeur, the unseen but observant spectator, a role in which he assumes, like Mercier, the autonomous position of critic and philosopher. However, this position is, in a manner that distinguishes Rétif from spectators of the earlier, daylight city, constantly at risk, for in the city after dark appearance had become an unreliable and at times a plainly misleading indicator, a catalyst not only of transgressive interaction but of subversive violence as well.

It is precisely such uncertainty that lends Rétif's anecdotes their appeal, for it is the deceptive appearances of their characters, their misconstruction, and their isolated, happenstance encounters and clashes that make the accounts so fascinating. Yet it is also such ambiguity that most consistently provokes Rétif's violent disapproval: misleading appearances are condemned as such a threat to the moral order that the police, Rétif suggests, should "prohibit masquerades of all kinds, including the delirium of the carnival" (*défendre les mascarades de toute espèce, et jusqu'au délire du Carnaval*).[22] It is no surprise, within such an uncomfortable economy of desire, that Rétif reserves his most violent expressions of alarm for his encounters with male transvestites, in whom he finds the archetypal image of both the nighttime city's corrupting pleasures and its brutal economy of sexual predation and victimization.[23]

These views of fashion culture, of the destabilizing influence of the Palais-Royal, and of the unsettled nocturnal city suggest the depth and severity of the social crisis experienced in Paris in the 1780s, and they indicate as well how the changing character of social performance both contributed to that crisis and articulated a clear sense of impending cultural change. Yet these records depict that crisis as it was made manifest and worked out within the eroding structure of ancien-régime society. The catalysts of political collapse—the actions and performances that would bring about the Revolution—would take a more popular form and find their articulation not in fashion, in leisure culture, or in pictorial aesthetics, all areas tightly bound up with high culture, but in the street and in collective acts of violence directed specifically against the symbolic and surveillant power of the monarchy.

In the 1780s, Rétif's journals began to record not just scenes of thievery and depredation but episodes of organized violence as well. In 1782, for example, he noted with alarm the outbreak of gang violence at the annual St. Jean's Day Bonfire. Although the scene is filtered through Rétif's luridly suggestive narrative, the action he depicted emerges with startling theatrical logic. The crowd

seemed tranquil enough at first. However, as I listened to the conversation, I realized that a group of goldsmiths' and clockmakers' workers from the Place Dauphine were forming a circle and deftly maneuvering pretty girls into its center to render them victims to their imprudent curiosity, which blinded them to what was going on. "Watch out!" said M. du Hameauneuf. Thus I observed the maneuver, which continued. I turned my attention to another group. This one worked differently: it encircled all the men who seemed likely to have money and watches: they would push them by a little wavelike motion, which they barely perceived, and the one who was pushing the most roughly was the one who complained, moreover, of the crush. This riffraff stayed honest until the last rockets.

"Watch out!" repeated Du Hameauneuf. "Without me you would have been carried along, but together we support each other." I noticed that the undulations were redoubling. I didn't watch the rockets at all, and I noticed that the pickpockets didn't either; it seemed to me that they would slip their hands into the pockets when the rockets shot up and pull out the hook during the cries and agitation excited by each spent shell. But I soon turned from that scene back to the other.

The journeyman goldsmiths were still at it. The imprudent women who were caught in the different circles they had formed seemed to be lifted one or two feet off the ground, others were lying horizontally across many arms; some of them were caught in the middle of a double circle and all of them were being treated in the most degrading manner, and sometimes the most cruel. Their cries went unheard, because the men chose the moments when the shells were falling or shouted themselves to drown out the shouts of their victims. Du Hameauneuf cut through the different circles like a knife and took me along. "Don't say a word!" he had told me. "We would be smothered." We saw some horrible things; in one instance, in the middle of a triple circle, a young girl with her mother, who was forced to be a witness and accomplice to the infamies done to her daughter. The hapless girl fainted . . . The rest of this story can't be told. Fortunately, the fireworks ended, and this time weren't resumed. The provost of merchants was informed of what we had seen, and our statement, together with another, was enough to stop to these dangerous pranks. The pickpockets and the hoodlums drained away like water, and the victims found themselves surrounded by entirely different men, who could imagine only that they had too tightly pressed.[24]

In comparison to the general character of Rétif's episodes, which encompass a multitude of real and probably imagined acts of sexual and criminal violence, the pickpocketing and even the gang assault upon young girls are not particularly remarkable. What distinguishes these events is their context and their method, for such acts customarily occur, in Rétif's accounts, quietly and under cover of darkness, in solitude and in isolation. The crimes of the bonfire, however, are carried out in full view, and they find their cover in the beguiling distraction and whistling, empty shells of a royal fireworks display, that most spectacular demonstration of the king's power to illuminate, and to control, the city. In fact, the bonfire had traditionally been ignited by the king himself, and the annual celebration was, if an occasion of permitted license, one controlled by higher rather than lower levels of surveillance and police presence.[25] And yet the acts that Rétif relates here are carried out not in secrecy and hiding but with studied impunity, in plain view, not desperately but with obvious premeditation and planning, and followed not by riotous retreat but by sudden, skillful evaporation into the press and flow of the crowd. Rather than marking, like most of the criminal scenes that characterize Rétif's episodes, attempts to evade royal authority, to play upon its liminal blind spots, such acts were political, openly defying that authority, relying upon and even declaring its absence, even upon a central stage and occasion of power. Rétif's colored narration, certainly, plays upon this implication, not least by drawing our attention repeatedly to the "*baguettes tombantes*" (empty rocket shells) that muffle the crimes, but it does not, if we credit even the outlines of his story, create it.

Such performances were fundamental to the formation of Revolutionary theatricality. Rather than simply imagining the monarchy's loss of power, these acts
staged that loss, asserting in the most visceral manner both the hollowness of absolutism's monumental vision of society and the local, contestatory failure of its
authority over public action, demonstrating—in a highly theatrical performance—
the manner in which its symbolic and political regime could be blinded, stripped
of its sight and thus of its rule. This is not to say that the sexual violence and petty
theft witnessed by Rétif constituted anything like self-conscious revolutionary acts;
yet these acts carried such implications, for they enacted not simply disorder but
organized, public, deliberately theatrical defiance of absolutism's rule.

We are apt, from a post-Revolutionary standpoint, to underestimate the degree
to which these gestures shocked contemporary observers, for we are accustomed
to thinking of Paris itself as a city marked by frequent acts of political violence.
Yet even in the middle of the 1780s, no less capable an observer than Mercier himself believed Paris to be a city and a community incapable of riot, unaccustomed,
like its English counterpart, to determined public expressions of discontent and
rebellion.[26] Though they were isolated, to be sure, these pre-Revolutionary incidents must have struck contemporaries as anything but incidental, for they
marked not only the government's loss of control but also the looming presence
and threat of the crowd—a presence and a threat suggested by Jean-Michel
Moreau's sweeping view of the massed audience of the 1782 fireworks held to
celebrate the birth of the dauphin. Here, royal spectacle seems already to serve
not as the centerpiece but as the backdrop for a now-unfolding spectacle of popular action.

We have seen, in the gang violence of the bonfire and the royal fireworks,
early articulations of political theatricality. In the last years leading up to the
Revolution, however, such performances seem to have changed, both in their
tenor and their claim, in their implication and their threat. Perhaps the most
telling phenomenon was fashion violence, which Rétif first observed just months
before the fall of the Bastille:

> On my way to the *Français*, I had noticed on one of the sidewalks of the Pont
> Henri what seemed to be a schoolboy who dropped to the ground each time a lady
> approached. I couldn't tell why, but finally I heard a young woman cry out: though
> I imagined that it was some kind of crude trick, I didn't stop to ask.
>
> That evening, as we set out for Mme. De M***'s, I saw the same young woman
> in a milliner's shop, and I asked the reason for the cry she had let out. "A nasty
> boy cut me with a knife, through my brand-new shoes! Since it was the second

time that's happened to me this year, I could tell what he was doing when I felt him touch me, so I screamed and he ran off."

"It's a new sort of trick," said a pretty woman nearby. "They cut them with a pocketknife. I was almost crippled by the same thing six months ago. People should be warned about this bizarre behavior"(*cette manie singulière*).[27]

This "new sort of trick" (*un nouveau genre de polissonnerie*), a decidedly odd one at any time, seems particularly so just months before the fall of the Bastille, and Rétif notes in the same episode that this odd phenomenon seems to have been related to equally unprecedented acts of dress slashing.[28]

On their face, such acts may appear far less overtly political than the riots of the same years, and to my knowledge no commentator has ever accorded them any political significance. However, in the context of what we know of the shape and tenor of spectacular tensions in the late-eighteenth-century city, they seem significant indeed, for they assert not the interruption of a gaze but the assertion of one, not a defiant, symbolic act of monarchial blinding but a violent, concretized act of unmasking. Fashion violence—for that, not just sexual predation, is what it was—was an act of rage not against the king but against what had become the prime symbol of the inequities of daily life, that libertine economy of pleasure that dominated city life and victimized its lowest and poorest denizens.

That economy was not without its promise of equity, for from it had emerged the utopian vision of a mobile, natural society and the model of a kind of identity that was fluid and changeable, founded upon performance rather than blood and action rather than property. However, as the observations of both Mercier and Rétif make quite clear, this promise appeared by the 1780s grossly illusory, as the city's decadent leisure culture emerged as the most pointed image and context of victimization, poverty, and commodification. Fashion violence, rather than merely striking out against inequity, asserted the illusory nature of this continuity. And it did so not through an act of ideological refusal, but through a subversive, threatening performance of antitheatrical violence—of unveiling, exposing, and destroying the artifice of privilege.

Publicity and Early Revolutionary Theatricality

Political performance in Paris, as I have suggested, was not invented with the fall of the Bastille in the July Days of 1789. The first of the Revolution's

Facing page: Jean-Michel Moreau, *Le Feu d'artifice, Fêtes données au Roi et à La Reine, par La Ville de Paris,* January 21, 1782.

great *journées*—a term reserved for those massive, extended episodes of collective violence that punctuate Revolutionary politics—would gain much of its force and resonance by playing quite consciously upon a theatrical logic that had by then developed its own conventions. Yet, if the collective performances of the 1780s and the fashion violence of preceding months would shape Revolutionary theatricality, they were still in a certain sense only gestures. Limited and indirect, meant to be suggestive rather than definitive, they carried the threat of revolution and developed its dramaturgy, but they were not, as the fall of the Bastille would be, the act itself.

That act has received more commentary than any other Revolutionary moment, and, with the exception of the executions of Louis and Marie-Antoinette, it is probably the only event of the French Revolution that survives in popular memory. Much of that reputation rests upon the event's apparent symbolism; more than simply marking the onset of popular revolution, the fall of the Bastille continues to be understood as a spontaneously theatrical gesture of liberation from the ancient weight of tyranny, a moment in which the long-suffering populace rose up in an authentic collective performance that gave expression, in exquisitely appropriate symbolic acts, to the nation's political unconscious. That its outcome catalyzed such gestures is certainly true; that its events were rapidly shaped to fit such a narrative is significant and will be discussed below. However, as historians have often observed, the actions of July 14 unfolded not as a concerted act of symbolic defiance but as a confused, collective response to the fear of attack, a fear shaped and driven by a series of unintentional miscues, alarmist rumors, and banal miscommunications. Rather than being concerned to set an example for history, the Bastille's "liberators" were concerned, perhaps rightly, for themselves and their own safety.

Less familiar are the immediate sequels to the Bastille's fall, which were by contrast deliberate acts of symbolic defiance. After the fortress was taken, Bernard de Launay, the governor of the Bastille, and Jacques de Flesselles, the provost of merchants, were executed in the street and decapitated, and their heads were then paraded on pikes to the Palais-Royal, apparently to great applause. On July 22, a week after the fall of the Bastille, a still-angered populace summarily seized Bertier de Sauvigny, the Intendant of Paris, and Foullon de Doué, his father-in-law, and executed them on the Place de Grève (the official site of criminal execution). More precisely, the crowd hanged Sauvigny and Doué from a lamp-iron mounted on the corner of the Hôtel de Ville and situated directly beneath a bust of the King. To demonstrate the people's authority over the public space of execution, and to carry out that execution immediately beneath the king's symbolic presence, was only part of the message being sent on July 22. More noteworthy was the decision to employ the city's single most prominent lamp-iron—the exemplar of absolutism's apparatus of public surveillance—as a ceremonial gallows.[29] For both participants and spectators, the executions enacted a highly theatrical displacement of the king's authority that went well beyond that of July 14: rather than merely implying liberation, they suggested instead a political version of "Changez-moi cette tête," a decapitation and usurpation of absolutism's surveillant power. The body of the nation was now to watch, and to control, its head.

The July Days thus constitutes a formative articulation of Revolutionary theatricality; however, its political performances suggest as well something of the limited composition of the political audience during the spring and summer of 1789, the manner in which Revolutionary politics was still, in these first months, shaped by and for local spectators. With the events of July, that audience suddenly expanded, for the establishment of the people's authority over Paris brought with it the sudden, explosive liberation of the French press.[30] In the six months that followed, French political journalism changed almost beyond recognition: state censorship and privileges for printers abruptly ceased to function, allowing not only the uncensored commentary of established journals but also the immediate rise of dozens of new, unlicensed ones. By Christmas, the few long-established journals of political commentary—all based, given the monarchy's hostility to criticism, outside of France—had been joined by more than a hundred new periodicals, most based in Paris itself.[31]

The efflorescence of this new political press was significant in itself, but even more noteworthy was its appropriation of a distinct position of surveillant power, a position borrowed not from absolutism, nor from the bourgeois model of a critically distanced observer, but from the performative violence of popular insurrection and from the theatricality of the July Days' most visceral spectacles. Camille Desmoulins, the orator whose fiery address in the Palais-Royal had catalyzed the fall of the Bastille, adopted the title "Procurator-General of the Streetlamps" as his editorial moniker, and in a celebrated pamphlet even adopted the conceit of addressing his readers as if he *were* a street lamp. Other adaptations of this kind of role were more indirect, but no less pointed. Jean-Paul Marat, before adopting his familiar title "*Ami du Peuple*," wrote simply as the "*Publiciste parisien*"; and Charles-Joseph Panckoucke, in founding the Revolution's most important journal of record, the *Gazette nationale*, appealed to the obviously surveillant position in the paper's subtitle—the *Moniteur universel.*[32] As Jeremy Popkin observed, the term *publiciste* in particular links Marat to the largely underground, pre-Revolutionary efforts to subject official activities to public scrutiny and discussion, but the discontinuity is perhaps more significant, for now Marat's invocation of the term is not resistant but authoritarian, a claim not of opposition but of power.[33]

With that explosion the performance of politics was placed before a much larger, very different sort of audience, and the October Days (Oct. 5–6, 1789), the next great *journée* of the early Revolution and a decisive moment in the evolution of its political culture, can be understood in part as a conflict fought precisely in terms of the authority of this expanded audience. Interestingly, the perfor-

"Discours de la lanterne aux Parisiens." Bibliothèque nationale de France.

mance that would initiate this *journée*'s several theatrical events was not popular at all, but one enacted at Versailles and before the eyes of the royal family.

On the night of October 1, in the Royal Theater at Versailles, the officers of the Royal Bodyguard held a private banquet for the officers of the Flanders Regiment, which Louis XVI had just recalled to the palace. The regiment's arrival had caused considerable anxiety in Paris, though its residents had reason enough already to feel uneasy. For almost two months the king had stubbornly withheld his approval of the abolition of aristocratic privileges, a measure passed by the National Assembly on the night of August 4 in the wake of enthusiasm and energy following the fall of the Bastille. While the July Days had prompted Louis to disperse the troops he had gathered about the capital in early July, the arrival of the Flanders Regiment in late September suggested that the king's recalcitrance as to the matter of privileges was not a sign of reluctance but a ploy and a prelude to open aggression. To make matters worse, the abolition of privileges had sparked, like the fall of the Bastille, yet another wave of emigration by nobles, and unemployment in Paris had risen considerably in July, August, and September, as the luxury trade plummeted. Poor weather conditions exacerbated the food shortage caused by the summer's unrest, fueling suspicions of an aristocratic conspiracy to starve the people into submission. Under such circumstances, the recall of the Flanders Regiment appeared to be a preparation for the reassertion of royal power over Paris and suggested to many that such reactionary elements were in the ascendancy at Versailles.

The banquet, which was tacitly understood to be a send-off for the troops, was an occasion of unrestrained revelry, and it appears to have devolved into an event of barely concealed political reaction. The boxes overlooking the stage were occupied by members of the court and, toward the end of the evening, the royal family joined the audience. The appearance of the king, the queen, and the dauphin in the royal loge prompted impassioned toasts to the king and to his family; as observers later noted, no glasses were raised to the nation. Black and white cockades, the badge of the *monarchiens,* were distributed among the guests, who promptly discarded the *tricoleur* badges of the nation. The queen's colors were raised and saluted, and in an impromptu display of inebriated loyalty, a few of the officers then scaled the boxes in a mock rescue of the monarchy. Finally, and this gesture seems to have been the critical faux pas, the same officers then returned to the stage and, allegedly, trampled underfoot the discarded colors of their imagined foe.

News of this event reached Paris on October 3, where it served as the catalyst for the second of the great performances of the October Days. Early on the morn-

Anonymous, "Banquet of the Flanders Regiment." Bibliothèque nationale de France.

ing of October 5, a crowd of between four thousand and seven thousand women, mostly market women from the faubourg Saint-Antoine and Les Halles, gathered in the courtyard of the Hôtel de Ville and set off in procession to Versailles. Bread was the ostensible goal, but since late August, radical leaders had been discussing a march on Versailles in order to relocate both the king and the National Assembly to Paris—a move that would ensure the city's safety and provide a boost for its struggling economy. The notion of a march to Versailles by the women of Paris had been raised the previous day in the Palais-Royal, and the return of the sovereigns to Paris had been proposed as one of the women's demands even before they set off that morning.

While the procession, which gathered arms along the way, was unusual simply by virtue of its composition, a number of additional factors produced an even more curious impression. Lafayette, at that time commander of the National Guard, responded to this armed insurrection with much-noted lassitude, apparently seeing no real danger in the action. As a result, he set out after the procession only hours later and only upon the insistence of the guards. Even more remarkably, the crowd included a significant number of men dressed in women's clothing—men who, far from blending inconspicuously into the crowd, seem to have been among the most vociferous of those urging the marchers to demand not merely sustenance but the return of king and queen to Paris.[34]

Encountering no opposition, the procession reached Versailles late in the afternoon. Louis received a deputation and promised to reprovision the city; his promise seemed to satisfy a good number of the protestors, and many women apparently departed for Paris. Shortly afterward, however, Lafayette arrived, too late to intervene but just in time for his National Guard of fifteen thousand (all wearing the *tricoleur*) to join those still encamped on the Place d'Armes. Shortly thereafter, Lafayette himself appeared before the king flanked by two *commissaires*, representatives delegated by Paris's governing Commune, who demanded that the royal family—for its own safety—return with them to the city. Presented with a fait accompli, Louis and his family departed from Versailles the following day and were escorted back to Paris in a triumphant, though rainy, processional.

It is tempting to read in that departure—and many have—the decisive collapse of the remote, absolutist system of monarchical authority so stunningly realized a century before by Louis XIV. Snatched from Versailles, the king had been pried loose as well from his insulated position at the center of the self-contained world of the royal court, a world in which the monarchy's political authority had emanated impersonally and absolutely from behind the veil of court ceremony and the physical grandeur and isolation of Versailles itself. However, to read in Louis's departure from Versailles a reversal of his position as absolute spectator is, in some sense, to fall prey to precisely the theatrical delusion that informed the behavior at the banquet. For the monarch and his supporters, the extravagant performances in the Royal Theater seemed to be just that—royal theater, subject solely to the spectatorial authority of the king. Yet, as the people's ensuing performances made clear, the actions that took place that evening were subject to the authority and approval not of the privileged monarchical spectator but of a new national public engendered by a newly empowered press.

It was the scrutiny of this audience in particular—an audience well-prepared to exploit such unruly behavior—that the banqueters on the private stage of Versailles neglected to consider. Perhaps more important, it was the aegis of this public gaze that conferred upon the march to Versailles its peculiar force. For the cross-dressed men who accompanied the initial procession were not, strictly speaking, attempting disguise; indeed, all accounts agree that they were easily recognized *as* men without difficulty. And such recognition (as their boisterousness suggests) was intentional, for the circumstances and the context of the march demanded not effective disguise but, to the contrary, a legible gesture, a blatant pose; transvestism here served not as a ruse but, like the bonfire unrest of the pre-Revolutionary city, as a mark of impunity, a theatrical reminder to the armed forces at Versailles that their actions were taking place in view of a larger public and that, insofar as that public was concerned, the crowd marching through the gates at Versailles was composed entirely of women. In this context the march was thus an overt challenge to the authority of the monarchical gaze, a theatrical assertion of the presence and the authority—even within Versailles itself—of the public gaze. Upon their arrival in Paris, Louis and his family were installed in the hastily refurbished Tuileries, from which, ironically, they displaced a troupe of actors. On this new stage, now one of the public's making, they would be subject over the following four years to increasingly intense, and increasingly hostile, scrutiny.[35] As Bailly, the mayor of Paris, had proclaimed as early as August, "Publicity," rather than any sort of material force, "is the people's safeguard."[36]

The first acts of political theatricality in the 1780s were distinguished by their particular disruption of sight, by their violation of the city's increasingly unstable relations between observer and observed. Those performances gained their dramatic force and their symbolic meaning by blinding royal authority, cutting off surveillance, asserting and unmasking, in public fashion, the absence of its power. This mechanism, the privileged and central gesture of the Revolution's early political action, would continue to play a fundamental popular role in the shape and development of Revolutionary theatricality, driving the obsession with plot and conspiracy, the insistence upon unveiling traitors and spies, the denunciatory frenzy of Paris during the Terror, and the savage violence of the September massacres. Revolutionary theatricality would, from the start, adopt this specific gesture—what might be termed the politics of publicity—as a central convention of its performance. It is the politics of publicity, and the gesture of unmasking specifically, that connects Paris before the Revolution to the violence of the Terror—or, to adopt Priscilla Ferguson's stronger claim, that "connect Paris in revolution to modernity."[37] Such politics define, as well, the theatrical conditions in which the languages and conventions of drama would contribute to the articulation of Revolutionary politics.

CHAPTER TWO

The Drama of the Revolution

The stage is a lie: its aim is to bring the lie close to the greatest
truth.

Louis-Sébastien Mercier (1773)

Pre-Revolutionary Acting and Theater

Despite a widespread desire for reform, French theatrical drama in the period
immediately preceding the Revolution remained tightly constrained by institutional regulation: only three theaters—the Opéra, the Comédie Française, and
the Théâtre des Italiens—enjoyed official support, and to them were granted exclusive rights over both dramatic repertoire and certain kinds of performance.[1]
During the latter half of the century, however, considerable pressures had been
brought to bear on this closed theater world, as the unlicensed theaters along
the Boulevard du Temple, in the Palais, and elsewhere attempted in various ways
to circumvent the strictures on both the legitimate dramatic repertoire and its
privileged performance modes.[2]

One way to do so was to exploit the legal separation between the aural and the
visual aspects of theatrical performance, for the monopolies held by the licensed
theaters were grounded in various ways upon theatrical speech: the Comédie was
the primary domain of spoken drama, the Opéra and the Théâtre des Italiens,
of song. Left to the fairground and boulevard theaters were the visual modes of
performance: acrobatics, jugglers, animal acts, and pantomime, as their per-
formers were barred from singing or speaking before the public. In their desire
to present plays, these theaters devised various ways in which to present purely
visual drama onstage, with offstage actors singing or speaking the parts. Puppet
shows were the most obvious means with which to accomplish such ends, but
pantomime, which had become popular in the city since the 1740s, offered an

even better solution.[3] In 1784, the Beaujolais, a "puppet" theater located in the Palais-Royal, began to employ child actors to mime the parts of plays taken from the repertoire of the Comédie, with adult actors speaking from the wings. This innovation was quickly picked up by competitors, and in 1787 the new Bluette-Comiques began having adult actors mime the parts onstage to offstage accompaniment.[4] The resulting hue and cry raised by the licensed theaters gave rise to what Marvin Carlson described as a "ludicrously complex set of police rulings," one result of which was the requirement, for the Bluette and another recent arrival, the Délassements-Comiques, that they hang a gauze curtain between the audience and the drama being mimed onstage.[5]

As is often noted, Plancher-Valcour, the director of the Délassements-Comiques, decided at some point soon after the fall of the Bastille to rip down the gauze curtain that had been prescribed for his theater, an act he accompanied with the cry "Vive la Liberté!" The act was clearly understood by contemporaries as the moment when the theaters of Paris were "liberated," freed finally of the absurd weight and ossified stricture of absolutism's institutional rule.[6] Critics have drawn from this implication the conclusion that the theaters then became a leading force in Revolutionary politics, and yet, as the work of recent theater historians has made clear, the Revolution did not give rise to a sudden richness of politically radical drama, for—as Plancher-Valcour must have sensed quite keenly after the great theatrical uprising of July 14—the theater proper had already been supplanted by the stages of Revolutionary politics.[7] In contrast, Marie-Hélène Huet reads in Plancher-Valcour's gesture a sign that "the theater provided models for public disclosure. The desire to " 'tear away the veil,' the forceful and passionate search for unmediated action," she notes, "was a constant theme of Revolutionary rhetoric."[8] However, if such a reading responds to the mode of the gesture, it misses what must have been part of its point. Certainly it is a sign of letting the public in, revealing all to its forceful and passionate eye, but it is also an act of opening the wall of the stage and letting the actors out. If Plancher-Valcour tore a veil of public disclosure, he also declared the opening of a Pandora's box of public performance, releasing into politics the entire resources of a repressed, long-oppositional theater.

Almost immediately, as Paul Friedland's recent work makes clear, large numbers of actors and dramatists turned from the stage to the streets and political platforms, emerging in some cases to prominence as Revolutionary leaders.[9] Actor-politicians included among their numbers some of the Revolution's most powerful political figures, including Collot d'Herbois, Fabre d'Eglantine, and Charles-Philippe Ronsin.[10] The advantages to be gained in the Revolution by

such capabilities as the stage provided were considerable, particularly in its earliest, most naively innocent phase; indeed, as one recent historian has observed,
Mirabeau, the leading figure of the first Revolutionary parliament, gained and
held power in part because he was the first to recognize clearly the theatrical
logic and conditions of the Revolution's new contexts of political communication
and representation.[11]

However, as contemporaries noted, the mixing of theatrical and political
representation raised from the start pressing questions as to the representational
authenticity of political performance. As one might expect, the pre-Revolutionary
period's rising sense of the artifice of social performance had been accompanied by an analogous crisis in the representational authority of acting: a crisis
defined by a fundamental shift, during the middle decades of the century, from
a notion of acting as persuasive metamorphosis to one of acting as persuasive imitation.[12] This shift, which Friedland describes as a move from the demands of
truth to those of truthfulness (from *vrai* to *vraisemblance*), altered in turn the
quality of antitheatrical prejudice, shifting its emphasis from the spectacular
threat of the actor's troubling self-transformation to the social threat of the actor's effective use of duplicity.[13] In so doing, it thus transferred the "burden of
belief" from the actor to the audience. The illusion of authenticity and the claim
to representational authority were no longer dependent upon the actor's successful metamorphosis; they relied, rather—not, perhaps, by 1750, or even 1770,
but certainly by 1789—upon the audience's acceptance of an imitation as real.[14]
This fundamental conceptual and perceptual shift, Friedland suggests, would
constitute an ongoing problem for Revolutionary politics, giving rise inevitably—
and throughout the Revolution—to accusations that actor-politicians in particular were not only false and unconvincing but also active agents of conspiracy
against the nation.[15]

The political culture that emerged with the convention of the Estates General,
in May of 1789, reflected, consciously or unconsciously, a fairly acute sense of
that problem, for it adopted in programmatic fashion a theatrical aesthetic—that
of the bourgeois *drame*—designed to overcome it. While conceptions of acting
changed, theatrical aesthetics had undergone a related process of transformation,
as the demand for theatrical *vraisemblance* called into question as well the representational authority of both neoclassical decorum and popular theatrical performance. However, rather than marking a move away from models of metamorphosis to models of imitation, the shift in theatrical aesthetics that took place
during the pre-Revolutionary period marked a shift away from a frankly theatrical stage—one that had traditionally acknowledged and foregrounded the

explicitly fictive quality of theater—to a stage devoted to the effective creation of a realist-illusionist theater, in which fiction became (or was to become) indistinguishable from life.

The move toward theatrical *vraisemblance,* once begun, proceeded by a logic that seemed, like the disillusionment of social theatricality, to be an irreversible plague of representational delegitimation. For rather than merely replacing the unconvincing with the convincing, *vraisemblance* proceeded by a strategy of comparative critique: to move toward a persuasive illusion, it drew attention to inconsistencies and flaws in the theatrical illusion, and particularly to the anachronism of theatrical representation.[16] More than merely striving for wholeness, the critique of *vraisemblance* thus also began to require the replacement of the past by the present, subjecting traditional modes of representation to the presentist demands of empirical reason.[17]

Yet, if the move toward *vraisemblance* in acting was imbued with the antitheatrical critique of late-ancien-régime society, theatrical *vraisemblance* was also tightly bound up, Friedland suggests, with the utopian desires of the rising bourgeoisie, for it made possible the establishment of the "fourth wall"—and with it the capability to use the stage as a self-contained space in which to imagine a new society.[18] Put slightly differently, theatrical *vraisemblance* can be understood both as a negative critique of ancien-régime society and an attempt to envision a theatrical scene, and through it a society, that did *not* participate in—in fact, banned and dissolved—that anxiety-producing economy of vision and desire that characterized both the space of the Palais-Royal and, through fashionable display, the public space of the city. Such a reading is consistent with the larger aesthetic concerns of the bourgeois *drame,* which aimed in many ways at transforming the theater into a transparent moral universe, autonomous of the corrupt society of court and aristocracy, in which virtue is shown to reign triumphant.[19] However, it is important to see this transformation as a steady process of disenchantment rather than a sudden rupture into utopia. The elimination of spectators from the stage was a crucial development in that process, but the move toward *vraisemblance* was carried out not as a sudden, wholesale rejection of one representational code for another but as a gradually accelerating process of shearing away the conventional authority of traditional theatrical presentation, of cutting off anachronism until the picture seemed "right" for a moment.

The particular strategies by which this aim was to be achieved were specific. To the elaborate costuming and extreme emphasis on declamation that characterized acting at the Comédie, Diderot opposed an attitude of absorption, in which the actor's engagement in a task would render him or her oblivious to observation, allowing the presentation of unfeigned, expressive gesture, and sober attire, clearly indicative of one's social function, freed from the ironic gesture and posturing of fashion.[20] Similarly, theatrical action—that is to say, the local movement and representation of dramatic action, independent of larger generic considerations—was to be structured in accordance with the functional and familial relations that obtained between the characters. This focus was to be accompanied by a correspondent shift in favored theatrical effects: the *coup de théâtre*, indicative of the changeable fortunes, arbitrary decisions, and superficial status of the court (and of ephemeral fashion), was to yield to the *tableau*, a moment of harmonious inevitability that clarified—visually—the connection between virtuous action and favorable circumstance.[21]

The specific logic of bourgeois theatrical *vraisemblance* would play a powerful role throughout the Revolution, but its influence is most apparent, as one would expect, in the performance of early and pre-Revolutionary politics, in which the impulse toward political change was still understood as a process of radical reform rather than violent revolt. The Abbé Sieyès's *Qu'est-ce que le Tiers Etat?* (Jan. 1789), the most influential pamphlet of the Revolution's formative political culture, described the task of the estates in terms strikingly resonant with the aims of the Diderotian theater: to neutralize the ill effects of the parasitic nobility, exposing and banishing from the stage those who are "without function and without usefulness" and, in so doing, to establish and reveal the "true relations" between individuals in society.[22] In fact, just these theatrical imperatives seemed to mark the success of these new actors' first performance, the procession that opened the Estates General; there, as Jean Starobinski pointed out, observers were scandalized by the glaring contrast between the plain, functional clothing and sober demeanor of the Third Estate and the ornate, insistently theatrical robes and silks of the nobility and the clergy.[23]

This early political appropriation of bourgeois theatricality, immensely powerful in 1789, reached its highpoint in Jacques-Louis David's attempt to commemorate the Tennis Court Oath, that moment in June when the delegates of the self-declared National Assembly, threatened with forceful dissolution by the king's troops, vowed to remain in permanent assembly until they had established a constitution for the nation.

No other event during the Revolution so satisfied Diderot's demands for a moment of harmonious inevitability that revealed true social relations, a moment that clarified the connection between virtuous action and favorable circumstance

Facing page: Jacques-Louis David, *The Oath of the Tennis Court*, June 20, 1789, preparatory drawing (1791).

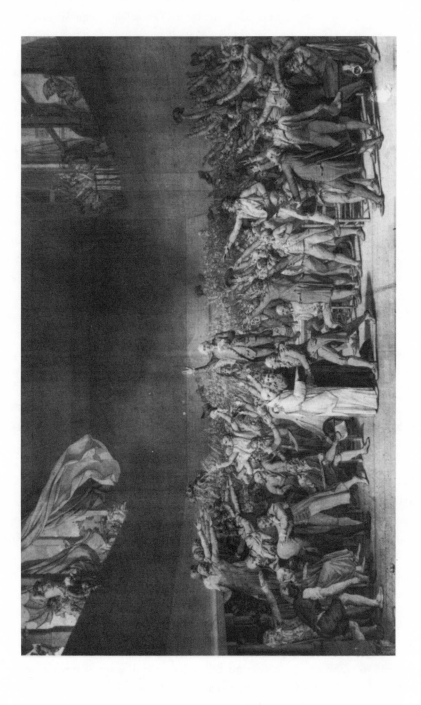

and, in so doing, conveyed the promise of a reformed society. In keeping with the title question of Sieyès's pamphlet, the Tennis Court Oath suggested that the Third Estate, in its constitution of the new nation, might in fact "become something."[24] Appropriately, David's rendering of the event was composed with exacting tableau logic, offering not only a journalistic record of the event but a precise image of its culminating theatrical moment.

Such strategies were not entirely persuasive, however. First, theatrical *vraisemblance*, as Rousseau had already pointed out, was still theater, and the theater, even if it displays images of virtuous action, does so through the false medium of actors. Acting, according to Rousseau, thus frustrates in practice any notion of a *vraisemblable* theater, for the actor, whether pursuing metamorphosis or persuasive imitation, cannot avoid duplicity.[25] In Rousseau's terms, the inevitable recognition that such scenes as *The Tennis Court Oath* involved theatrical representation, the fact that these figures stand not as themselves but as surrogates for others, as *representatives*, frustrated the sense of authenticity they attempted to produce.[26] By requiring some acknowledgment of that audience on whose behalf political action was being carried out, the politics of theatrical *vraisemblance* was fatally flawed, if not oxymoronic, for it attempted to yoke a social philosophy of virtue and transparency to a medium and a practice fundamentally productive of deceit and immorality.[27]

From Rousseau's perspective, the way to avoid this problem was to discard "theater" altogether or to change the very nature of theatrical performance. The solution (one that would resonate deeply in the political culture of the Revolution) was to eliminate the very concept of *rôles*, to collapse the distinction between actors and audience, to replace the theater, in short, with the public festival. "Let the spectators become an entertainment to themselves," he urges, "make them actors themselves; do it so that each sees and loves himself in the others so that all will be better united."[28] Rousseau's concept of the festival as a means of testifying to communal unity would of course find direct application in the spectacular public festivals of the Revolution.[29] However, his argument suggests as well some of the troubling contradictions that the political culture of the Revolution would face, for Rousseau insists here not on *vraisemblance* but on absolute theatrical transparency, on the elimination of any substantive divide between public and private identity, between actors and audience.

But the tableau of the Tennis Court Oath—as an event, not only as a picture— raised other problems as well, problems having to do with the temporal mechanism of the tableau and its relation to the larger trajectory of Revolutionary politics. If the Tennis Court Oath was a moment that was to have revealed the true relations of the various members of the new Nation, it was also a moment that testified to the uncertainty, provisionality, and incompleteness of those relations, for the oath itself marked not the achievement of a natural political community but the announcement of a moment when "everyone" expressed a shared desire for such an achievement. The vow offered by the representatives was to remain in session *until a constitution was established.* In this sense the scene became visible not as a tableau of autonomous constitution and dramatic closure, not a moment of Diderotian denouement, but as a moment of defiance—a seizing of the stage or, more specifically, the announcement of a new, *vraisemblable* theater of politics, set in self-imposed exile from its assigned spot at Versailles, in which would be staged the new drama of a Revolutionary nation. Indeed, David's dramatic rendering of the delegates is not quite a self-contained *tableau.* It testifies, in the outward gaze of the spectators situated in the upper left corner and in the barely discernible lightning bolt visible through those windows, to the external presence and power of the king—a power now relegated to the background and outside the frame and space of action but nonetheless still very present.[30] In this gesture of defiance, the Tennis Court Oath, and indeed the larger Diderotian rhetoric of politics leading up to the autumn of 1789, participated less in a constitutive politics of national identity than in the establishment of what Thomas Crow has aptly described as a culture of disruption.[31]

Within months, David's tableau would become obsolete, its apparent *vraisemblance* marred, in Friedland's terms, by "vestiges of the old theater" that had become "glaringly apparent." In the foreground, for example, is the figure of Mirabeau, then the leading orator and exemplary representative of the Assembly. By the time this drawing was exhibited, viewers would have been aware of his secret correspondence, even then, with the royal family.[32] But the problem was not merely the duplicity of Mirabeau: if the Tennis Court Oath rendered obsolete, within its Diderotian logic, the now-distanced spectacle of royal power, the fall of the Bastille—as we have seen in the preceding chapter—displaced in turn such an intimate, relatively controlled theater of Revolutionary politics.

These events provide more than a clear delineation of the particular problems and challenges that would face the Revolution's political actors; they also define, in fairly precise terms, the initial formation of the Revolution's political theater. However, they are in themselves incomplete, for what they do not address are the conditions and problems that would inform Revolutionary efforts to shape such theatrical events into narratives of meaningful—that is to say, historical— action. To understand those, it is necessary to take a closer look at two additional transformations in pre-Revolutionary France: first, the period's changing conception not only of theater but also of drama, both as a form and in its "dual sense," to adopt Michael McKeon's terms, "as a formalistic genre and as a mode of representing the world";[33] and, second, the period's altered conception of history and of historical change.

Pre-Revolutionary Drama and History

The central thesis of Paul Friedland's work is the hypothesis that the French Revolution can be understood as having involved two coincident "revolutions," one theatrical and the other political, in representational authority. These complementary revolutions, Friedland asserts, were themselves "manifestations of an underlying revolution in the very categories of perception, in the way that individuals made sense of the world around them."[34] What I am suggesting here is that this "underlying revolution" involved a second, similarly dialectical pair of revolutionary transformations in contemporary perceptions of drama and history. These revolutions can be understood as related in many ways to the theatrical and political revolutions, for they were shaped and driven by similar forces of change and were articulated, moreover, by the same radical thinkers.

As Claudio Guillén observed, literary genres, including most prominently those of the drama, were "until the Romantic or pre-Romantic age" understood "as occupying a terrain whose components evolve over centuries, as ever-changing models for which we must find a place in a literary system or polysystem that sustains a definite moment in the evolution of poetic forms."[35] This conception of genres was "historical and dynamic," but change was understood as slow variation within a "historically given" structure, as Wellek pointed out when he noted (citing Boileau as his example) that neoclassical criticism felt little awareness of the need to provide a typological rationale of genre.[36] Rather than being understood as "rationalist constructions," genres were instead considered as "established and conditioned social complexes," what Wellek, adopting Kant's terminology, described as "a 'regulative' concept, some underlying pattern which is real, i.e. effective."[37] In this view, genre is effective in part "because it actually moulds the writing of concrete works."[38] However, Guillén gets closer to the mechanism of genre's force before romanticism when he suggests that "pragmatically, or from the point of view of the reader (or, more accurately, readers: the public), genre implies not only contact but contract. It is what Hans Robert Jauss has named deftly . . . [a] 'horizon of expectations.'"[39]

As the work of Reinhardt Koselleck suggests, between about 1550 and the middle of the eighteenth century, history was understood in closely homologous terms. The rationalist political prognostication of the seventeenth-century, he notes, had "a static temporal structure insofar as it operated in terms of natural magnitudes whose potential repeatability formed the cyclical character of its history."[40] History was understood as dynamic, but "to the extent that the past [could] only be experienced insofar as it contain[ed] an element of that which is to come (and vice versa), the political existence of the state remain[ed] trapped within a temporal structure that can be understood as static movement."[41] That is to say, things changed, but only within a structure that remained fixed. Rather than being understood as rationalist constructions, constitutional forms were instead considered to comprise—like genre—a closed set of historically given possibilities, and politics "consisted in evading a threatened natural decline through a just combination of forms."[42] Until the eighteenth century, history maintained an exemplary value based upon "an assumed constancy of human nature": "If there occurred a degree of social change," Koselleck observes, "it took place so slowly and at such a pace that the utility of past examples was maintained." Thus, "the temporal structure of past history bounded a continuous space of potential experience."[43] Like genre, history was thus understood as a regulative concept, a set of exemplary forms whose efficacy was demonstrated by their "repeatability" and whose force relied upon their ability to provide a plausible horizon of expectations.

During the eighteenth century, however, "progress opened a future that transcended the hitherto predictable, natural space of time and experience."[44] The "future of this progress" was characterized by two primary features: its increasing speed and its unknown quality—unknown, Koselleck notes, "because this accelerated time abbreviated the space of experience, robbed them of their constancy, and continually brought into play unknown factors, so that even the actuality or complexity of these unknown quantities could not be ascertained." The "bearer of the modern philosophy of historical progress" was "the citizen emancipated from absolutist subjection and the tutelage of the Church: the *prophète philosophe*, as he was once strikingly characterized in the eighteenth century . . . Lessing has described this type for us: he often 'takes well-judged prospects of the future,'" but he nonetheless resembles the visionary, 'for he cannot wait for the future. He wants this future to come more quickly, and he himself wants to accelerate it . . . for what has he to gain if that which he recognizes as the better is actually not to be realized in his lifetime?'"[45]

The product of this acceleration was a fundamental shift from history understood as a collection of exempla to history understood as difference. What was common to all historical theory between 1760 and 1780 was "the destruction of the exemplary nature of past events and, in its place, the discovery of the uniqueness of historical processes and the possibility of progress . . . Nature [the unchanging, given structure of the world] and history could now conceptually part."[46] Bringing about that separation, working "through the past as quickly as possible so that a new future could be set free," was, as Koselleck points out, "the declared objective of the *Encyclopédie* . . . 'Once, one knew exempla; today, only rules,' said Diderot."

The development of dramatic genre in the late eighteenth century can be understood in similar terms. Just as progress opened a future that transcended the "natural space" of time and experience, so too did it reveal a widening gap between the character of lived experience and the "established and conditioned social complexes" articulated in traditional dramatic form. And just as the philosophes were the bearers of the modern philosophy of progress, so too were they the bearers of the modern concept of dramatic genre. If historical theory between 1760 and 1780 shared an active commitment to the destruction of the exemplary nature of past events, dramatic theory during the same period shared an active commitment to the destruction of the exemplary nature of traditional genre.

In what amounts to the manifesto of the bourgeois *drame*, the 1773 essay *Du Théâtre*, Mercier asserts that the goal of this new drama is to provide a clear idea "of the stamp of our characters, the turn of our imaginations, of the manner in which, finally, we envisage the throne and court, and the lively and transient revolutions (*les révolutions vives et passagères*) that emanate from it" and thus to offer "the picture (*tableau*) of our actual ways of living."[47] In part, this goal was to be attained by an adjustment of class perspectives, a reorientation of dramatic focus on the domestic culture of the bourgeoisie and a closer adherence to the experience of daily life. As recent scholars have shown, this effort functioned as the dramatic complement of theatrical *vraisemblance,* bringing the drama's action within the more familiar sphere of familial action, reconfiguring dramatic crisis in terms of personal and social conflict and contributing, in so doing, to that greater sense of intimacy and authenticity toward which theatrical reform was aimed.[48]

While such a focus was understood in part as an effort to produce a new positive form of drama, its procedure and effect, like that of theatrical *vraisemblance,* involved not the sudden rejection of one representational code for another but a gradual and accelerating process of undermining and exposing as unrealistic the conventional aspects of traditional genre—a process of interrogating the limits and anachronistic social complexes of tragedy and comedy especially.

Hence Diderot, in his *Discours sur la poésie dramatique* (1758), explains that in *Le Fils naturel* (1757) he had tried to "give an idea of a drama that was between Comedy and Tragedy" and in *La Père de famille* (1758) to interrogate the space "between the serious drama (*le genre sérieux*) of the *Le Fils naturel* and Comedy," and that, if he had the time and courage, he would write a play that would stand "between the serious drama and Tragedy." Whether or not his audience enjoyed the works was of secondary value for Diderot; what mattered was that the plays demonstrate "that the gap . . . between the two established genres," like the in-between social complex of the emergent bourgeoisie, "is not imaginary."[49]

As was the case with the effort to establish theatrical *vraisemblance,* the desire for dramatic truthfulness became bound up not only with social and class gaps but also with temporal gaps, and in that sense late-eighteenth-century drama can be thought of as an effort to subject genre to the scrutiny of time, drawing it into consonance with the present. Such efforts certainly predate the later eighteenth century, as Voltaire's historical tragedies make obvious, but it is in the period leading up to and immediately preceding the Revolution that the accelerating drive toward contemporaneity—this "working through the past as quickly as possible so that the future might be set free"—begins to take on its full radical potential in the drama, and it is in Beaumarchais's *Le Mariage de Figaro* (1784), especially, that the political force of such strategies becomes most evident.

Today, the politics of *Le Mariage* seem to many not only questionable but doubtful.[50] As many have pointed out, this is, after all, a play that frames its politics within a comedy of intrigue. It contains some radical statements (such as Figaro's famous soliloquy on the chance nature of social status), but these are unexceptional for the time, and the social structure and interaction of the play belong firmly to the world of the ancien régime. Figaro is a revolutionary character in a formal sense, but he is not on the face of it a political actor; his concern, rather, is to prevent his master, Count Almaviva, from taking advantage of Suzanne, his fiancée. Desire, not politics, drives the action, and most of the characters, including Almaviva, Rosine (the countess), Suzanne, and Chérubin (Almaviva's page), are wholly wrapped up in a dizzying game of frustrated and uncontrollable love. By comparison to the play's many scenes of masquerade and disguise, assignation and evasion, domestic intimacy and traditional comic festivity, its few moments of outright social drama seem both limited and secondary. Even the play's most obvious antagonists—the scheming Bartholo (the doctor), Bazile (the countess's music instructor), and Marceline (the household maid)—are presented not as representatives of any sort of political regime but as anachronistic schemers drawn from the ridiculous world of Italian comedy.

The count's threat to exercise his *"droit du seigneur"* (a feudal lord's legendary right to supplant his servant in the marriage bed on the wedding night) carries some symbolic political force, but it serves primarily as a catalyst for a delightful series of amorous evasions and pursuits. Similarly, Marceline's threat to exercise her legal right to Figaro's hand in marriage (on the basis of an unpaid debt) can be viewed as a political comment, and Marceline is certainly given some lines of direct political critique, but that threat evaporates midway through the play, and her radical commentary on gender inequality was cut at the insistence of the actors.

Yet what is so interesting about such evaluations is, not least, the degree to which they clash with contemporary assessments, even those three epigrammatic judgments that have become commonplaces in critical introductions: Louis XVI's flat statement that "the Bastille would have to be pulled down before such a play is staged"; Danton's remark, that "Figaro killed the nobility"; and Napoleon's assessment of the play as "the Revolution in action." Not only were these not lighthearted remarks, but together they offer a fairly precise, serious description of the play's political force as it was anticipated, recognized, and retrospectively assessed during the Revolutionary era.[51] The most interesting for my purposes is the last of these comments, that of someone who could hardly be called a refined drama critic but who embodied, for contemporaries, the idea of the Revolution "in action." Why describe *Le Mariage* in such terms, as the Revolution in *action* rather than the Revolution in idea, or spirit, or message? Napoleon's remark foregrounds *performance*, not theme: it stresses the play's dynamic rather than its voice. Examined in terms of the argument I have been developing, the plot's action not only implies revolution but—like the theatrical gang violence of the St. John's Day bonfire—also demonstrates it. The means by which Beaumarchais achieves this effect is precisely that of temporal acceleration—by driving the action of the play relentlessly into the present moment and, in so doing, bringing the horizon of revolutionary expectation into the span of a day.

The principal method by which Beaumarchais gains acceleration in *Le Mariage*, as in *Le Barbier de Séville* (1775) is simply pace: his return to plot-driven comedy is the underpinning structural engine in these two of the trilogy's three plays especially, and recognition of the effect of such a choice upon contemporary audiences should not be underestimated.[52] However, the temporal compression of *Le Mariage* is magnified, both internally and in relation to both *Barber* and *La Mère coupable* (*The Guilty Mother*, 1792), by Beaumarchais's *dynamicization* of the dramatic narrative. That is, *Le Barbier* modifies internally from farcical to romantic comedy, *Le Mariage* from romantic to social comedy, and *La Mère Coupable* from social comedy to *drame*.[53] Beaumarchais's generic assignments are sometimes taken to be ambivalent, as if the point were only uncertainty, but the narrative trajectory of the trilogy, linked through each play, is pointedly progressive and historical, articulating a foreshortened move through the history of dramatic form.

Beaumarchais's well-known dynamicization of character—the manner in which he employed a group of characters who appear or are mentioned in all of the plays but change with them—is linked to this narrative technique, but it is generally understood to signify the characters' growth and development. Less often noted is the manner in which the dynamicization of character highlights the successive failure of anachronistic, and particularly patriarchal, models of authority, and the manner in which the plays thus highlight not the growth of individuals but generational changes in social and political authority.[54] Bartholo and Bazile are only the most obvious examples of that critique, which extends, arguably, in *Le Mariage*, to the monarch himself. In this second work, moreover, we see not simply the same group again, but one now situated within a larger society, and the characters added are drawn as sketches of types from everyday life.

Such characterization in turn allowed Beaumarchais to foreshorten the dramatic depiction of social practice and custom. The *droit du seigneur*, of course, is deliberately anachronistic—less a reference to a real legal threat than a gesture toward Almaviva's archaic idea of patriarchal right. Against it is set practices of extreme contemporaneity: the play is driven by fashion—costumes change continually, cross-dressing is constant and identity (and authority) determined throughout by appearance. The focus is pointed and political. The play opens with a lord idly pursuing skirts, hiding behind an invalid's chair piled with dresses, displaced and trading places with a wanton boy who is both a cross-dressing actress and an ironic figure of uncontrollable, indiscriminate lust. The resonances are playful, but at the time they must also have strongly echoed the problems and threats of the city's social life. That Beaumarchais chose to conclude with a fireworks gone wrong is more pointed yet; the tone may be playful, but what we are shown is a crowd in the dark, misrecognitions right and left, and more than a few corrective acts of retributive violence.

Such social proximity is in itself a threatening gesture, but to it Beaumarchais added a similarly close, foreshortened picture of politics. From the implied indictment of libertine excess in act 1, the play moves by act 3 to a literal indictment of the king—or his portrait, which surmounts that act's action and serves as the implicit target of all its address. To it are directed, by implication, Figaro's repeated profanity as well as his scathing description of politics as sordid intrigue carried out by hapless, blinkered, cowering hypocrites, a description that must have seemed—given the play's very performance—to come close to a public denunciation of Louis XVI (III.v).

It is here that a censor could simply have stopped stop reading; however, Beaumarchais goes further, for the trial not only reveals the corruption of the courts but also serves to give Figaro power. Recognized by his scar (saved by the noble standard of epic recognition), he becomes immune to the threat of the law. By the play's end, he serves actively as the lord of the estate, his status apparent both in his busy management of the other servants and in Suzanne's closing assumption of the countess's dress (and the countess's less-expected adoption of her servant's). Confronted by Almaviva in act 5, he mocks him by aping fear ("It's my Master!" [V.x]) and, shortly after, yields to the count's demand for answers only because he can't see anyone with the authority to exempt him from such a demand (V.xii).[55]

In this light, Figaro's act 5 soliloquy (V.iii), considered by many to be an overlong autobiographical reflection, may be recognized as a highly contemporary, even anticipatory, reflection—addressed to the audience—on the political moment: "Everybody starts arguing," but who's in control? "It's you, it's him, it's me, no, it's not us, so who is it then?"[56] Power is vacant, or dictated by a distinctly *ephemeral* chance ("sometimes master, sometimes servant").[57] Finally, Figaro's question is not "Why did this happen" but "*How* did it happen?"[58] And, significantly, "Why these things and not others?"[59] Why, for example, did this play happen, and not (yet) the fall of the Bastille? A "fantastic series of events," as he puts it.[60] In a formal sense, then, Napoleon was right: Beaumarchais's play was the revolution in action, offering in its movement from the past to the present a dynamic image of social collapse.

The political implications of Beaumarchais's play were tied directly, I think, to this compressive critique of the past. As Koselleck notes in his discussion of the historical idea of revolution, by this time the concept, "originally naturalistic and as such transhistorical," had "extended its partially metaphorical meaning: each and every thing was comprehended through it. Movement abandoned its naturalistic background and entered the reality of everyday life." Novelty and change, in a temporal sense, had become *daily* phenomena, making plain the obsolescence of historical exempla and radically constricting the horizon of expectation produced by events. The effect of this widening gap "between previous experience and coming expectation" was that "lived time was experienced as a rupture, as a period in which the new and the unexpected continually happened."[61] In short, by the time of *Figaro,* history had come to seem similarly dynamic, and revolution to be seen, like Beaumarchais's drama, as the possibility or the follies "of a day," as the play's subtitle and closing song put it. As such, it suddenly fit the narrative scale of the drama, and the possibilities offered by the performance of history merged with those implied by the performance of Beaumarchais's play. Put differently, Figaro's questions were, for their audience, pressing and real. If these things could be acted, why not others? If this play could be staged, who could possibly be in charge?.

Revolutionary Drama and History

If the development of history before the French Revolution militated against the authority of traditional drama, the onset of the Revolution, almost paradoxically, reversed this situation. That is, the authority of traditional drama suddenly became an asset rather than a constraint. For in the Revolution's upending and reversal of representational authority, and with the establishment of a Revolutionary theater of action governed by the politics of publicity, the need for common, broadly recognized narratives of performance became pressing. In short, the representational crisis that had characterized pre-Revolutionary political culture was replaced by a representational void. "The characteristic feature of the Revolution," François Furet pointed out, "was a situation in which power was perceived by everyone as vacant, as having become intellectually and practically available."[62] Moreover, as Lynn Hunt observed, "There was no Revolutionary Bible that could serve as a source of confirmation and sanctification of Revolutionary practice."[63] What was needed was not merely an appropriate rhetoric of Revolutionary politics; like both drama and historical exempla, the language of Revolutionary action had also to provide a plausible horizon of expectation. In Mona Ozouf's succinct formulation, "the most urgent task," once the Revolution had begun, was "to decide on the narrative of the Revolutionary events."[64]

Doing so was, even by October of 1789, a difficult task for the Revolution's political actors, for as we have seen, the October Days had registered a profound shift in the discursive context of political action. By now, certainly, Huet's reading of Plancher-Valcour's torn curtain rings true, for after October the public stage of Revolutionary politics was certainly marked by an insistence upon public disclosure. With startling rapidity, the Revolution's new leaders found themselves acting not before the limited sphere of informed opinion, an audience apt to sympathize with the Diderotian theater of the Tennis Court, but before a much larger and more diverse audience, and one now informed by a press that was well prepared to critique—and even to try to script—the performance. "Whatever historians may think," Popkin reminds us, "the journalists of the time did write as if the newspapers could set out scripts and guidelines to prepare the actors on the Revolutionary stage for their parts," and there are numerous examples of such scripting in Revolutionary history, both by French papers and—as I show in Chapter 4—by the foreign press.[65]

Despite the rise of the press, however, Revolutionary politics and the scripting of a Revolutionary narrative were still tied fundamentally to performance rather than to journalism: Hunt has pointed out, for example, that "the spoken word retained its supremacy" at least "to 1794, and perhaps to 1799," not least because of the central importance, in such an anxious discursive context, of performative speech.[66] In consequence, the expansion and scrutiny of the theater of politics was accompanied by a concomitant intensification of the performance of Revolutionary politics: the common gestures, characters, conventions, and forms of the theater became even more fundamental to political performance, constituting together one of the very few languages of political action and social critique shared by a substantial cross-section of French society. And this expanded audience was not merely situated at second hand, through the press; the Assembly itself, now relocated to Paris, had begun to draw such substantial audiences that it was blamed by contemporaries for having detrimental effects on the theater.[67] To a degree that distinguished it markedly from the Estates General, the National Assembly began consciously to adopt the ways of the theater: representatives began to play to the galleries, to provide transcripts of their speeches to the press in advance, to hone their gestural skills and their oratorical delivery through lessons with professional actors.[68] Such efforts were often disparaged by political commentators (including, ironically, Edmund Burke), but they also attracted in certain instances genuine admiration; the actor Molé, Angelica Goodden notes, "greatly admired Mirabeau, and regarded him as having a profound, not a trivial, feeling for dramatic performance."[69]

It is in these conditions that the drama of the French Revolution may be understood as having begun. The problem of shearing away the past had been overcome; the follies of a day had become the fall of the Bastille, and with that breakthrough into Revolutionary performance history had now become dramatic. This was not only a metaphorical relation; like the relation between theater and politics, that between drama and history during this period is better understood as a conceptual merging. More specifically, it seems to have been the product of what might best be understood as a temporal convergence, a brief period during which the accelerating foreclosure of historical time, and thus of exemplary historical action's potential horizon of expectation, passed through the durational window of a day—and thus into, and through, the space of drama as a narrative form.

At the same time, however, it is equally important to recognize that the same process of accelerated change had stripped the drama of its own capability to carry exemplary authority. As Beaumarchais had shown, the drama, and not only history, had now become the matter of a day. In Diderot's terms, there were, by the Revolution, "no examples; only rules."

Comedy

> The comic poet . . . will unmask before our eyes the rogue and the
> hypocrite, showing them to us in their true character; he will put
> the honest, decent man in the various crucial situations of life,
> and he will take care to place him in a light that will fill us high
> regard and affection for him.

> *Johann Georg Sulzer, s.v. "Comédie,"* Encyclopédie *(1755–1780)*

> The only way to save the State and the nascent constitution is to
> put the King in a position which will permit him to form an im-
> mediate coalition with his people.

> *Mirabeau, secret correspondence with the royal family,*
> *October 15, 1789*

If the reconfiguration of the political theater in October of 1789 makes evident the strength of the radical desire to "tear away the veil" of political artifice, it suggests nothing of the popular strength of the desire—among moderates, and nationally—to repair rather than rupture the political fabric of the nation.[70] It should not be surprising, then, that Revolutionary politicians responded to 1789s crisis of political and theatrical representation by appropriating that most quotidian and reassuring of dramatic genres—comedy—as the guiding structure and principle of political action. Such a genre appealed for obvious reasons, not least the simple fact that most people, including the nation's political leaders, had difficulty imagining how the Revolution might be ended and the new Nation founded in the absence of the king. In 1789, and until the summer of 1791, reconciliation was the overwhelming impulse of the day.

The theater offers overwhelming evidence of such sentiment. In stark contrast to what we might expect after *Le Mariage de Figaro* had so thoroughly deconstructed traditional comedy's patriarchal obsolescence, both the legitimate and the illegitimate theaters turned strongly toward inherited form.[71] Not only did the comedies of Molière and Marivaux enjoy renewed appeal, but contemporary dramatists produced work that looks, in comparison to *Figaro*, almost reactionary—and not only in its embrace of patriarchal authority. *Nicodème dans la lune* (1790), a "folly in prose" by Beffroy de Reigny, was the period's most popular drama, and it offers a telling contrast to Beaumarchais's sharply contemporaneous work.[72] Rather than driving the stage into the moment, its action is displaced to the moon, and the society that is encountered there is not that of Revolutionary Paris but that of the ancien régime, still intact, governed by an emperor whose rule remains untouched by political revolt or even rebellious unrest. That the play refers everywhere to France's current situation is obvious— indeed, de Reigny's subtitle is "The Pacific Revolution"—but its political message is almost nostalgic in its sensibility: to restore peace, the emperor need only heed the counsels of *"honnêtes gens"* (decent gentlemen) and reunite himself with the humblest of his subjects. More than merely testifying to a desire to turn back the clock, *Nicodème* evinces everywhere a desire to draw away from the sort of explicitness and immediacy of *Figaro;* it is not a pointed critique but a delicate allusion, not a scathing realistic portrait of a corrupt government and impotent monarch but a soothing fantasy of a more distanced, more reassuring construction of royal power.

Political performance pursued a similar course. Lynn Hunt has suggested that "in the first months of Revolution, most rhetoric was unconsciously shaped by what Northrop Frye terms the 'generic plot' of comedy."[73] In a sense this observation seems right; the markers of comic characterization and structure permeate the rhetoric of the early Revolution, and all the patterns of Frye's archetype can be easily found.[74] Moreover, there is not in the rhetoric of this period, as there would be much later, when politics turned tragic, any use of explicit dramatic exempla; no prominent dramatic roles are invoked as personae, no well-known dramas brought into rhetorical play. However, to conclude from such signals that this shaping was "unconscious" seems difficult to accept, given what we have seen of the context of rhetorical performance. It is true, for example, that Mirabeau does not say, in his correspondence with the royal family, that a comedy must be staged; but it is difficult to imagine that his injunction to "put the king in a position which will permit him to form an immediate coalition with his people" was an unconscious appropriation of comedy's rules and possibilities.

Instead, I suggest that this "shaping" of the Revolution's political comedy was—like the theaters' move away from Beaumarchais's distance-collapsing aesthetic—deliberately implicit, and it was understood that it had to remain so in order to work. For the king, explicitness would have meant admitting what could not be admitted: his willing participation in a humbling play. For the Revolution's leading actors, it would have meant announcing not only that politics was scripted and staged but also that the leaders of the people had chosen to participate in, and to help stage, a restoration of traditional master-servant relations. For both, as for the public, it would have shown the mythic structure of the nation—the familial conjunction of the king and his people, the idea of the *corpus mysticum* upon which the nation's royal authority was grounded—to be a theatrical choice, not a natural state. In consequence, the early Revolution's comedy had perforce to be tacit: not unconscious but implied.

At the same time, what such a comedy meant and how it would be played out were seen differently by each of these parties. For the king, a successful comedy was a necessary condition of survival, for without it the monarchy would have no place in the household of the nation. For the right, the appeal of comedy meant much the same thing: if the king could tumble, then perhaps he might not fall. For progressives and radicals, however, the prospect of a comic roll was perhaps more consequential—not merely a traditional comic correction, but, like *Le Mariage de Figaro*, a means by which to set the anachronism of monarchy in relief and thus to hasten the lessening power of patriarchal authority. Such a reading is supported by Gumbrecht's observation that Mirabeau, in persuading his colleagues on July 16, 1789, to "thank the king—in the face of all contrary evidence—for having proved himself a true father of the people," did so primarily to put the king in a position in which he could not *refuse* to accept a humbling reunion with the nation.[75]

There was another reason for such delicacy. Like all comedies, the Revolution required, for its resolution to be attained, the unveiling and expulsion of a blocking figure—in this case the aristocracy—that stood between the natural people and their head, impeding the gaze and operation of justice, standing in as the catalyst and source of disorder and serving as the sacrificial totem of a renewed relation of originary harmony. The gesture of unmasking a deceitful aristocracy, a gesture as vaguely and opportunistically defined as one might expect, was in such a situation a forceful use of comedy's possibilities.[76] For the Revolution's political leaders, that move could be cast as the tearing aside of a constraining veil, much like the curtain of the Délassement-Comiques, so as to achieve a clear view of power; for the monarchy, it could be represented as the removal of a parasitic imposter by the reasserted gaze of the just king. In short, a comic expulsion of the aristocracy offered both sides a way to avert the threat of their own unmasking—but again, such a move precluded any recognition of politics as theatrical play.

In a sense, the comic drama of Revolutionary politics can be understood then as raising very much the same problem of representational authority as that produced by the Tennis Court Oath, namely, producing an illusion of authenticity by means of the exposure of artifice. The comic Revolution's exemplary expression of that problem is found in a similarly theatrical moment: the Festival of Federation, held on the first anniversary of the fall of the Bastille and dedicated to the immediate reunion of the king and his people.[77] On the one hand, the festival is understood to have been the closest thing the Revolution produced to a Rousseauist ceremony of transparent communion. The people themselves prepared the ground for the event, digging an enormous amphitheater in the Champ de Mars for the spectacle. Louis XVI assisted in those efforts, and his participation was taken to be a clear indication of his genuine desire for reconciliation.[78] By all accounts the impulse for such communal harmony was strong, and the festival produced a powerful illusion of community.

On the other hand, like the Tennis Court Oath, the Festival of Federation seemed unable to avoid the implications of its own negative critique. First, the anthem of the event, the *Ça ira*, undercut such easy ideas of peace and harmony, for its leading verse ("Ça ira, les aristocrates à la lanterne! Crèvent les aristocrats" [The aristocrats to the lantern! Die aristocrats]) was a constant reminder of the troubling problem of who possessed spectacular authority in this new community.[79] Moreover, the king's own participation in the event begged precisely the same questions, for his central role in the festivities could not but frustrate the communal transparency of the event. As Gumbrecht observed, the participant of a festival "experiences the respective other as 'sovereign' but at the same time he also imagines himself in precisely this role. This experience, according to Rousseau, is blocked in the collective receptive situation of the theatre because it draws the attention of all the spectators to the events on stage and puts its fictional situation as an 'obstacle' between the spectators' gaze, which, in the festival, 'becomes transparent' to one another."[80]

Such tensions must have been apparent to the participants, for the king's role in the festival was, ironically, a repudiation of the claims of the people's absolute gaze: they could not see through to each other, despite their rhetoric about aristocrats and lanterns. The only way the festival could be seen as a success was to restore precisely those hierarchical relations that the lantern executions had contested and claimed to reverse. Put more simply, the illusion of the Festival of Federation—and that of the comedy of the Revolution—depended upon the perceived authenticity of the king's role as "father of his people." Otherwise, he was nothing other than another impediment.

Moderates and conservatives, in particular, attempted to maintain the viability of this comic rhetoric as long as possible, as it offered the strongest grounds upon which to bring the political changes of the Revolution to a stable conclusion. In a circular letter of April 1791, the foreign minister, de Montmorin, explained to the ambassadors of France how they should interpret the king's role in the Revolution's events:

> His Majesty convoked the Estates General of His kingdom . . . This provisional legislative act . . . sufficiently announced His Majesty's wish to reinstate to the nation all its rights . . . The Estates General assembled and adopted the name of National Assembly; very soon, a constitution, fitting to serve the happiness of France and the monarch, replaced the ancient order of things, in which the apparent power of the monarchy had covered but the actual power of the abuses of certain aristocratic corpses . . . What is called Revolution is nothing but the annihilation of the heap of abuses which had been accumulating for centuries through the errors of the people or the power of the ministers, which had never been the power of the kings; these abuses were not less lamentable for the monarch than they were to the nation . . . they no longer exist . . . this is the French Revolution.[81]

The potential popular appeal of de Montmorin's narrative is obvious, and it was by no means at odds with prevailing opinion in the National Assembly and among propertied citizens, whose perspective was more skeptical. For most moderates, the Revolution had, with the adoption of the constitution, reached its logical conclusion; social change could be instantiated in due time, in an orderly fashion, but the most pressing need was the establishment of stability. Such convictions were lent greater strength by further changes in the theatrical organization of Revolutionary politics, for the dominance of the Assembly was, by the summer of 1790, already being challenged by the popular societies and clubs that had arisen in the wake of the July Days, and in these the Revolution's radical voices gained strength.

The flight to Varennes, however, made such a resolution incomprehensible. The detailed circumstances and actions of the Varennes episode are fascinating in themselves, and they have been explored by many historians, but even the basic outline of events makes clear how and why this moment had such a decisive impact on the Revolution's politics.[82] On the night of June 20, 1791, the royal family attempted to flee the country—more specifically, they attempted to escape to the eastern border, where there had gathered the assembled forces of the nation's unseated aristocracy. Tragically or fortunately, depending upon one's viewpoint, this effort was carried out with almost farcical incompetence, and the royal carriage was stopped in Varennes after Louis, thoughtlessly sitting at an open window, was recognized. The royal family was seized and, the next day, escorted under armed popular guard back to Paris, along a road apparently lined in force by a silent, now unforgiving people.

With Varennes one can follow, Michel Vovelle suggests, "the stages of a gradual process of emancipation, seen by the actors themselves as a tragedy, in the development of the image of the king. This image changed from that of the king as a father-protector, to whom the *cahiers de doléances* were respectfully addressed, to the image of the king as an enemy, whose symbolic death, anticipating the real event, was expressed by the glacial silence which greeted his return from Varennes, before becoming the subject of a fundamental debate in the Convention."[83] This shift, from comedy to tragedy, was decisive. After Varennes, attempts to stage anew, and convincingly, any reconciliation between the monarchy and the nation were bound to fail, for such a dramatic language was now revealed to have been merely a seductive fiction. Rather than definitively repudiating the play's necessary blocking figure, the king had attempted to break with the people. Comedy, as a dramatic genre of political change, could no longer produce any plausible horizon of expectation.

This loss of authority had immediate political consequences, for it forced the Assembly to consider an issue it had carefully avoided; namely, defining the nature of the king's powers in the new constitutional state. Prior to Varennes, the Constituent Assembly had conceived the metaphor of a "religious" or "respectful" veil to be thrown over the question; the status of the king, they agreed, was to remain outside the bounds of discussion. In a certain sense, that veil had been the political corollary of the tacit political comedy being played out. However, the flight to Varennes, as contemporaries realized immediately and as commentators have never since failed to note, had "torn the veil" from this convenient fiction: Louis would never again hold the trust of his audience, and he was to be treated henceforth with a level of suspicion and distrust hitherto reserved for those of lower station.

However, the effect of Varennes on the status of the Assembly was no less pronounced, for it called into question not only the trustworthiness of the king but also that of all those who had helped to produce the illusion of comic resolution. In consequence, many of the most prominent moderates in the Assembly now lost whatever claim they had made to political *vraisemblance.*[84] Not coincidentally, it was at this time that David abandoned his painting of the Tennis Court Oath.

Antitheatricality

Varennes, then, marked a critical moment not only of political change but also of theatrical and dramatic disillusionment; in so doing, however, it also raised disturbing questions of just how the increasingly radical course of Revolutionary politics could be brought to an end. Rather than simply calling into question one available and powerful dramatic language of political resolution, the episode raised doubts about the entire representative theater.[85] The radical voices of the political press stepped up their efforts to tear such veils away and to clear the stage of a troupe now viewed as imposters.

For Hunt, what happened next was merely a shift from one archetypal form to another: "the generic plot," she suggests, "shifted from comedy to romance."[86] However, the problem is that these genres do not belong to the same mode, and that shift—from presentation to inscription—reveals what amounts to a temporary collapse of the primacy of speech, performance, and particularly drama within the political theater. Instead, the press becomes primary; the moment of Mirabeau becomes that of Jean-Paul Marat, a great actor gives way to a great critic. This shift produced exceptional tension: the press, if it could easily arbitrate judgment, could not act, did not exercise representative authority. Rather, its authority was derived from, and operated within, the virtual space of public opinion.

The crucial moment in this transformation occurred just a year after Varennes. By then, it looked to contemporary observers as if the monarchy stood some chance of stopping and even reversing the tide of political change, for it had succeeded in persuading (or, rather, provoking) an Austro-Prussian coalition to invade France. For the Girondins and the left, war offered, at last, an opportunity to strike out offensively at the émigré forces of the nobility gathered just over the Austrian border and in so doing to force a decisive test of the king's loyalties. For the right, as well as for Lafayette, then in command of the army of the center, the declaration of war was supported because it was seen as an opportunity to institute martial law, stifling radical political activity and bringing the revolution to a quick close on a more conservative basis. The Assembly, perceiving this threat, on June 6 passed a measure to establish outside Paris an army of National Guards. Louis, happy to foster internal weakness as he awaited restoration by force, vetoed the measure and dismissed his adversarial cabinet. On the twentieth, the Tuileries was invaded by angry demonstrators, who cornered the king in a window embrasure and demanded that he retract his veto and restore the dismissed cabinet. Louis refused, speaking to the crowd for nearly three hours and showing calm, patience, and composure throughout, until the crowd dispersed. It was remembered as his finest political performance of the Revolution; certainly, it was his most successful, revealing the capabilities he might have had in a more personal political milieu. With the Austrian and Prussian forces gathering for invasion, the king seemed to have scripted things just as he wanted: Lafayette, prompted by the demonstration to turn his troops against Paris, could offer no resistance to external invasion; the moderates, removed from power, sat lobbying behind the scenes; and the right, content to be in power as a crisis approached that would justify martial law, remained carefully mute.

It was this complex and profoundly duplicitous situation that Marat addressed in the July 9 issue of his incendiary *Ami du Peuple*. By the time of this crisis, his radical political commentary had earned him enormous popularity and notoriety in Paris, and he set out here to explain to this broad urban audience the true nature of the scene unfolding before them. Pessimistic about both the Revolution's future and his own (for he was at the time evading arrest), Marat addressed his readers as if they were sitting in a vast theater, watching the closing moments of a failed play.[87] "Before leaving the performance," he asked, "let us consider the stage for a little while longer from the back of the theatre where we are situated; let us examine the acting of the players, the responses of the spectators, and let us seek the principal reasons for the opposition to the establishment of liberty among us, after we had momentarily overcome despotism."[88] The problem, according to Marat, was not that the novel play of Revolutionary politics had been ineffectual but that its novelty had proven to be superficial. In the view of the friend of the people, the "theater of State" in the summer of 1792 was no different than it had been three years before: "only the decorations have changed, but there are still the same actors, the same masks, the same plots, the same forces." Girondist or Feuillant, Marat suggested, made little difference; from his vantage the political actors were all filling customary roles in an all-too familiar drama of *courtly* politics. There was, he pointed out, "still a despot surrounded by collaborators, still vexatious and oppressive ministers; still a single legislator, still unfaithful and prevaricating agents of authority; still greedy, fawning, oppressive, and scheming courtiers; still petty careerists, brazen intriguers, cowardly hypocrites; still men consumed by the thirst for gold and deaf to the call of duty, of honor, and of humanity."[89]

The Revolution is here a dark, anachronistic comic theater, a stage populated by the same old comic villains. But even those actors and that odious stage were not, for Marat, where the real problem lay: "Today," he asserted, "the principal actors are behind the curtain; it is there that they plot at their ease with those who play the parts before our eyes." The Assembly and cabinet, he suggested, were not representatives at all, but mere puppets, "new actors" who had filled "the same roles" and who would "likewise be replaced, without anything having changed in the play of the political machine." From Marat's perspective, the play of the Revolution, the proper drama it demands, would be possible only when the audience acted against these *hidden* impresarios, the "cheats who deceive them . . . the scoundrels who have deluded them."[90]

This was not simply a critique of the particular political drama being enacted; with Marat, the Rousseauist critique of theatricality came into its own, and the result was an extended assault on the political stage. From August 10, 1792, when popular insurrection and an attack on the Tuileries forces a suspension of the monarchy, until September 5, 1793, when a demonstration in the Convention forces the adoption of terror as "the order of the day," Revolutionary politics was marked by a series of purges. In September 1792, rumors of the imminent arrival of Prussian troops in Paris prompted the September massacres, five days of popular tribunals executing summary justice on the aristocratic "traitors" (who were, in fact, mostly petty criminals) being held in the city's prisons; in January 1793, the king was tried, and sentenced, as a traitor to the nation, after first being shorn of his title and his status as a symbolic, supraindividual actor. This radical revolution directed itself as well at the remaining actors and stagehands of the failed national comedy; in June, the Girondins—leaders of the left only a year before—were arrested, for like the Feuillants before them they had risen to power only to enter into misguided secret correspondence with the royal family, seeking a suitable way to draw political change to a harmonious close.

However, the enormous process of theatrical disillusionment articulated by the events of 1792 and 1793 was not complete. The stage was swept of many of its most prominent early actors, but the changes catalyzed by Marat's scathing critique of political representation also gave rise to new and more intimate stages of political theatricality: the tribunal and the committee, arenas in which the exuberant rhetoric of early Revolutionary politics was subjected to a colder inquiry and in which questions of politics became, explicitly, questions of law.[91] Mirabeau's sentimental oratory, magnificent as it was, would have been thoroughly obsolete in this milieu; instead, it was the cool analytical discourse of the

Jacobins that began to dominate the political stage. On July 13, 1793, Marat was assassinated, and two weeks later Maximilien Robespierre was elected to the Committee of Public Safety. In September, a demonstration in the Convention provided the pretense for the declaration of Terror as the order of the day. And in those events—in the violent rise to ascendancy of the Jacobin regime—we find the beginnings of a second attempt to bring the Revolution to a moment of dramatic conclusion, though now through the language and rhetoric, and the epistemological frame, of tragedy.

Tragedy

> Man falls into peril and into misfortune through a cause which is
> *outside him,* or *within him. Outside him,* it is his destiny, his situa-
> tion, his duties, his bonds . . . *Within him,* it is his foibles, his im-
> prudence, his penchants, his passions, his vices, sometimes his
> virtues . . . This distinction of the causes of misfortune, either *out-
> side us,* or *within us,* marks the divide between two systems of
> tragedy, the ancient and the modern.

> Jean-François Marmontel, s.v. *"Tragédie"* Encyclopédie
> (*1755–1780*)

On July 27, 1794, a date known in the Revolutionary calendar as the Ninth of Thermidor, Robespierre marked the moment of his own downfall by shooting himself in the jaw. The irony of this self-wounding, aside from the intriguing question of whether it was a suicide botched by fear, intervention, or intent (or even a suicide attempt at all), is extreme, for Robespierre's act would render the Revolution's most effective orator a notably *mute* witness to his own hasty indictment and grotesque execution the next day. Unlike Danton and Desmoulins, unlike even the most common victim of the Terror, unlike the king, whose last phrases at the moment of his execution have been noted, questioned, disputed, and mythologized, Robespierre never had his last words, never delivered the parting scaffold speech in which contemporaries often found the most significant image, the unveiled character of those figures they had condemned. The trial and execution of the king had been a careful public spectacle, an open and reasoned demonstration of natural justice; in contrast, that of Robespierre was the hurried slaughter of a dangerous beast.

Three days later, the French National Convention rescinded the Law of 22 Prairial (June 10), which had, by eliminating virtually all judicial guarantees for the accused and by allowing the Revolutionary Tribunal no choice other than acquittal or death, served as the legal instrument of what is known as the Great Terror. In the previous fifty-one days, 1,376 persons had been executed in Paris, and the magnitude of that increase becomes clear when we bear in mind that the guillotine had claimed only 1,251 victims over the preceding fifteen *months*. The fall of Robespierre and the cessation of the Terror marked a crucial moment in Revolutionary politics, for they mark not only the collapse of radical revolution but also the decisive moment in the longer collapse of tragedy as a way of thinking, acting, and ordering historical experience.

The particular situational appeal of the "stern classical traditions of the Roman republic," as Marx called them, was strong. In part, that appeal was based on familiarity, for the Jesuit pedagogy of pre-Revolutionary France, in which classical recitation played a prominent role, had provided many of the delegates to the Estates General with a shared language of political allusion.[92] As the Revolution became increasingly radical and as its leaders struggled to locate legitimate models for political action and authority, the language of classical politics, and of Roman tragedy in particular, emerged as a fundamental, even ubiquitous element in the rhetoric of the Revolution's political culture.[93] "There was scarcely a significant Revolutionary politician," Gumbrecht notes, "who was not celebrated as 'Brutus' or 'Cato,' nor castigated as 'Cataline' or 'Tarquinius.'"[94]

It wasn't until the summer of 1793, however, and particularly with Robespierre's rise to power, that the language of tragedy emerged as the central dialect of Revolutionary politics. If before that time that dialect had been a rhetorical convention it then became a doctrine, and the Revolutionary government instituted a regime of censorship and rhetorical propaganda that was more restrictive than anything that had been experienced under the monarchy.[95] On August 2, similar measures were taken against the theaters: the Convention decreed the regular performance, at state expense, of the tragedies *Brutus, Caïus Gracchus,* "and other dramatic plays that retrace the glorious events of the Revolution and the virtues of the defenders of Liberty."[96] The purpose of this program seems not merely to have been the elimination of dissent; rather, it was in a sense an effort to prepare the stage for a proper Revolutionary performance—an action that might finally serve as an example of virtue rather than a testament to deceit.

The genre, of course, was to be tragedy: but more specifically, ancient tragedy. As Marmontel suggested in the *Encyclopédie,* the "advantage" of ancient tragedy over modern was that "In a republican state exposed to great dangers, [populated by] a mass of men prepared for anything and resolved to do anything, [such tragedy] brought them to see that all men were equal under the rule of destiny . . . That is what it was important to inculcate in a free people."[97] The focus on ancient tragedy was of course already characteristic of the Revolution's tragic rhetoric, but with Robespierre's rise the model of that virtue it produced was made a central feature of the political definition of the state. As Marx pointed out, Robespierre in his February 5 "Address on the Principles of Political Morality" explicitly defined virtue ("the *fundamental principle* of a democratic government . . . the mainspring which supports it and gives it motion") as that "public virtue which worked such prodigies in Greece and Rome."[98] Similarly, Saint-Just's report on the arrest of Danton was "composed in the ancient style and directed against *Danton* as against *Cataline*," and his report on the general police was similarly framed in terms of the Roman republic.[99]

Many historians have suggested that the conventional nature of such rhetoric, and hence its status as mere metaphor, was plain. However, Blanchard has argued that this sort of oratory did more than simply offer a figurative context in which the historical process of the Revolution became comprehensible; rather, it installed Revolutionary action within an imaginary stage setting, producing "the illusion of playing *History* in a magically summoned scene, in which men no longer keep their name but take, like actors in the theatre, the traditional names of the heroes of Greece and Rome."[100]

It is precisely this sort of transfer that we find in Robespierre's address on political morality, as he considers the possibility that the French people may not in fact be a wellspring of Republican virtue: "When the government alone lacks it, there remains the resource of the people's virtue; but when the people themselves are corrupted, liberty is already lost . . . What does it matter that Brutus has killed the tyrant? Tyranny still lives in the people's hearts, and Rome survives only in the person of Brutus."[101] Robespierre (like Saint-Just) had been elected to the National Convention on September 5, during the third day of the September massacres; his tenure was opened by the abolition of the monarchy and punctuated, exactly four months later, by the execution of Louis XVI.[102] From the start, he had been a prominent advocate of execution, and in a straightforward manner it is the tragic identity of Brutus that Robespierre assumes here. Yet, even as he assumes that exemplary role, Robespierre raises the possibility that his Brutus inhabits a solopsistic world—and by extension the possibility that the Republic of Virtue might exist only in the mind of Robespierre himself.[103] And such a suggestion raises problems: if the Republic of Virtue might exist only within the mind, can the tragedy then be an exemplary, ancient tragedy? Or would it be, as Marmontel suggested, modern tragedy—merely the creation of an internal passion?

Over the course of the spring of 1794, Robespierre seems to have become increasingly isolated within just this sort of tragic echo chamber. In March, the Jacobins struck out first against the radical Hébertist left (which had enjoyed the popular support of the Paris *sections*) and then against the Dantonist core of the moderate left (which had been gaining support for an end to the Terror), eliminating in a period of just under a month all apparent opposition. In consequence, Revolutionary politics became characterized almost immediately by a scrupulous univocality, and one reinforced and extended by the rapid restriction of the Revolutionary press, the implementation of massive internal propaganda efforts, and the average person's obvious desire (in the midst of the Terror) to remain unnoticed. Having eliminated all vocal opposition, the Jacobin regime found itself suddenly in an environment in which the only response to statements from the center, both in Paris and from the provinces, was a kind of imitative and camouflaging mimicry. "The artificial character of such messages," Bouloiseau observed drily, "soon became apparent."[104] At the center, such echoes could only have reinforced a sense of solopsism and heightened the necessity for careful self-scrutiny.

In May, Robespierre appeared before the Convention to make his second major policy address, his report on religious and moral ideas. With the very first line, his inward focus becomes apparent: "It is in prosperity," he muses, "that peoples, as well as individuals, should, in a manner of speaking, retire within themselves to listen, with passions stilled, to the voice of wisdom."[105] No longer certain enough to invoke the sort of popular Republican virtue to which he had appealed even in February, Robespierre here seems more concerned with convincing *himself* of the very possibility of a Republic founded on virtue. "The moral world," he puzzles,

> far more even than the physical world, seems full of contrasts and enigmas. Nature tells us that man was born to be free, yet the experience of the centuries shows us man enslaved . . . The human race reveres Cato, yet bows beneath the yoke of Caesar. Posterity honors the virtue of Brutus, but allows it only in ancient history. The centuries and the earth are given to crime and tyranny; liberty and virtue have endured for only an instant on a few points of the globe. Sparta shines like a flash of lightning in immense darkness . . . But do not say, O Brutus, that virtue is a phantom![106]

That Robespierre's peculiar direct address to Brutus was, in a manner of speaking, a question asked of himself seems obvious. That he had determined upon playing the role of a tragic martyr is made explicit: "O sublime people!" he would add, "Receive the sacrifice of all of my being: happy is he who is born among you! Happier still is he who can die for your well-being!"[107] However, the remarkable gesture here is his plea that Brutus "not say . . . that virtue is a phantom," as if the truth of virtue depends not upon its demonstration but upon the stoic refusal of an illusory Brutus—of Robespierre *as* Brutus—to admit that it is all merely a creation of the mind. The stakes involved in this illusion were, to say the least, enormous. Two days later the Law of 22 Prairial was passed, and the Great Terror began. Robespierre's well-known doctrinal justification of Revolutionary terror, from his address on political morality in February, makes clear just how much the Revolution now relied upon such theatrically summoned affirmations of virtue: "If the driving force of popular government in peacetime is virtue, that of popular government in revolution is both *virtue and terror:* virtue, without which terror is fatal; terror, without which virtue is powerless. Terror is nothing other than justice that is prompt, severe, and inflexible; it is thus an emanation of virtue."[108] Terror, then, gains its legitimacy not from the voice of popular acclaim but from the silent reflection of virtue.

By the middle of July it had become apparent that opposition to Jacobin rule had grown enormously; both the remaining moderates, who feared that they would next be arrested, and a number of the radical left, who sensed that they might be blamed for the excesses then taking place, had good reason to attack. On July 27, the Ninth of Thermidor, Robespierre and his closest associates were, in accordance with a carefully orchestrated plan, rapidly denounced and arrested in the Convention. However, the guards who were to convey them to prison released their prisoners, and the Robespierrists fled to the Hôtel de Ville, where they began to gather support for a popular coup; the Convention responded by outlawing the group. Late in the night of 9 Thermidor, what remained of the Paris *sections* gathered at the Hôtel de Ville and awaited Robespierre's call to rise against the Convention. Robespierre himself, however, seems finally to have lost faith in the authority of his tragic illusion. Asked why he would not call the *sections* to revolt, Robespierre asked simply, "In whose name?" Brutus's phantom presence, it seemed obvious, could no longer serve as a touchstone of legitimacy; yet to act as an individual, in his *own* name and without office, would have been to enact not an ancient but a modern tragic fall. Without leadership, those who had gathered before the Hôtel de Ville melted away, and Robespierre and his compatriots were arrested without opposition.

It is important to realize that the tragic confrontation toward which the Revolution was aiming *failed to transpire*, despite all efforts to the contrary. Robes-

pierre had no stern tragic confrontation with his accusers, and there was no decisive moment of conflict; events seemed less to tend concertedly in one direction than to waver, stall, and evaporate, ending in a botched suicide and a sordid
execution. The most tragic element of those events lies precisely in the spectacle
of that failure and the implication—grasped immediately by contemporaries—
that tragedy was not an epistemological ground of justice but just another self-
deceiving rhetoric of power, and one inextricably linked to violence. That spectacle (see Chap. 4) had a decisive effect on subsequent drama; it also, however,
had a decisive effect on history, for with the failure of tragedy as a rhetoric of political action the drama also ceased to provide historical action with any forms
that could offer a plausible horizon of expectation. As both Marx and François
Furet have pointed out, Thermidor marked not simply a change of regime but
also the "reassertion of civil society over the illusion of politics."[109] The drama
was over.

Afterword: Melodrama

With that final generic collapse, the divide between history and drama was
re-established, if at first only weakly. In the immediate wake of Thermidor, the
theater offered a wave of plays that restaged the overthrow of the Jacobin
regime, though like early Revolutionary comedy those dramas tended to avoid
too close a look at the central figures and events of that act. Instead, the stage
offered at first simple comedies in which Jacobin villains were joyously unmasked and expelled or bourgeois dramas in which virtuous protagonists over-
came evil tyrants. Fairly quickly, however, official discomfort with even such
abstracted spectacles as these led to a suppression of all explicit dramatic references to Revolutionary history.[110] It was in the wake of that suppression, and in
a sense as a formal response to it, that melodrama arose.

The origins of melodrama have always been linked to the French Revolution.
However, modern literary historians have tended, at least since Peter Brooks's influential work, to understand that connection as an indirect consequence of shattered religious belief—to see melodrama as a reflection of the Revolution's evacuation of the "traditional Sacred" or as a replacement for a "Christian religion
that had been discredited."[111] However, as Frederick Brown suggested some time
ago, contemporaries understood the connection to be both more direct, less epistemological than ontological, and related not to the loss of religious belief but
to the end of the radical revolution. Brown's assertion is supported—and derived
from—Charles Nodier, who claimed in his critical introductions to the plays of

Charles Pixerécourt that melodrama was the necessary and direct product of Revolutionary experience:

> The entire people had come into the streets and the public spaces to perform the greatest drama in history. Everyone had been an actor in this bloody play, everyone had been a soldier, a revolutionary, or an outlaw. To its solemn spectators who had smelled gunpowder and blood, there was a need for emotions analogous to those from which they had been cut off by the re-establishment of order . . . There was a need to be reminded anew of the framework, always uniform in its result, of this great lesson that comprehends all philosophies, supports all religions: no matter how low, virtue is never without recompense, crime never without punishment. Make no mistake! This was not melodrama! It was the morality of the revolution.[112]

For Brown, Nodier's commentary suggests that melodrama "ritualized the Terror," providing contemporaries with a theatrical re-enactment of the extreme events to which they had become accustomed. However, I wonder if it isn't possible to push things a bit closer, for Nodier's language makes Pixerécourt's melodrama seem not merely a re-enactment of the experience of the Terror but a dramatic articulation of its principles. "Virtue is never without recompense; nor crime without punishment": this is not the action of the Terror, which by its collapse was associated more with blind violence than blind justice, but its doctrine. It was, as Nodier says, "the morality of the Revolution," a term that (curiously enough) was for contemporaries associated not with the action of Terror but with Robespierre himself, the "mouthpiece," Furet notes, of the Revolution's "purest and most tragic discourse."[113]

Could it be that Pixerécourt's melodrama refigured not the broad violence of Terror but the ancient tragic rhetoric, the illusory version of history claimed by the voice of Robespierre? Nodier's commentary makes such a reading seem possible. In a sentence that probably informed Brooks's understanding of melodrama's religiosity, Nodier claims that "Pixerécourt's theater, in the absence of worship, made up for the rules of conduct laid down by a *mute pulpit* [my emphasis]."[114] But is Nodier speaking of a religious pulpit that has fallen mute? As is now well known, muteness was a privileged category in melodrama and the mute a character more exemplary within melodrama than any other. "No one," Brown writes, "brought tears to Boulevard eyes more readily than he who had been, in Pixerécourt's pompous expression, 'deprived of the Word.' "[115] What is the mute, indeed, but the hero himself turned round about? Where the hero's name has the force of magical incantation, the mute's aphonia translates his anomia: speechless, he is nameless. Where the hero administers justice summary and absolute . . . , the mute's inability to plead his case, to make himself heard, to answer his accusers, is a nightmarish precondition of justice summary and absolute."[116]

I am not trying to suggest here that early melodrama is somehow all about Robespierre. Rather, I want to consider the possibility that in melodrama muteness becomes the tacit sign of the Revolution's dramatic collapse or, put differently, the sign for its final evacuation of the notion of performable history. In that sense, the mute testifies not only to the failure of Revolutionary ideals but also to the historical condition of post-Revolutionary modernity—a condition in which speech has ceased to exercise historical agency and in which all tragedy has become modern.

Mona Ozouf concluded in her landmark study of Revolutionary festivals that "the Revolution's mania for festivals is the story of an immense disillusionment . . . Far from utopia's providing the French Revolution with a mirror in which it recognized itself for what it was, it was the Revolution that held up the glass in which utopia could see its true features."[117] Certainly, we must recognize a similar process of disillusionment in the Revolution's complex appropriation of theatrical conventions and dramatic forms—all were attempts to impose on the political public an acceptable narrative with which the actions and ideas of the Revolution might be made legible, advanced and established, and brought to a close, and all were efforts that resulted instead in the invalidation of the appropriated forms.

The outcome of this process was the destruction of the exemplary nature of traditional dramatic genre and, in its place, the emergence of a historical poetics of the drama. That process was by no means begun with the Revolution; as I have tried to show, one can see in the history of late-eighteenth-century drama its accelerating approach and crisis and in the period of the Revolution its completion. To suggest as much may appear to recapitulate the perspective of traditional literary history; Hegel marked the rupture there, and such a conception seems to come rather close to Steiner's and Brooks's understanding of the French Revolution as a crucial "epistemological moment" in the history of the drama. However, for all three the Revolution stands outside and above that process of formal development, driving it by altering through other means—that is, historical action—the larger implicatory framework in which the drama participates.

What I hope to have suggested here is that the Revolution's historical action, the manner in which it negotiated and reshaped history and historical consciousness, was instead intimately bound up with that "revolution" in the drama—that these two revolutions were dialectically paired and that their interpenetration marked a brief convergence, driven by modernity, of history and drama.[118] That convergence would not recur. As Furet observed, "the true break in continuity [that the Revolution] wrought between 'before' and 'after'" was "a change in the ways of legitimating and representing historical action," a shift from "the idea that history is shaped by human action" to the recognition that it is instead the product of a "combination of existing institutions and forces."[119]

CHAPTER THREE

The Revolution and British Theatrical Politics

The British Revolution

In consequence of the Revolutionary explosion of the international news press, the events and actions of the French Revolution were experienced by outside observers with a sensible force and a temporal immediacy without precedent. Nowhere was this phenomenon more intense than in Britain, and particularly in London, where an already well-established news press was rapidly transformed into the first mass news medium, and daily news of international events came suddenly—as many contemporaries would note—to dominate not only the conversations of London coffeehouses but also those of remote village greens. The dramatic events of the Revolution were, to be sure, quite local in their action, and often private in the extreme, but they were also, and for those just across the Channel especially, disconcertingly, breathtakingly near, in a manner that nothing in history had been before. It was this effect, and not merely the exceptional quality of the Revolution's action, that prompted what seems now the oddly vivid imaginative engagement of contemporary observers.

However, the Revolution that took place in France was not the Revolution seen in Britain, for even at its most efficient that press coverage was, by our standards, exceedingly erratic, outrageously biased, and directed from the outset to manipulate and not merely inform its audience. Moreover, these powerfully mediated, often mangled representations were taken in by spectators who possessed their own theatrical and political languages, accepted very different conventions of social as well as dramatic action, and held other assumptions, attitudes, and ideas of identity and its relation to performance, so that even events reported accurately from France took on, in Britain, different and often unintended meaning. To understand such transformations and translations—to understand, in short, the reception and impact of the French Revolutionary crisis of dramatic form in Britain—one must first take a look at that rather different context of British theatrical politics, at the manner in which it made use of spectacle and dramatic rhetoric and the ways in which it related theatrical to political performance.

One significant difference between the French and British contexts may be found in the nature and character of public space in the their respective capital cities. Unlike Paris, London was not shaped by absolute planning, and its development and expansion were not marked by the same predominance of great public projects and grand axes of spectacular authority. Instead, the rapid expansion of London into and through the eighteenth century proceeded in "irregular waves of building activity stirred and halted by economic fluctuations," and the creation of public spaces was "made and animated by a culture of sociability driven by the commercialization of leisure."[1] Rather than creating those broad, monumental expanses of public space on which the Revolution would later enact its ceremonies and its conflicts, London developed patchwork patterns of smaller squares—less monumental civic spaces than neighborhood parks, and parks kept carefully free of unwanted commercial activity and unwanted assembly.[2] In contrast to the surveillant organization imposed upon Paris by absolutism, London developed, Miles Ogborn has suggested, as a network of commercial traffic, a largely abstracted civic space defined not by the presence of royal authority but by the circulation of goods and services.

One illuminating point of comparison between the two contexts is offered by Schivelbusch: locks, rather than *lanternes* distinguish London of the late eighteenth century from Paris.[3] Although the British city was even larger than Paris during this period, its logic was in this sense more local and more private. London's streets, rather than constituting public space ordered and regulated by the symbolic gaze of the monarch, were empty borders between private jurisdictions, jurisdictions enforced by security rather than surveillance. This is not to suggest that London was unmarked by public and political unrest or that it was freed from the spectacular and theatrical tensions that so strongly marked the eighteenth-century French metropolis. However, these tensions were certainly less polarized, for they were not driven by the same pressurized conflict between spectacular power and transgressive action. Indeed, Marc Baer has argued that disorder and theatricality in Britain contributed to social stability and helped to maintain rather than challenge the status quo.[4]

In similar fashion, London's theaters seem also to have alleviated rather than fostered social tensions, becoming over the course of the century larger, more inclusive, and less focused upon a hierarchically arrayed gathering of audience

notables than upon shared accessibility to the dramatic performance.[5] It would
be a mistake to overemphasize the democratizing character of such changes, for
with this increase in inclusivity came greater political surveillance and control.
The Licensing Act of 1737, for example, had instituted rigorous political regulation of the drama, subjecting most plays to preperformance censorship, suppressing traveling players and confining theatrical activity to licensed stages, and to
a great degree eliminating the capabilities of those stages as a platform for even
mild political commentary.[6] Moreover, the price of tickets instituted an effective
form of censorship in this public space by limiting the ability of the lower classes
even to attend and consigning them largely to the pit. Such economic and political restrictions constrained the British theater's function as an adequate arena in
which community, both social and political, might be negotiated. Nonetheless,
theatrical disorder in eighteenth-century London carried nothing like the compressive charge of theater politics in France at the same time, and the contest
between legitimate and illegitimate theater was in Britain a struggle marked
less by rigidity and repression than by a pragmatic process of adaptation and
accommodation.[7]

Finally, the political press and the mass public created in France at the time
of the Revolution already existed in Britain, and in a much more stable, institutionalized, and regulated form. Here, too, commercial interests combined with
limited government control to produce a press that understood its role in terms
not of the surveillance of power but rather of the management and shaping of
public opinion and the expression and promotion of the diverse discourses that
together constituted England's public sphere.

In such a context, the events of the Revolution, shaped as they were by a more
politicized, radical set of relations between drama, theatricality, and politics,
appeared not only as foreign spectacles that challenged comprehension but also
as threatening performances that challenged England's own carefully modulated
culture of political theatricality. The Revolution, in short, forced British culture
to confront new ways of performing politics, and it was through the negotiation
of that confrontation, I suggest, that the Revolution changed British drama.

The Importance of Plumage:
Burke's Dramatic Discourse and History

Edmund Burke's *Reflections on the Revolution in France* were published in
January 1790, just months after the October Days. The *Reflections* articulate a
scathing critique of the political developments of 1789: Burke condemns the

Estates General, asserts that the Revolution's introduction of paper *Assignats* will bring economic chaos, and expresses his terrible grief that Europe did not—as one—dash to the defense of France's outraged monarchy. Over the course of the *Reflections* Burke weaves together a resonantly persuasive if occasionally contradictory cluster of implied as well as explicit, figurative as well as literal, arguments against the Revolution. His appeal to the dramatic values of his readers, one of the most important of the *Reflections'* rhetorical strategies, begins almost immediately; indeed, it is to the conventions of the theater that Burke appeals as he frames his initial description of the phenomenal impact of events across the Channel. "All circumstances taken together," he asserts,

> the French revolution is the most astonishing that has hitherto happened in the world. The most wonderful things are brought about, in many instances by means the most absurd and ridiculous, in the most ridiculous modes, and apparently by the most contemptible instruments. Everything seems out of nature in this strange chaos of levity and ferocity, and of all sorts of crimes jumbled together with all sorts of follies. In viewing this monstrous tragicomic scene, the most opposite passions necessarily succeed and sometimes mix with each other in the mind: alternate contempt and indignation, alternate laughter and tears, alternate scorn and horror.[8]

The Revolution, Burke suggests, is an illegitimate political performance because it is an aesthetic monstrosity, its actions and representations a violation of those principles of genre which bring action into harmony with the order of nature. He will play upon this trope of illegitimacy repeatedly throughout the *Reflections.* However, it is not merely an external chaos that Burke evokes, nor is it merely a generic argument that he invokes against the strange spectacle taking place across the Channel. Burke grounds his judgment as well upon the suggestion of a consequent internal chaos, a disorderly confusion of passions that "necessarily" arises in the mind of the theatrical spectator—and a confusion that testifies sensibly to the truth of his assertions about the disorderly political drama being enacted in France. It is the British spectator's *reaction* upon which Burke anchors his argument, translating the debate over France's political conflict into a question of spectatorial response.[9] "To some," he notes with mock dismay, referring to the members of Britain's Revolution Society, "this strange scene appeared in quite another point of view," eliciting "no other sentiments than those of exultation and rapture."[10] To support the Revolution is, in these terms, a mark of both spectatorial incompetence and personal intemperance, both a failure of proper sentiment and an irrational, uncontrolled indulgence in the excessive (religious, sexual) passions of "exultation and rapture."

It is after having thus positioned his audience—having, in a sense, established his readers' appropriate awareness of proper spectatorial sensibility—that Burke then reverses his tactics, extending in subsequent pages his image of Revolutionary France as a political theater wholly given over to monstrous theatrical and spectatorial excess. The representatives of the National Assembly, he asserts, "act like the comedians of a fair before a riotous audience; they act amidst the tumultuous cries of a mixed mob of ferocious men, and of women lost to shame, who, according to their insolent fancies, direct, control, applaud, explode them, and sometimes mix and take their seats amongst them, domineering over them with a strange mixture of servile petulance and proud, presumptuous authority. As they have inverted order in all things, the gallery is in the place of the house."[11] From the mixture of opposite passions to the violence of a political theater turned topsy-turvy, the emotional, aesthetic, social, and political disorder of revolution are for Burke of a piece; the implication, one that would become almost an obsession in British reactions to the Revolution, is that there is no clear boundary between a revolt of the imagination and riot in the streets.

And with this implication in mind, Burke then sets out a very different drama: a royal tragedy, in which the isolated order of French monarchical rule offers, within the confusion of Revolutionary upheaval, a haven for the British spectator's dangerously disordered passions. He begins, appropriately, by rewriting the October Days in such a manner as to clarify the contrast between peace and revolt, between order and chaos, between stately tranquility and intemperate passions. "History will record," Burke writes,

> that on the morning of the 6th of October, 1789, the king and queen of France, after a day of confusion, alarm, dismay, and slaughter, lay down, under the pledged security of public faith, to indulge nature in a few hours of respite and troubled, melancholy repose. From this sleep the queen was first startled by the sentinel at her door, who cried out for her to save herself by flight—that this was the last proof of fidelity he could give—that they were upon him, and he was dead. Instantly he was cut down. A band of cruel ruffians and assassins, reeking with his blood, rushed into the chamber of the queen and pierced with a hundred strokes of bayonets and poniards the bed, from whence this persecuted woman had but just time to fly almost naked, and, through ways unknown to the murderers, had escaped to seek refuge at the feet of a king and husband not secure of his own life for a moment.[12]

The March of Women becomes the rapacious mob, those same "ferocious men" who threaten the National Assembly, the riotous audience now disturbing the repose of royal order, violating the indulgence of nature itself, and driving both queen and reader toward a refuge that is itself under siege. And, critically, Burke pauses his narrative here, stepping away and into an analogous refuge of memory to set out a contrasting image of the queen, an image that has ever since served as a focal point for debates over Burke's aesthetic representation of the Revolution. "It is now sixteen or seventeen years," he muses, "since I saw the queen of France, then the dauphiness, at Versailles, and surely never lighted on this orb, which she hardly seemed to touch, a more delightful vision. I saw her just above the horizon, decorating and cheering the elevated sphere she just began to move in—glittering like the morning star, full of life and splendor and joy. Oh! what a revolution! and what a heart must I have to contemplate without emotion that elevation and that fall!"[13]

Rhapsodically figuring Marie-Antoinette as a celestial beauty newly risen, as a morning star gracing royalty's harmonic spheres, Burke lifts his readers, too, out and away from the threat at Versailles. Turning back history, he elevates the queen to idealized abstraction, restoring in the process the virtuous innocence of a woman whose reputation had by 1789 brought her firmly within the realm of earthly passion. In so doing, Burke constructs for his audience a tragic heroine— the heroine around whom he then figures his larger Revolutionary tragedy. Returning to October, and relating the royal family's installment in Paris's Tuileries Palace, he assures his readers that the queen had felt the horrors and faced the perils of her situation "with the dignity of a Roman matron." Like Lucretia, she will, Burke is certain, "in the last extremity save herself from the last disgrace." No monstrous tragicomedy shall be played by this queen, for the natural nobility of monarchical government insists even unto death upon tragedy: if "she must fall," he declares, "she will fall by no ignoble hand."[14] Here is generic order; here, Burke suggests, dramatic and political sensibility are proper.

Despite the *Reflections'* enormous success, Burke's idealized portrait of Marie-Antoinette was received even by his friends as almost indigestibly sweetened.[15] Yet Burke's dramaturgy managed two crucial tasks: first, it acknowledged and even intensified the fear that Britons felt in response to the violent popular unrest taking place in France, and, second, it offered a powerful framework—the experience of the theater—within which to make sense of what seemed beyond sense. If the tragic heroine at the center of Burke's drama seemed forced, that representation was made considerably more palatable in conjunction with the *Reflections'* vividly rendered threat of violent and vicious insurrectionary mobs.

The influence of the *Reflections*, almost immediately and ever since, has been extraordinary, not simply as an articulation of political theory and a commentary on Revolutionary politics, but also as a specifically *dramatic* representation of the Revolution. Contemporary critics focused on this aspect of Burke's argument immediately: "Mr. Burke," complained Thomas Paine in his *Rights of Man* (1791), "should recollect that he is writing History, and not *Plays*."[16] Such objections have not abated. The factual distortions of Burke's account, its poetic justice or gross inappropriateness, the manipulative strategies of its rhetorical appeals, its knowing incorporation of his influential theories of aesthetics, its unabashed expression of his gendered politics have all received much attention in ensuing centuries, as countless commentators have joined in Paine's outraged accusation or struggled to defend Burke's picture.[17]

However, both sides of this debate have tended, until recently, to maintain an accompanying misperception—the notion that Burke *imposed* the lens of the drama upon "History." Following Paine's lead, and despite critical awareness of the contemporary currency of the theater as a figure for political and social action, historians—and even historians of the drama—have presented Burke's dramatic representation as an anomalous, even inaugural act of literary refiguration. As one scholar of romantic drama recently asserted, summing up quite accurately the traditional assumption, "Among the many contested habits of mind unleashed by Burke's *Reflections on the Revolution in France* is the propensity to view the French Revolution as theater."[18]

It is in some sense not at all difficult to account for the rapid formation and enduring appeal of such a misperception. If Burke's royal drama seemed forced and anomalous in 1790, it appeared, after the execution of Louis and Marie-Antoinette in 1793, to have been predictive and, after the Terror, to have offered a prescient critical model for a tragic reading of Revolutionary history. By the middle of the next century, viewed through Marx and Hegel, through romanticism and its deep sense of the tragedy of Revolutionary experience, Burke's dramatic rendering seemed less conventional than proleptic.

Yet, to pry Burke's tragedy loose from its local context—to shift its status from that of a contemporary political gesture to a dramatizing "habit of mind"— elides its engagement in, and indeed effaces, the emphatic, contested theatricality of politics in both France *and* England during this period. A desire for such effacement clearly informed Paine's critique of the *Reflections*. Burke, Paine argues, "is not affected by the reality of distress touching his heart, but by the showy resemblance of it striking his imagination. He pities the plumage, but

forgets the dying bird. Accustomed to kiss the aristocratic hand that hath purloined him from himself, he degenerates into the composition of art, and the
genuine soul of nature forsakes him."[19] Attacking Burke's tragedy as artifice,
Paine seems to suggest by contrast that revolutionary history—revolutionary
politics—is unmediated by such theatricality, that the Revolution is, and could
be apprehended as, a natural, direct manifestation of the people's will. Of course,
Paine's is an equally distorting claim, as the preceding chapter's discussion of
revolutionary culture suggests. Yet, if Burke is frequently taken to task for the
distortion of his Versailles tragedy, Paine has hardly been held so accountable
for this equally distorted suggestion that Revolutionary politics eschew such
theatricality.[20] Why?

One explanation is that Paine's critique, his assertion that Burke's dramatic representation masks and distorts some atheatrical political reality, is more attrac-
tive to the political sensibilities of modernity. Certainly his antitheatrical political rhetoric anticipates quite strongly the nineteenth century's increasing distrust
and eventual turn away from that self-consciously theatrical exercise of power
which had marked the culture of monarchical and aristocratic politics.[21] If Paine's
radical politics proved out of step with the early nineteenth century's conservatism, his "plain-spoken" critique fit it well. Conversely, if Burke's *Reflections*
offered in its conservatism a political judgment on the Revolution that the early
nineteenth century would find compelling, that very popularity reinforced the
subsequent desire to refigure as mere metaphor Burke's invocation of the theatrical sensibility of an obsolete and aristocratic organization of power—despite
its consonance with contemporary theories of aesthetic response.

In accordance with such impulses, British political culture more generally
during the period has been, until recently, similarly treated. As I have suggested
in preceding chapters, historiography long foregrounded the spectacular theatricality of French Revolutionary politics, if only to dismiss it, as Carlyle did,
as the "foisonless, unedifying" spectacle behind which the perceptive viewer
might just discern, with Burke, the motions of a larger tragic conflict. By contrast, England's politics during this period appeared to be soberly, pragmatically
atheatrical, and even those elements that were undeniably so received little
recognition by comparison. Yet, a number of recent studies have made evident
the inaccuracy of such perceptions, and taken together they suggest that Burke's
dramatic *Reflections* might be better understood not as an exception or an anom-
aly but as a culminating statement of a British discourse of political theatricality that had been developing, by 1790, for almost twenty years.[22] To understand

how this is so, it is helpful to take a closer look at the rather different construction of relations between politics and theater in Britain's public sphere.

"Habitual Native Dignity": The Theater of British Politics, 1770–1794

In contrast to the almost exclusively political French press created with the onset of the Revolution, Britain's newspaper industry had its origins in the free-ranging discussions, gossip, and rumor of the coffeehouses, and it had from the start recognized the appeal of papers that ranged over a broad variety of political, commercial, cultural, and social topics.[23] By the 1780s, papers were typically diverse in their choice of topics for news and commentary, touching upon everything from the latest rumors of governmental matters to commodity prices, social gossip, and even literary reviews and announcements.[24] The theater, in particular, occupied even by the 1770s a prominent role in both the news coverage and the economics of many London dailies. It offered a regular source of advertising revenue, a daily source of cultural news, and a steady source of revenue-producing gossip, rumor, and scandal—for the British press was even in these early stages first and foremost a commercial pursuit. *Puffing*, or paid promotional mention, as well as extortion, paid agreement *not* to mention, were both common practices of professional journalists during the period, and practices directed with equal enthusiasm against well-known figures in theater and the arts, commerce, court, and parliamentary politics.

As such practices suggest, the British press of the late eighteenth century developed in an environment of considerably greater political and commercial freedom than its French counterpart. As with the development of London's theaters, however, it would be a mistake to overlook the strictures that were devised to monitor and regulate such openness, for the British papers did not at any time enjoy the virtual impunity possessed by the French news press during the early 1790s. England's political journalists were subject throughout this period to substantial laws against seditious libel, laws given real force by occasional and at times heavy-handed application. It wasn't until the early 1770s, in fact, at the time of the "Junius" controversy, that the British press successfully asserted the right, de facto if not de jure, to report directly upon parliamentary debate.[25] Even after having established that right, the press found itself at substantial risk if it engaged in overly pointed or direct criticism of the government or, particularly, of the royal family; as a result, many of the major journals in London had by the latter decades of the century allied themselves in various ways and to various degrees with political parties.[26] Such patrons were not in themselves, however, a reliable guarantee of safety for members of the press; quite to the contrary, politicians could and occasionally would use a newspaper as a convenient cover from which to libel an opponent, leaving the paper's proprietor to hang in the wind if charges were leveled.[27] The threat of such prosecution did not stifle political commentary, but it prompted newspapers to work through implication and suggestion and to develop over time "an allusive style and an allegorical approach, rich in innuendo and code words and letters."[28]

The theater was an obvious source of reference for such oblique commentary, not least because it constituted in its own right one of the most prominent and voluminous subjects of news. Not only did it provide a rich, continuously changing, and immediately available set of conventions and allusions for indirect commentary on political events, but the very proximity of theatrical and political news on the page contributed to the evolution of an interpenetrating, combinatory discourse in which political and theatrical journalism began to overlap and even form a sort of juxtapositive web.

One significant mechanism of such development was the formal layout of British newspapers: unlike today's papers, which characteristically devote a discrete section to each area of the news, many of the dailies of the 1780s and 1790s mixed items together in a seemingly random fashion.[29] Political, social, and theatrical items were set side by side and mixed together in columns, so that one might read in 1793, for example, an item on the birthdays of the king's children followed by a report of political maneuvers in Parliament followed by a critique of the latest Covent Garden production and then a brief mention of optimism in the campaigns against the French. At times political items would be figured as theater news, as was the case at the end of April in 1794, when the *Times* offered a two-part commentary on parliamentary matters, including a critique of its patron party, that took the form of a fictitious battle of the theaters.[30]

But there were more subtle resonances between the two realms as well, for the *Times* offers frequent examples of both intentional and coincidental juxtapositions of theater and politics, juxtapositions in which larger meanings seem evident even from our position of cultural and historical distance. As one might expect, some of the most suggestive of such moments were something more than coincidental but rather less than deliberate—juxtapositions that seemed to find in the theatrical news a microcosmic expression of public political opinion. One exemplary instance of such combinatory logic, in the context of this discussion, is the *Times* of July 1, 1789.

The paper's second page (that on which the most important news was offered) devoted the greater part of its four columns to Louis's emphatic declaration and speech to the Estates General of June 23, in which he condemned the combinatory defiance of the Tennis Court Oath, ordered the three estates to return to their separate chambers, and insisted that distasteful, interfering spectators thenceforth be prohibited from observing the estates' proceedings from the galleries. Seemingly by chance, the *Times* reported on the same page no fewer than three separate incidents of theatrical unrest: an invasion of the Crown Gallery of the Covent Garden Opera House by ruffians, a rude ejection of gentlemen and ladies from their boxes at Covent Garden Theatre by individuals falsely claiming rightful possession, and a near duel between two gentlemen in the theater's Crown Gallery. Just below those items, the paper repeated its report that Louis "expressly forbids that any strangers should in future be admitted to the Galleries of the National Assembly. Some persons were so indecent as to clap and applaud some particular Member . . . while others again were hissed."[31] It is little wonder that Burke, undoubtedly a reader of this ministerial journal, and certainly attentive to the importance of theatrical effect and response, would just a few months later conflate these items, suggesting that the National Assembly acted "amidst the tumultuous cries of a mixed mob of ferocious men, and of women lost to shame, who . . . sometimes mix and take their seats amongst them," and thus conclude, famously, that "the gallery is in the place of the house."[32]

However, it was not only through allusion and juxtaposition on the page that the newspaper brought the theater and politics together in late-eighteenth-century Britain. The newspapers contributed as well to the unusual formation in the 1770s of a common rhetoric of public performance; a set of conventions of both public speech and spectatorial response, shared by the discursive spheres of Parliament, court, and theater and characterized by the conjunction of spectatorial sensibility with oratorical taste. This rhetoric constituted the language of Burke's theater of politics, and it is in terms of this language that Burke's dramatic representation of the October Days was composed, received, and contested.

The establishment of parliamentary reporting in 1771 had changed politics in a manner as unfamiliar to the public as it was uncomfortable for politicians. Public opinion, an entity that existed largely through and in the press, replaced the limited galleries and the benches of Parliament itself as the implicit audience of much parliamentary oratory. Politicians were forced to address a larger audience, and they were forced to do so through the press; some even blamed the loss of Britain's American colonies on the deleterious effects of such a radical shift.[33] The audience, for its part, was no less unaccustomed to parliamentary debate,

The King's Declaration
· That the Three Estates
Retain Their Separate
Identities and Chambers
· That No Spectators
Be Present to Disrupt
Their Deliberations

The King's Speech
· His Command
That the Gentlemen
Return to Their
Separate Chambers

A Riot Attempted
at the New Covent
Garden Opera House
by Men Who Had
"Found Their Way
Into the Crown Gallery"

Ladies and Gentlemen
"Rudely Thrust Out
of Their Places"
at Covent Garden Theatre

A Duel Nearly Occurs
in the Crown Gallery
That Same Evening

The King's Stricture
Against "Strangers" in
"the Galleries of the
National Assembly"
is Repeated
as a Society Item

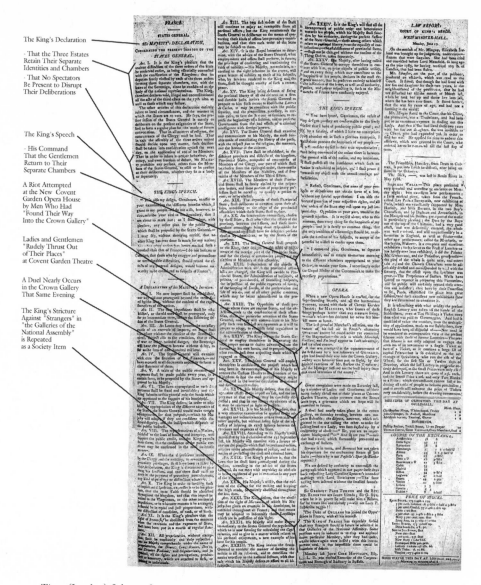

Times (London), July 1, 1789.

and, as in France three decades later, the theater offered politicians a common set of conventions, expectations, and criteria for effective public speech. Such practices were reinforced by the involvement of many political journalists, who were of course the conduit through which parliamentary oratory reached the pages of the press, in the theater. Lucyle Werkmeister's profile of individuals linked to the fourteen London dailies of 1792 offers a useful sample: Thomas Harris, one of the paymasters who arranged for the Treasury's political press subsidies, was also the manager of Covent Garden; the prominent playwright James Boaden was one of two editors of the *Oracle, or Bell's New World;* the actress Mary Wells was a frequent contributor to and occasional editor of the *World;* William Cooke, a Treasury writer who reported the debates in the House of Lords for a number of papers, was also a noted playwright and critic, having published in 1775 his *Elements of Dramatic Criticism.*[34] As even this list suggests, the British appropriation to politics of the languages of the drama was very different than that which took place in France in the opening months of the Revolution; rather than playing to a radical press and full galleries in an atmosphere of strict publicity, British politicians spoke in effect to an audience composed of representatives of the party-supported press—representatives who were also members of a theater industry that was itself carefully controlled by the government.

Sheridan's rise to political prominence exemplifies the new criteria of effective political action in such a context. Sheridan first gained his reputation as a dramatist with *The Rivals* (1775) and *The School for Scandal* (1777), and he became part-owner and director of Drury Lane in 1776. In 1779 he came out with *The Critic,* a satire of the theater industry itself, including its reliance upon paid support in the press. The next year Sheridan was elected M.P. for Stafford, and he rapidly gained a reputation as one of the most capable orators in Parliament. He was named under-secretary of state for foreign affairs in 1782, became secretary of the treasury the following year, and in 1788 was made a member of the Privy Council, all the while retaining his position at Drury Lane and managing, to a large degree, the opposition press. As William Cobbett, one of Sheridan's most determined critics, complained in 1804, "There is and always has been in this country a natural alliance, a sort of family compact between the press and the theatre; and therefore when the chief of the latter happens to deal in politics as well as plays, his political adversaries, unless they have the good luck to deal in plays, combat him at a fearful disadvantage."[35]

Precisely what enabled Sheridan to so master these three realms seemed rather mysterious to Cobbett, who attributed his control of the press to "some quality I suppose, more than commonly amiable."[36] Yet, there is a continuity that runs through Sheridan's career, one that is, I think, a fundamental component in any effort to understand properly the theatricality of British politics during this period. Sheridan was widely considered to be the most eloquent man of his generation, at a time when the art of rhetoric had come to be seen as of great value in this expanded, if still controlled, public sphere of politics. His 1788 address on the impeachment of Hastings was, in Byron's estimation, "the very *best* oration . . . ever conceived or heard in this country," and it created the sort of sensation usually associated with a theatrical premiere.[37] Peter Davison offers a description of the event worth quoting in full, if only to gain some greater appreciation of the appreciation that attended upon Sheridan's oratory:

> People, many of them 'peeresses in full dress', waited for hours to hear Sheridan's onslaught on Warren Hastings . . . and some of them paid up to £50 for a seat. The rush 'to get convenient seats, nearly proved fatal to many'. Yet they might simply have been treated to a repetition of his five-hour speech on the same topic given to the House of Commons in the preceding year, itself described by the *Gentleman's Magazine* as 'the most astonishing effort of eloquence, argument, and wit united, of which there is any record or tradition'. His speech at the trial was spread over the afternoons of 3, 6, 10, and 13 June, 1788; and on the first afternoon alone he spoke for 4½ hours. He was taken ill on the tenth, and at the end of his peroration on the thirteenth he collapsed in Burke's arms and had to be assisted to a chair. It was undoubtedly a remarkable *performance*, though whether the collapse was or was not the work of an actor (as Gibbon supposed) is a moot point.[38]

Significantly, Sheridan's oratorical virtuosity was not grounded in striking originality of figure, spontaneous insight, or electrifying delivery; he tended rather to work out his figurative comparisons carefully and well in advance, to speak with "calm dignity" rather than great energy, to have been noted for his "good sense, ingenuity, and temper" and to speak in public with a clarity and elegance of style, elocution, and gesture not generally observed in his private speech.[39] In all of these traits, Sheridan was the very exemplar of the Elocutionary Movement, a philosophy of rhetorical training that enjoyed enormous influence at the time and whose most influential proponent was his father, Thomas Sheridan.

In contrast to classical rhetorical training, the elder Sheridan's *A Course of Lectures on Elocution* (1762) emphasized not reasoning, figures, or arrangement but "the just and graceful management of the voice, countenance, and gesture in speaking."[40] Supported by both Jonathan Swift and Lord Chesterfield, Sheridan promoted the Elocutionary Movement largely as an educational philosophy, and one very much concerned with linking the period's increased educational opportunities to social advancement. As Sheridan (an ex-actor) repeatedly emphasized in his lectures, speech patterns denoted social position, and education that failed to address proper speech failed as well to provide gentlemen with real opportunities to rise. All dialects other than that of the court were, he noted, "sure marks either of a provincial, rustic, pedantic, or mechanical education; and therefore have some degree of disgrace annexed to them."[41]

The education of a gentleman, if it were to prepare one for a career, had therefore to teach elocution associated with the cosmopolitan manners of the court. In training his students, Sheridan was thus concerned not merely with enunciative clarity but with what might better be described as the entire "manner" of declamation, or the way in which the speaker's verbal and gestural performance conveyed both a discernment of sense and, perhaps more important, a proper sensibility. Tone, gesture, and countenance were, as Thomas Conley noted, perceived by Sheridan to be the "languages of passion and imagination"; far from constituting a mere façade, manners revealed, expressed, and conditioned sensibility, and sensibility was in turn indicative of taste, civility, and breeding.[42] Grounded in manners, such oratory appealed less to logic than to taste as its basis of sense and judgment, exemplifying what Conley describes as a more general transformation, within rhetoric at this time, from "'common sense' as an epistemological warrant" to "'taste' as a mode of social redemption."[43]

Begun as an educational movement, the Elocutionary Movement had become by the 1770s the basis of a much more extensive and normative convention of public performance, a convention that along with the newspaper press helped to define what could be described as a nascent, continuous space of public performance and public identity—a space in which political, theatrical, and court life all participated in a shared culture of public speech. Both Sarah Siddons and John Philip Kemble, for example, had been students of Thomas Sheridan's methods. Sheridan had in fact been Siddons' primary acting teacher, and both of these leading actors adopted Sheridan's practice of holding "Attic evenings" devoted to recitation.[44] Their restrained, declamatory style of acting thus mirrored on the stage of Drury Lane the courtly oratory of R. B. Sheridan, succeeding and contributing greatly (along with the aesthetic theory of Reynolds) to the rapid eclipse after 1776 of Garrick's "natural acting."[45] Theater, Parliament, and Court, the three discursive spheres most strongly imbricated in the pages of the newspapers, thus came increasingly to share the same performative language of public speech. As one might expect, in such a situation aesthetic, political, and courtly values came increasingly to overlap and complement each other, defining not simply a shared public sphere but also that theater of political action in which both Sheridan and Burke gained prominence. It was, in 1790, precisely that interlocking network of theatrical, political, and chivalric values that defined what we may describe as Burke's theater of politics, and it was certainly that interlocking network that lent Burke's *Reflections* its rhetorical coherence.

British liberties, Burke notes early in the *Reflections*, have "from Magna Charta to the Declaration of Right" been claimed and asserted "as an *entailed*

inheritance derived to us from our forefathers."[46] To some degree his concern
here is to differentiate the British conception of rights, founded in the common
law tradition, from that abstract conception of rights asserted by the Revolution
and derived from natural law theory and the logical tradition of Roman law.
Yet Burke's purpose extends beyond questions of legal philosophy; the treatment
of rights as an entailed inheritance, he notes, has carried with it certain civilizing benefits as well. "Always acting as if in the presence of canonized forefathers,
the spirit of freedom . . . is tempered with an awful gravity. This idea of a liberal descent inspires us with a sense of habitual native dignity, which prevents
that upstart insolence almost inevitably adhering to and disgracing those who are
the first acquirers of any distinction." Burke's language is familiar: "upstart insolence" here appears very like Sheridan's plague of noncourtly dialects, potentially "adhering to and disgracing" those who first rise to some distinction. The
analogy is a useful one, for in Burke's schema the very notion that rights are a
sort of entailed inheritance serves, like the Elocutionary Movement, to socialize
and civilize the upwardly mobile, gentlemanly bourgeois. Just as Sheridan's elocutionary training provides one with a proper courtly demeanor, so too does the
"idea of a liberal descent," according to Burke, inspire "a sense of habitual native dignity." British liberty becomes "a noble freedom. It carries an imposing
and majestic aspect. It has a pedigree and illustrating ancestors. It has its bear-
ings and its ensigns armorial. It has its gallery of portraits, its monumental in-
scriptions, its records, evidences, and titles."[47]

The effects of such liberty are more than merely elevating, for that dignified elevation fosters in turn sentiments of "veneration, admiration, and attachment" to
the state.[48] "Reverence to our civil institutions," Burke suggests, is procured in accordance with the same principles "upon which nature teaches us to revere individual men," for in his figurative schema it is civil institutions that hang in the portrait gallery of liberty's noble descent.[49] Such personalized civil affections had in
Burke's view a critical role in the conduct of political action, for they soften and
strengthen, in the mutual observance of dignified civil discourse, the cold authority of law. Such discourse, of course, is itself structured by "manners," or the theatrical conventions of tasteful address, countenance, and gesture through which the
sympathetic bonds of community are enacted and affirmed. And, indeed, one can
easily imagine how for Burke, in his own upward mobility to parliamentary prominence, this model might have seemed persuasive: manners, he declares, are those
"pleasing illusions, which made power gentle and obedience liberal, which har-
monized the different shades of life, and which, by a bland assimilation, incorporated into politics the sentiments which beautify and soften private society."[50]

The "origin" of "this mixed system of opinion and sentiment" was "ancient chivalry," which, "without confounding ranks, had produced a noble equality and handed it down through all the gradations of social life. It was this opinion which mitigated kings into companions and raised private men to be fellows with kings." Chivalry thus becomes for Burke a kind of ancient form of the Elocutionary Movement, extending to all a civilizing courtly manner that elevated, dignified, and preserved liberty: "Without force or opposition, it subdued the fierceness of pride and power, it obliged sovereigns to submit to the soft collar of social esteem, compelled stern authority to submit to elegance, and gave a domination, vanquisher of laws, to be subdued by manners."[51] Liberty, chivalry, and manners are therefore of a piece—all mutually reinforcing aspects of Britain's native freedom. It is within this rhetorical framework that Burke both structures and defends his tragic reading of the October Days, for he extends to both the institution and the persons of the French monarchy, and particularly to the queen, a place in that sphere of sympathetic manners and chivalric sentiment: "I thought ten thousand swords must have leaped from their scabbards," he famously exclaims, "to avenge even a look that threatened her with insult."[52]

Burke's argument here thus played well to the conventions and attitudes of a culture defined by the elocutionary intersection of theater, politics, and court. Yet Burke goes too far, claiming for his sentiments and the theatrical aesthetic they imply a status that far exceeds such cultural particularity. Why, he asked, "do I feel so differently" from those who exalted in the October Days? "For this plain reason: because it is *natural* that I should; because we are so made as to be affected at such spectacles with melancholy sentiments upon the unstable condition of mortal prosperity and the tremendous uncertainty of human greatness; because in those natural feelings we learn great lessons; because in events like these our passions instruct our reason; because when kings are hurled from their thrones by the Supreme Director of this great drama and become the objects of insult to the base and of pity to the good, we behold such disasters in the moral as we should behold a miracle in the physical order of things." Indeed, for Burke the theater becomes a sort of litmus test of such a reaction. It is "a better school of moral sentiments than churches," for in the theater "men follow their natural impulses" and "would not bear," much less exult, to see the sufferings of France's royal family—to see, as he put it, "the crimes of a new democracy posted as in a ledger against the crimes of an old despotism."[53]

And yet this is precisely where Burke declares his own obsolescence, for by 1790 neither the discursive consensus to which he appealed nor the theatrical sensibility he invoked could claim the normative status of a "natural" response.

The Revolution's impact had already been felt in Britain, and against Burke's appeal to chivalric sentiment there argued not only a different political rhetoric but a political rhetoric that entailed as well a different, and ultimately dominant, theatrical sensibility. It was Wollstonecraft and Paine who most capably articulated an opposing rhetoric of politics, albeit one that encountered great opposition as the Revolution turned to violence. However, it was Sheridan, ironically, who brought to prominence the new theatrical sensibility that such rhetoric entailed, and that sensibility, as I hope to show, came rapidly to define a new relation between politics and theater in Britain.

"The Real Prisoner of Misery": British Political Theater, 1789–1799

It was specifically in response to Burke's claims of an "inborn," "natural" tragic sensibility that Paine, in the *Rights of Man*, sarcastically describes him as "accustomed to kiss the aristocratical hand that hath purloined him from himself," for such claims were a kind of absurd self-denial from such an obviously self-made man. Through such denial, Paine suggests, Burke is forsaken by "the genuine soul of nature" and "degenerates into the composition of art."[54] For Mary Wollstonecraft, too, precisely this naturalizing aspect of Burke's argument is most objectionable.[55] "What do you mean by inbred sentiments?" she asks in her *Vindication of the Rights of Men* (1790): "From whence do they come? How were they bred? Are they the brood of folly, which swarms like insects on the banks of the Nile, when mud and putrefaction have enriched the languid soil? Were these *inbred* sentiments faithful guardians of our duty when the church was an asylum for murderers, and men worshipped bread as a God? when slavery was authorized by law to fasten her fangs on human flesh, and the iron eat into the very soul?"[56]

Focusing on Burke's characteristic claim that "vice lost half its evil, by losing all its grossness," Wollstonecraft attacks Burke's appeal to a gendered and aristocratic sense of taste as a natural basis for his moral judgment of the Revolution. "What a sentiment to come from a moral pen!" she observes. "Your politics and morals, when simplified, would undermine religion and virtue to set up a spurious, sensual beauty, that has long debauched your imagination, under the specious form of actual feelings."[57] Far from offering a basis for moral judgment of the Revolution, Burke's sentiments were, for both Paine and Wollstonecraft, exemplary of just those social attitudes that made revolution necessary, for it was precisely the "romantic and chivalric spirit" that allowed the privileged classes to ignore the suffering of the poor and the violence of slavery in favor of the sentimental woes of queens.

And in this critique Burke's appeal to the theater becomes central: "Misery, to reach your heart," rebukes Wollstonecraft, "must have its cap and bells; your tears are reserved, very naturally considering your character, for the declamation of the theatre."[58] Paine, too, charges Burke with requiring as his hero or heroine "a tragedy-victim expiring in show," and both authors counter Burke's "showy resemblances" of distress with their own "reality of distress,"[59] those "continual miseries" of the poor over which Burke's theatrical imagination "throws a veil."[60]

Yet, what both authors offer is something rather different from a complete rejection of Burke's theatrical rhetoric of sensibility, for both Paine and Wollstonecraft, even as they appeal to the rhetoric of antitheatricality, invoke the pathetic figures of a competing drama. As Paine asserts, Burke's "hero or his heroine must be a tragedy-victim expiring in show, and not *the real prisoner of misery, sliding into death in the silence of a dungeon*" [my emphasis].[61] For Wollstonecraft, Burke mourns "the empty pageant of a name" while "the sick heart retires to die in lonely fields, far from the abodes of men." If Burke invokes sympathy for an idealized queen, Wollstonecraft and Paine invoke similar sympathies for characters drawn with equally theatrical extremity: "the sick wretch, who can no longer earn the sour bread of unremitting labour [and] steals to a ditch to bid the world a long good night—or, neglected in some ostentatious hospital, breathes his last amidst the laugh of mercenary attendants."[62]

These "prisoners of misery" emerge in nineteenth-century melodrama as stock figures more familiar even than tragic queens. Even in 1790, however, the type had already become quite well known to British audiences, for the prisoner of misery was a critical part of those gothic fictions that first articulated popular sentiment against France's feudal aristocratic and religious institutions. More particularly, and almost certainly the source of Paine's image, the fall of the Bastille had translated into the symbolic practices of popular insurrection just such aestheticized sentiments, and for many Britons the fall of the Bastille was experienced most spectacularly as a kind of gothic theater. Even as they explicitly attacked the explicit theatricality of Burke's *Reflections*, then, both Paine and Wollstonecraft implicitly asserted a competing dramatic rhetoric of politics. And while Burke's invocation of tragedy appealed, as we have seen, to the discourses of Britain's "legitimate" theater of politics, the "real prisoner of misery" appealed rather to the conventions of the popular spectacular theater.

Just sixteen days after the July Days, Astley's Royal Amphitheatre advertised the introduction of two "extraordinary scenes of the BASTILE, External and

Internal."[63] News of the prison's fall had arrived only a week before, and Astley's was the first theatrical establishment to take advantage of London's exceptional curiosity about the stunning events in Paris. Having entertained its audiences with tumbling, rope dancing, and equestrian extravaganzas for three years, Astley's was well suited to this novel sort of current events spectacular.[64] The following week, however, Palmer's Royal Circus of St. George's Fields trumped Astley's utterly, announcing to the public "an entire new and splendid Entertainment, founded on the subject of the French Revolution, called The TRIUMPH of LIBERTY; Or, The DESTRUCTION of the BASTILE." The Royal Circus claimed for itself comprehensive accuracy in its exhibition, "including, amongst a Variety of other striking matters incidental to the event, the whole of the plan, attack, storming, capture, and demolition of that horrid sepulchre of a people—the Bastile—massacre of the citizens that passed the drawbridge—the execution of the Governor and Mayor—the whole of several Military engagements, and processions on that and other occasions; together with the proceedings that gave freedom to the empire of France."[65]

The production was an immediate and overwhelming success, and the opening explosion of the French Revolution enjoyed a phenomenal run of seventy-nine successive nights at the Royal Circus.[66] There is little doubt that for a great many Britons the fall of the Bastille as it was enacted at Palmer's was a vivid and formative experience. What is particularly remarkable, however, is the degree to which that event had been rewritten for the stage: the production changed known facts and altered the flow of events, dropped in references to England and its envied liberties, and, most significantly, grafted the titular, historical event onto the narrative frame of a patriotic romance.

In John Dent's published version of the play, the fall of the Bastille becomes the story of Henry Dubois and Matilda, whose love is stymied by the prison's governor. Matilda's father, we learn in the play's opening moment, has been unjustly imprisoned for years, fading into weakness (or, as Paine would put it, "sliding into death in the silence of a dungeon") and facing certain doom unless Matilda agrees to marry Henry's hated rival. Yet, as the play opens drums are beating in anticipation of the people's siege of the hated fortress, and Henry, sensing an opportunity to liberate Matilda's father, places himself at the head of the patriotic crowd. The action unfolds as both a spectacular "documentary" recreation of the siege and a heroic rescue drama, including a striking scene of confrontation between Henry and the governor himself, a gothic "monster" who embodies the cruel and arbitrary power of France's feudal tyranny.

It is plausible to assume that this spectacle was for many in England their first view of the Revolution in action, and the impact of its depiction of the July Days as a youthful, heroic romance seems to have been powerful. Even Wordsworth seems to allude to the currency of such generic fantasies at the time, famously recalling in the *Prelude* the impression of the Revolution "as it appeared to enthusiasts at its inception":

> Bliss was it in that dawn to be alive,
> But to be young was very heaven!—Oh! times,
> In which the meagre, stale, forbidding ways
> Of custom, law, and statute, took at once
> The attraction of a country in romance![67]

One fascinating aspect of the Revolutionary romance at Palmer's is that it changed slightly over time to accommodate accounts, rumors, and myths of the fall of the Bastille. Most notable among these shifts was the play's incorporation, a few weeks after opening, of a scene of the alleged discovery in the prison's dungeon of a skeleton locked in an iron mask. The story of "the man in the iron mask" had been around for some time, having been given its most recent impetus by Voltaire. The customary interpretation was that the prisoner was of royal blood, for only a prisoner whose face would have been widely recognized need have been masked, and only the visage of the king (so the story's fairly compelling logic runs) would have been widely recognized. In fact, no such skeleton had really been found in the Bastille, but both the London papers and Palmer's were happy to accept such rumors as a basis for revision. For the audience at the Royal Circus, as for the French revolutionaries, the actual existence of the skeleton was in some sense less important than its compelling symbolic force: the man in the iron mask represented the very archetype of feudal tyranny, with its gloomy dungeons and arbitrary powers of imprisonment. The man in the iron mask was, in short, the specific exemplar of Paine's "prisoner of misery": "To put the very face of man in chains!" exclaims Dent's heroic Henry,

> No crime's alledg'd!—his lips with death are seal'd,
> And who he was can never be reveal'd.
> Down let us trample on these Hell-born laws.[68]

The imaginative power of such a figure was considerable, and by October John St. John had written an opera on the subject. Yet, even in the fall of 1789 the British government had begun to grow uneasy about the representation on stage of subjects drawn from the Revolution, and St. John's opera was refused the licenser's approval on October 21. Kemble himself evidently edited the manuscript and gained approval for a much more politically moderate work, but the political trends had already become fairly clear. Over the next year representation of the Revolution on British stages became far more difficult, and by 1791, Jeffrey Cox has suggested, censorship under the Licensing Act had clearly taken on an added dimension, beginning with the interdiction of plays that espoused revolutionary sentiments.[69] By 1792, the radicalization of the Revolution and fears of the spread of popular violence to England prompted even tighter control over the stage: censorship extended not only to plays that appeared to support the Revolution but also to works that, however indirectly, seemed to allow the Revolution a presence on stage. Tyrannicides, rebels and rebellions, demagogues and mobs, whether contemporary or ancient, historical or fictional, glorified or condemned, were not to be shown to the public.[70] It was perhaps the only period since their composition that any of Shakespeare's works were banned from the British stage. The rationale for such measures was simple: as Cox explains, "The official fear in England (in France, the official hope) was that the theatrical recreation of revolutionary events would lead to their re-enactment on the streets, a fear not wholly unfounded in an era of theatrical as well as political riots."[71] The "romance" of the Revolution in the theaters of Britain was, with fair rapidity, brought to an end.

Yet if the depiction of Revolutionary events and even of Revolutionary sentiments seemed dangerous to the authorities, there was one figure at least who recognized in the spectacular rhetoric of Palmer's stage romance an exceptional language of national heroic theater. Sheridan, as a celebrated orator and playwright, as well as a theater manager and manager of the press, was both well placed institutionally and inclined politically to appropriate to the British stage some of the generic conventions and spectacular conventions, if not the radical political action, of the Bastille drama. In spectacular romance he recognized a powerful means through which to link great historical action to common individuals, and he set about, in the 1790s, producing in Britain a political theater that would succeed in more popular form the Burkean model of theatrical politics. What is fascinating about this effort is that Sheridan himself was the very model of the Burkean orator, and even in his development of a new, popular political theater it is possible to recognize the continuing influence of that political culture.

One reason that Sheridan was perhaps so attracted to such a project is that he shared with Paine and the radicals a clear sense of the relation between popular action and belief, on the one hand, and the representation of power by those in power, on the other. In his critique of Burke, Paine argued emphatically that the violence of the July and October Days (when insurrectionary crowds had murdered and then brandished aloft the heads of various governmental representatives) was due, not to a monstrous absence of that "habitual native dignity" which Burke saw in the English, but to the crowd's misguided imitation of their own government's spectacles of power. The people learn violence, Paine asserts, "from the governments they live under, and retaliate the punishments they have been accustomed to behold."[72] In February of 1790, Sheridan famously split with Burke over precisely this issue. The rift seems to have stemmed from Burke's speech to the Commons on February 9, and Jack Durant's description of the episode is worth quoting at length:

> What seems most to have troubled Sheridan about Burke's speech that night was that it inveighed against social excesses in revolutionary France without properly fixing the blame for them. Blame belonged, said Sheridan, not to the National Assembly, where Burke seemed to place it, but to the despotic government of pre-revolutionary France, a government that "set at naught the property, the liberty, the lives of a subject," one "that dealt in extortion, dungeons, and tortures; that *set an example of depravity to the slaves it ruled over.*" It was not to be wondered at that a people liberated from such oppression should be guilty of excess, that it should act "without those feelings of justice and humanity, which the principles and the practices of their governors had stripped them of." [my emphasis][73]

It seems unsurprising, then, that Sheridan, who also felt considerable sympathy for the Revolution's ideals of universal fraternity, would attempt to appropriate the civic rhetoric of the Revolution itself to the self-representation of British power.

His first exercise in such theatrical propaganda was a "theatrical entertainment" commemorating Lord Howe's June 1, 1793, naval victory over the French. *The Glorious First of June* was composed in just three days at the end of that month and staged for the benefit of the widows and children of the men killed in the action. The piece revives all the characteristics that made Dent's *Bastille* so popular, including the narrative frame of a romance and the central spectacle of the recent battle enacted in all its scenic grandeur. Sheridan wrote some fine speeches for the piece, thus carrying into the theater his celebrated oratory, but the tone of *The Glorious First* was emphatically popular, with broad humor and a number of rousing songs. Its production was an enormous success, deemed by the *Times* "a national tribute to national heroism," and it sparked a wave of song writing that continued for some time in the press.[74]

Most fascinating is the manner in which this piece's popular theatrical aesthetic is matched by a remarkable thematic acknowledgment and even endorsement of the great popular appeal of revolutionary sentiments. Its climactic song, *Conquer to Save,* offers an almost bizarre amalgam of British nationalism and Revolutionary enthusiasm, and the piece scripts into the very conflict with France itself the ideology of romantic rescue. When, for example, the tri-colored ensigns of France appear on the horizon, "With three cheers they're welcom'd by each British tar"; and yet,

> Whilst the Genius of Britain still bids us advance,
> Our great guns like thunder bid defiance to France.

And yet again, once the French ships go down, "they no longer are foes":

> To snatch a brave fellow from a wat'ry grave,
> Is worthy a Briton, who conquers to save.

Similar sentiments are assigned even to Lord Howe, "who the man and the hero unites":

> The friend to the wretched, the boast of the brave,
> He lives still to conquer, and conquer to save.

Rather than opposing the Revolution, then, Sheridan's political theater suggests that Britain, in a role appropriated from the early ideology of revolutionary romance, is fighting to *rescue* the French, to snatch the "wretched" from sliding in silence into a "wat'ry grave."

The Glorious First of June, however, is a mere prelude to Sheridan's extravagant 1799 production of *Pizarro,* a spectacular heroic drama that he adapted from Kotzebue.[75] By this time the radical Revolution was long since over, and Bonaparte was in the ascendancy, threatening even the possibility of an invasion of England. *Pizarro* is, appropriately, an invasion play, and the political resonances are fairly obvious: the cruel conquistador is Bonaparte, while the innocent Peruvians stand in for the Britons themselves.

As romantic spectacle, *Pizarro* was unprecedented; Sheridan poured expense and energy into its design, and from all accounts it struck audiences as the most magnificent visual production to date. Its most astounding set piece occurred at the height of the third act, as Rolla, the sympathetic hero (played by Kemble), escapes across an Andean chasm on a precarious rope bridge, carrying in his arms the baby of the heroic Alonzo and Cora (played by Sarah Siddons), Alonzo's wife and the woman Rolla loves. Just as Rolla crosses the bridge collapses, and the resulting effect was so dramatic that it inspired Kemble's famous portrait as Rolla, holding the baby in the air.

As oratory, too, *Pizarro* was remarkable. In all of his plays, Sheridan's rhetorical presence in his characters is quite evident: as Davison remarks with some flourish of his own, "whereas in the best plays of two or three of the Restoration dramatists (and famously in Congreve), each character's speech is his own, in Sheridan, all is Sheridan. If this is so, it cannot but be a limitation—but it may also be that in Sheridan's greatest plays, something peculiarly reflective of the power of the man's use of language still comes through to us today."[76] Despite its hyperbolic reappropriation of Sheridan in the tradition of genius, the observation captures well one of *Pizarro*'s attractions as a theatrical event. As was quite well known, Sheridan had even on the day of performance not yet completed the script, and the overflowing crowds that evening were apparently aware that Sheridan was still writing *during* the performance, sending lines to Kemble and Siddons between scenes. The play's reviewers would note that *Pizarro* was somewhat expansive that night, as if Sheridan were speaking *ex tempore* on the floor of Parliament. With a story taken from Kotzebue, the audience had little doubt of the direction the play's action would take; what they did not know was how well Sheridan would articulate those actions, and so the greater source of tension on this occasion was not Rolla's dramatic fate but Sheridan's oratorical performance. In so combining these performances, Sheridan, too, was bringing together in a remarkable way the political theater of Parliament with the theatrical spectacular of *Pizarro*.

Yet the most notable aspect of this production was the play's climactic ceremonial scene, in which the Peruvians gather at the Temple of the Sun to obtain a blessing for their people before impending battle with the Spaniards. Combining the production's most imposing visual and oratorical moments, the scene had enormous impact as political theater. The patriotic speech that Sheridan composed for Rolla was thought by critics to be a model of political inspiration, contrasting emphatically the motives and spirit of the French (Spaniards) to those of the British (Peruvians): "THEY, by a strange frenzy driven, fight for power, for plunder, and extended rule—WE, for our country, our altars, and our homes.—THEY follow an Adventurer whom they fear—and obey a power which they hate—WE serve a Monarch whom we love—a God whom we adore."[77] And at the height of the scene the actors engage in an invocation to that "pow'r Supreme," performing a ritual procession of priests and virgins clothed in white, a lighting of the sacred altar, and a communal giving of thanks. Such a ceremony was unusual on the British stage, and Price goes to some trouble linking its theatrical effects to Beaumont and Fletcher's *The Tragedy of Bonduca* or to "Rowe's *The Ambitious Step-Mother* (1701)."[78] Of course, to Sheridan's audience, much more recent and evident precedents were available: the festivals of Revolutionary France. Such resonances were not entirely absent from Rolla's harangue, either. The Spaniards, he declares, boast that "they come but to improve our state, enlarge our thoughts, and free us from the yoke of error! . . . Be our plain answer this: The throne WE honour is the PEOPLE'S CHOICE—the laws we reverence are our brave Father's legacy—the faith we follow teaches us to live in bonds of charity with all mankind, and die with hope of bliss beyond the grave."[79]

This ironic reversal of populist sentiment, in which England is presented as acting in defense of a monarch chosen by the people, was not lost on contemporaries. Yet, remarkably, Sheridan seems less to have made some definitively recognized political statement than to have played perfectly to all parties. One contemporary noted that Sheridan had managed to offend both the violent Ministerialists and, from the very loyalty of the play, the violent oppositionalists. At the same time, not only did the royal family attend and apparently approve quite heartily of the play, but so too did the political reformer William Wilberforce, who had not attended the theater in almost twenty years. *Pizarro* was by some accounts the largest grossing theatrical production of the century, and it seems to have brought together, in a remarkable way, many of the diverse political and theatrical currents running through Britain's culture at the end of the Revolutionary decade.

Joseph Donohue notes, in *Theatre in the Age of Kean*, that "the Theatre Royal in Covent Garden was destroyed by fire in the morning of September 20, 1808. The fire was thought by contemporaries to have been ignited by wadding from a gun fired during a performance of Richard Brinsley Sheridan's spectacular romantic tragedy *Pizarro*."[80] It seems ironic that it would be Sheridan's play that would cause such a loss, for one might well argue that *Pizarro* also marked the destruction of that Burkean theater of politics which so deeply informed British culture for the two decades leading up to the Revolution. That destruction seems, too, to have been a kind of erasure, for with the emergence of spectacular melodrama, the subdued theatricality of British politics—carried out on the floor of Parliament and in the pages of the newspapers—seems almost to have vanished.

Recognizing the theatricality of that culture, and placing Burke's *Reflections* within that context, has been one of the primary concerns of this chapter. However, my second concern is in some ways more pressing: if Burke's culture of political theatricality seems to have been forgotten, the theatrical rhetoric of British pro-Revolutionary politics has long been neglected in the embrace of

Paine's antitheatrical critique of Burke. What I am suggesting here is that such emphasis on Paine's antitheatricality has prevented full recognition of the contribution to Britain's political culture and theatrical history of the spectacular, proto-melodramatic theater of early, pro-Revolutionary politics—a radical theater that emerged in Sheridan's triumphant *Pizarro* (1799) as the dominant theatrical discourse of British national identity.

The significance of *Pizarro*, accordingly, is not as an endpoint, for it offered the first exemplary model for the spectacular plays that came to dominate the British theaters of the early nineteenth century. The populist potential of those later dramas has been recognized already.[81] What interests me about this prehistory of the form is that it suggests a much stronger continuity between such nationalist spectacles and French Revolutionary politics than has yet been recognized.

CHAPTER FOUR

The Fall of Robespierre
and the Tragic Imagination

Robespierre: What! did th'assassin's dagger aim its point
Vain, as a *dream* of murder, at my bosom?

Coleridge and Southey, The Fall of Robespierre, *I.ii.6–7*

As a critical gesture, this chapter can be understood as an effort to close a current discontinuity between romantic studies of the impact of the French Revolution on British tragedy and eighteenth-century scholars' work on the representation of the Revolution in print. There is good reason for staging an encounter between these two areas of inquiry. Through the work of George Steiner, Ronald Paulson, Mary Jacobus, Jeffrey Cox, Julie Carlson, Terence Alan Hoagwood, Reeve Parker, Marjean Purinton, and William Jewett, for example, we have gained a much clearer sense of the broad trajectory and characteristic tenor of the British romantics' reactions to the Revolutionary experience: their initial enthusiasm for its cause; their sympathetic identification with its participants and their close imaginary participation in its events; their recoiling horror at the Revolution's subsequent violence; and the manner in which that psychological trauma prompted the romantics' characteristic abstraction and historical displacement of Revolutionary themes and concerns.[1] In romanticism's engagement with tragedy, that literary form most closely associated with both; indeed, revolution, as an abstract theme, permeates romantic tragedy to a degree unmatched in other genres, but the French Revolution, in its historical particularity and local immediacy, appears almost nowhere. Such pressurized displacement is so pronounced in romantic tragedy that it has been described by Terence Hoagwood as "the central fact about romantic drama."[2]

However, in its investigation of romanticism's engagement with the Revolution, literary scholarship has tended until recently, and to some extent even still, to reiterate that act of displacement, treating the romantics' experience of the Revolution, in accord with romantic representations of Revolution, as immediate and imaginary, as a single, prolonged moment of sublime horror rather than as a profoundly mediated, emphatically material, and highly local process of reception, apprehension, and negotiation. Indeed, this was precisely the critique leveled by David Jordan at Ronald Paulson's otherwise immensely useful *Representations of Revolution*. Although Paulson there offers a comprehensive view of contemporary aesthetic responses to the Revolution, he treats the Revolution itself, in Jordan's estimate, as "some vast, abstract, and amorphous upheaval that calls forth primal images of sex and generation and death and cruelty."[3] The problem is less pronounced, but no less evident, in the more recent work of Jacobus, Cox, Carlson, Hoagwood, and Jewett. There, the local negotiation of the romantics' responses to the Revolution, the complexities of those responses' imaginative and textual articulation, and their change and development within the Revolution have been more amply explored. In such work, the romantics' engagement with the Revolution has gained particularity and discreteness, but the assumption remains that the Revolutionary experience was, for the most part, unmediated: that the romantics (indeed, all revolutionary spectators) somehow possessed direct, comprehensive knowledge of events unfolding in France, that their meditations upon its philosophy responded directly to the articulation of those ideas in France, and that their nightmare visions of its violence and action were prompted by some direct view of its spectacle. Paulson's tendency to treat the Revolution as amorphous and undifferentiated has been overcome, but it remains for the most part an abstract creation, displaced from the partiality and imperfection of material culture.[4]

At the same time, however, Jeremy Popkin, Jeremy Black, and other scholars of Revolutionary print have made it quite apparent that the lived experience of the French Revolution was profoundly mediated, to a degree and in a manner that distinguish it from all earlier history.[5] They remind us that the vast majority of the Revolution's spectators, and indeed even its actors, experienced the Revolution not in person but through the medium of an exploding international political news press, an enormous system of journalistic transmission and broadcast that arose directly with the French Revolution and that changed entirely, over the course of just few years, the basic conditions and discursive contexts of historical action and political event. From the start, the events of the Revolution were not only conveyed by this expanding apparatus but also shaped by it, for it was in the newspaper, more often than on the street, that Revolutionary events were given initial narrative and dramatic coherence and assigned meaning and import, and it was in the rapid establishment of that paradigmatically modern cycle of the news day, too, that one finds the gradual formation of the Nietszchean nightmare of modern history, as historical action begins to be meted out, disenchanted, and bounded by the day-to-day particularity of the daily news.

Indeed, George Steiner noted some time ago that it was the explosion of international news journalism during the Revolution, and not merely the discrete events of Revolutionary politics, that "plunged ordinary men into the stream of history," eliminating the viability of tragedy both in the theater, where the audience now sat distracted, and in politics, where historical action increasingly took on the continual rhythms of the everyday and of the banal.[6] This deeper shift in apprehension and in consciousness is apparent everywhere in the post-Revolutionary period—perhaps most concretely in the history-defying violence of Napoleonic aggression, but also in the period's almost definitive literary and philosophical concern with the possibilities of heroic action in a postheroic age.

If it is possible to see in the romantics' displacement of Revolutionary events a traumatic recoil away from the corporeal violence of Revolutionary action and the philosophical collapse of Revolutionary ideals, we must also recognize in such displacement an effort to flee—indeed, to deny, to elide, to escape—this deeper, apprehensive, and ontological experience of historical disenchantment. And if we are to understand that experience, to understand the manner in which that fundamental apprehensive shift affected and found expression in romantic drama, we must look not only at the romantics' own images of revolution and the events in France, but at the hazy space in between the two—at that emergent apparatus of journalistic representation through which those events were experienced by and made known to their international audience. In this chapter I explore one particularly significant moment in that indirect experience of Revolutionary history: the fall of Robespierre, as it unfolded in the pages of the London *Times* in the spring and summer of 1794.

Robespierre and Coleridge's Tragic Imagination

M A C B E T H : Is this a dagger which I see before me,

    The handle toward my hand? Come, let me clutch thee:—

    I have thee not, and yet I see thee still.

    Art thou not, fatal vision, sensible

    To feeling, as to sight? Or art thou but

    A dagger of the mind, a false creation,

Proceeding from the heat-oppressed brain?

I see thee yet, in form as palpable

As this which now I draw.

Thou marshal'st me the way that I was going.

Macbeth *II.i.36–39*

Even in 1795, after the horrific violence of the Terror, Kant could gesture toward the shared ideals of the French Revolution and note that, in terms at least of its tendency toward freedom, the Revolution "finds in the heart of all spectators . . . a wishful participation bordering closely upon enthusiasm."[7] He was describing nothing new, for such "wishful participation" in the Revolution's aspirations had been a marked phenomenon of foreign spectatorship from the very outset of political unrest in France. Indeed, for Wordsworth the extraordinary aims articulated in the early days of the Revolution had not only prompted imaginary participation but had raised as well, in their sudden and apparent attempt to realize such abstract political ideals, the thought that perhaps the imagination itself had begun to emerge from the realm of mere fantasy to imprint its shape upon reality. In 1789, such a possibility seemed welcome, for "all those who had fed their childhood upon dreams," Wordsworth felt, might now realize those fantasies "not in Utopia . . . but in the very world."[8]

As the Revolution turned toward violence, however, the very possibility of some connection between the dreamt and the real—between the imaginary, sympathetic participation of men of feeling and the horrific violence of actual events—became increasingly troubling to those watching the Revolution from afar. If the Revolution suggested the imagination's material power, had sympathetic participation somehow contributed to Revolutionary violence? Had it lent support to, or even pushed to extremes, a cause that might otherwise have stopped short of regicide, of the Terror? If the radical Revolutionaries were regicides in act, were not their foreign spectators accomplices in mind?

Mary Jacobus has suggested that it was in relation to fears of just such a connection that *Macbeth* became such a highly charged play during this period. Not only did the tragedy confront first-generation romantics with a disturbing, offstage regicide, a regicide thus "acted out" in, and by, the spectator's mind; it also raised, in Macbeth's troubled vision of a murderous dagger, the specter of the potentially murderous power of the imagination. What, after all, is the relation between Macbeth's imagined dagger and the real weapon he draws forth? Does his "dagger of the mind" merely reflect ambitious desire, or does it, as Macbeth fears, usurp the rule of conscience, "marshalling" him toward his murderous crime?[9] For Wordsworth, who speaks in *The Prelude* of feeling an involuntary "sympathy with power" even during the height of the Terror, *Macbeth* clearly offered a resonant model for the guilty imagination of Revolutionary sympathy.[10] How could one control such disturbing dreams? How could one dispel them? Jacobus and other commentators have argued that Wordsworth, in *The Prelude,* turns to his model as a kind of solution, crying out Macbeth's "Sleep no more!" in his remembrance, displacing his own sense of complicity in a narrative gesture that at once acknowledges and dispels the guilt of his imagination.[11]

For Coleridge, however, such a sense of imaginative complicity was unusually acute and uniquely enduring. Julie Carlson, in perhaps the most insightful reading of his drama to date, argues that "Coleridge's is a body wracked by its inability to distinguish phantom from reality; and his is a mind recovering from, by covering over, a jacobin past. Not genius but guilt is what distinguishes Coleridge from his romantic fellows in terms of the politics of theatre. Unlike the second-generation poets, who did not experience the French Revolution as young men, or Wordsworth, who invokes Shakespeare to relieve his terror, only the genius of Coleridge is arrested at the stage of his youthful dreams."[12] If such "arrest" is extreme, it is also exemplary, for it is precisely Coleridge's recurrent concern with such feelings that, in Steiner's view, makes plays such as *Remorse* and *Zapolya* paradigms of romanticism's troubled dramatic imagination. It is in Coleridge's sustained "thematic concern with remorse," Steiner notes, that one finds the clearest expression of "that evasion of the tragic which is central to the romantic temper."[13] One might well read in such evasion a more nuanced version of the displacement that Hoagwood finds so fundamental to romantic drama and thus link the displacement of romantic drama to such cultural anxieties of complicity in the Revolution's violence—anxieties that Coleridge expressed more powerfully, perhaps, than his contemporaries. However, what Steiner doesn't address at all, and what Carlson treats only in passing, is how Coleridge's sympathies arose and how they were broken. What sort of wishful participation, and what experience of disillusionment, gave rise to such an enduring dramatic concern with remorse? Put differently, what sort of trauma brought about the arrest of his genius?

For Carlson, Coleridge's imaginary participation in the politics of the Revolution is historically diffuse, consisting in nothing more specific than the "youthful dreams" of the poet's early radicalism, of those "days of support for revolution, France, and Napoleon, the times when no apologies are needed for the poet or the man of action—or for the poet as the man of action."[14] This was the period, Carlson reminds us, when Coleridge first began to work out his influential distinction between absolute and commanding genius.[15] Men such as Macbeth, the French revolutionaries, and Napoleon were in Coleridge's view commanding geniuses, men impelled to "impress their preconception on the world without." From such men of action Coleridge distinguished absolute geniuses, poet-philosophers who "rest content between thought and reality, as it were in an intermundium."[16] While Coleridge's imaginary participation in revolution—his "youthful dreams"—conjoined him to commanding genius, his differentiation and privileging of absolute genius, Carlson argues, defined precisely the shift to that enduring refuge in the imaginary which would later mark Coleridge's poetic and dramatic work. That refuge, she points out, is defined fundamentally in Coleridge's later drama, in which the meditation of poet-philosophers is privileged over action—action that itself seems threatening to Coleridge.[17] Thus, in Carlson's reading, Coleridge appears to have maintained his sympathy for and imaginary participation in radical causes until very late in the 1790s.[18]

Yet the very delineation of such categories already marks a conscious concern with the problem of imagination's relation to action, and if Coleridge's dramatic imagination is so strongly marked by lingering guilt it seems unlikely that such guilt would arise *after* the poet had established a self-consciously critical attitude toward the power of the imagination.[19] The initial articulation of that concern with imagination, and in some sense the moment of Coleridge's sympathetic disillusionment, is earlier, more particularly defined, and already delineated in some detail by Nicholas Roe. It was Coleridge's "self-recognition in Robespierre" during 1794, Roe suggests, that first prompted his consideration of the relation between imagination and action generally and of the connections between imagination and Revolutionary violence in particular.[20] For Coleridge, he explains, it was Robespierre himself who first offered a version of the heroic rebel, a kind of ur-form of commanding genius. Unlike Britain's Pitt, Robespierre was in Coleridge's estimate a leader whose energy and intellect enabled the realization of his imagination "in the very world." Yet, the chilling abstraction which structured that imagination ("justice," "virtue," "reason") and the impatience of Robespierre's mind were in Coleridge's view fatal flaws, leading the Jacobin leader to rationalize murder. For Roe, the primary articulation of this portrait—and one that will prove significant later in this chapter—appears in Coleridge's "Introductory Address" to his *Conciones ad Populum* (1795), the published version of lectures that Coleridge delivered at Bristol during that year.

"Robespierre," Coleridge asserts there, "possessed a glowing ardor that still remembered the *end*, and a cool ferocity that never either overlooked, or scrupled, the *means*. What that *end* was, is not known; that it was a wicked one, has by no means been proved. I rather think, that the distant prospect, to which he was travelling, appeared to him grand and beautiful; but that he fixed his eye on it with such intense eagerness as to neglect the foulness of the road."[21] However, this image of Robespierre as a flawed visionary, as a too-eager genius whose "cool ferocity" leads him to neglect the horrors of the Terror, itself echoes an earlier Coleridgean portrait of Robespierre—a portrait sketched in the very opening speech of *The Fall of Robespierre* (1794). There, in lines written by Coleridge just days after Thermidor, the wavering anti-Robespierrist conspirator Barère muses in soliloquy over his fear of "the Tyrant's *soul*,"

> Sudden in action, fertile in resource,
>
> And rising awful 'mid impending ruins ;
>
> In splendour gloomy, as the midnight meteor,
>
> That fearless thwarts the elemental war. (5)[22]

In its basic outline of the flawed, heroic rebel, this portrait anticipates that offered in the *Conciones:* this soul carries the same incandescent ardor, the same unhesitating ferocity, the same determination to soar upward toward a sublime end. However, this version is also markedly more sympathetic, for the unscrupled means and the "foulness of the road," those indirect references to the murderous violence of the Terror, appear in this precedent portrait as fertile resources enlisted to overcome "elemental war." Far from showing Robespierre as a self-deluded genius overlooking base means, Coleridge here represents the architect of the Terror as a tragic hero battling creatively against imminent catastrophe.

Such a portrait raises pressing questions. Here, indeed, is a marked "sympathy with power," a moment of imaginary identification with commanding genius, and an experience that seems directly to prompt Coleridge's first considerations on imagination and violence. Here as well, in Coleridge's first and anomalously direct dramatic examination of the Revolution, is his only dramatic valorization of commanding genius's impulsion to realize the imagination. "There is no danger but in cowardice," declares Coleridge's defiant Robespierre, giving voice to an urge toward action that stands distinctly at odds with the meditative heroes of Coleridge's later dramas. For Roe, Coleridge's 1795 meditations on Robespierre's character indicate that he had discovered in the Jacobin leader "an alarming, distorted version" of himself; this 1794 portrait, however, seems to emerge from a position marked less by the distantiation of alarmed self-recognition than by sympathetic identification. What prompted such sympathy, and what gave it such form? What about it could have engendered such enduring guilt, and why would such feelings have been exemplary rather than anomalous within British romanticism?

Part of the difficulty in answering such questions derives from the oddity of the circumstances of the play's composition: Coleridge and Southey wrote *The Fall of Robespierre* immediately, as a half-serious wager, upon receiving news of the Thermidorean coup. As Southey recalled, the project "originated in sportive conversation at poor Lovell's, and we agreed each to produce an Act by the next evening—S.T.C. the first, I the second, and Lovell the third. S.T.C. brought part of his; I and Lovell, the whole of ours. But L's was not in keeping, and therefore I undertook to supply the third also by the following day. By that time S.T.C. had filled up his." The primary source of information for the authors, and their primary source of inspiration, was the London *Times*. As Southey puts it, he wrote acts two and three "as fast as newspapers could be put into blank verse," and it is not only the quality of that verse that suggests the honesty of his account. Southey's acts are clearly, even awkwardly drawn almost directly from the pages of the *Times*, so the action of those latter acts follows quite accurately the manner in which the events of Thermidor unfolded. Act 2 opens with Robespierre mounting the Convention's tribunal to demand that his opposition declare itself, and he is denounced from the floor along with his associates. Saint-Just arrives and attempts to speak in defense of both Robespierre and himself, but he is denounced in turn, and the act ends with their arrest and departure under escort. In the play's final act, the action remains situated in the Convention: as the representatives rejoice at Robespierre's downfall, a messenger arrives with news of his release and repair to the Commune. The fearful representatives learn of Henriot's muster of support for the Robespierrists, of his seizure in the streets, and of the dispersal and collapse of Robespierre's armed following. The play concludes with Tallien, Lecointre, and Barère, the leaders of the anti-Robespierrist conspiracy, rejoicing over France's newfound freedom. Southey borrows all these events wholesale from his journalistic source.

Yet, if Southey's acts seem merely to recapitulate the news, Coleridge's first act does nothing of the sort. Rather than concerning itself with the depiction of public action and political oratory, his contribution offers a darkly atmospheric fantasy of the conspiratorial tensions that precede Robespierre's denunciation— and one apparently derived from literary rather than journalistic sources.

Roe aptly observes that in Coleridge's dark Robespierre we can just discern "Milton's 'dread commander' in *Paradise Lost*": "Robespierre's awful stature recalls Satan's towering presence, his 'disastrous lustre' the obscured glory of the fallen archangel... Like Satan he retains traces of his 'original brightness' in his resourcefulness and swiftness to action."[23] There is, too, a definite sense that Coleridge recalls in this act something of the portentous atmosphere of Rome in

Shakespeare's *Julius Caesar*, a darkened city shaken by "tempests . . . dropping fire" and supernatural prodigies announcing a "strange impatience of the heavens."[24] "The tempest gathers," announces Barère in his first line, and much of the act is occupied with the clandestine meetings and encounters of the conspirators and the suspicious planning of Robespierre and his associates. At the close of Coleridge's act this allusion is made explicit, as Tallien declares that

> —If the trembling members
> Even for a moment hold his fate suspended,
> I swear by the holy poniard, that stabbed Caesar,
> This dagger probes his heart! (16)

Unlike Southey, then, Coleridge seems to offer, in act 1, a scene more concerned with the creation of dramatic atmosphere than with the accurate depiction of historical event. In its allusions and private scenes, the work seems evidently a product of Coleridge's imagination, and for that reason—as well as the problem of Southey's clanking verse—commentators have tended to locate in Coleridge's contribution the greater part of the play's literary value and significance. Moreover, these characteristics reinforce the sense that Coleridge wrote this act from a position of considerable sympathetic identification with Robespierre, for the consistent conflation here is precisely between the fearful atmosphere of the city and "the Tyrant's *soul*." If Coleridge paints the world of the conspirators, it is a world ruled, "in splendor gloomy," by the "midnight meteor" of Robespierre's defiant, commanding genius. Rather than depicting Paris as it is revealed in the news, Coleridge shows us a city dominated by the figure of the Jacobin leader and most expressive of his imaginative conflict with the Revolution's elemental darkness.[25]

What might have prompted such a powerful identification with and realization of Robespierre's own imagination by Coleridge remains, for Roe, uncertain, and for good reason.[26] What neither he nor any other commentators seem fully to have appreciated is the degree to which Coleridge's perception of the Revolution was, in the summer of 1794, mediated by the press—and particularly by the *Times*. Since June, Coleridge had been in relative isolation from the media, being engaged upon a walking tour of some six hundred miles; he arrived in August in Bristol, where he met up with Southey, and it was there that they learned, through the *Times*, of events in France. And if one takes a closer look at *that* experience of Thermidor, as it was shaped in the pages of the newspaper, one finds an extraordinary imaginative drama—not Coleridge's alone but a collective fantasy—of Robespierre's fall. In that imaginative experience, I suggest, one finds not only a record of the catalyst to Coleridge's self-identification in Robespierre but also a remarkable trace of the impact of the Revolution on the evolution of tragedy in the British cultural imagination.

"Perish the Tyrant!": The *Times* and Thermidor

The London *Times* was established only in 1785, and among the British newspapers in existence at the outset of the French Revolution it was thus a relative newcomer. By the summer of 1794, however, the *Times* had firmly established itself as the most timely and reliable source of continental news among British newspapers, an achievement that had much to do with the generous subsidies and privileged information that the paper received as the favored organ of the Pitt government.[27] However, such status was more directly the result of the unusual network of correspondence and transmission that such patronage enabled. The Revolution had increased enormously and immediately the demand for prompt and reliable coverage of events across the Channel, and the *Times* was unusual in its early and consistent devotion of resources to such coverage. Even in July of 1789, just as the dismissal of Necker set off in Paris the insurrection that would culminate two days later in the fall of the Bastille, the paper had immediately asserted the superiority of its reporting: "It is an act of justice which we owe to ourselves," the editors declared on July 15, "to call the attention of the public, to the peculiar authenticity which accompanies our foreign intelligence. While others' prints express themselves in hints and surmises, we speak boldly as to facts."[28] As in subsequent years, the paper's "peculiar authenticity" was founded upon exceptional speed: "The Messenger who brought the dispatches yesterday from France," the paper noted, "made the quickest journey ever known, having come from Paris in 38 hours."[29]

By 1794, after five years of revolution, the *Times* had set up a network of regular correspondents both within and around France; it had also developed established routes and couriers along which the news from Paris and from the rest of the Continent could be quickly transmitted to London. Within Paris the paper maintained a special correspondent, who dispatched reports and a packet of the latest French newspapers several times a week, sending them northward through Flanders to Oostende, where they would be bundled with military dispatches for rapid transit across the Channel.[30]

This system, unrivaled by any other source of news, proved over time to be quite reliable. At the beginning of 1794, reports from Paris arrived in London about three times per week, with an average transmission time of eight or nine days—which, given the necessity of crossing a contested military frontier, is quite impressive.[31] As a result, the *Times* offered a new installment of events and proceedings in Paris several times each week, with single installments sometimes amounting to several pages of information.

The superiority of the paper's resources and coverage gave it considerable power to shape politically the initial British experience of events in France. As it received copious amounts of material more rapidly than other sources, the *Times* could, and did, influence the order and the timing with which its audience learned of goings-on in France; it fragmented events, buried facts, and frequently engaged in outright political distortion. However, more interesting for my purposes here is the manner in which the systemic operation of the paper's transmission network, and the ostensibly neutral conventions of the paper's formal composition, affected the rhythms and the dramatic structure of Revolutionary events, shaping in characteristic ways the way those events were experienced by the *Times* readers.

Among the most notable distortions created by the paper's transmission practices was a recurrent sense of temporal acceleration and dramatic compression that came to be associated with especially important occurrences. News of such events was customarily sent and published with additional haste, and such acceleration and compression added considerably to the dramatic impact and immediacy of such moments. In January 1793, for example, during the trial and in the few days leading up to the execution of Louis XVI, the paper was able to increase the speed and frequency with which it received reports to such a degree that it stopped distinguishing events in Paris by date, instead referring them simply by the day of the week and, on the day of the king's execution, by the hour as well.[32]

Such practices could also, however, magnify shock and confusion, as they did in the spring of 1794. On March 25, the *Times* had offered its readers breathless news of the execution—just five days before—of the militant Hébertists, the first of the erstwhile radical allies to be purged by the Jacobins.[33] All told, the arrest, trial, and execution of Hébert and other leaders of the radical Revolution's left wing had been completed in just eleven days, a necessity given the enormous popular support enjoyed by both Hébert and his associates. Such rapidity was magnified by the *Times*'s accelerated receipt of the news, but that acceleration also made it particularly difficult for the paper to comprehend and account for this first of the Jacobin purges, for the paper had not yet received any news of the days just preceding the Hébertists' denunciation. It surmised, as did many observers, that this strike to the left betokened some abatement of the violent course of Revolutionary politics: not only did the execution of the Hébertists mark the first time that the more moderate of two struggling parties had prevailed over the more radical, it was also the first time since 1789 that such a contest had been carried out entirely within the institutional structure of the standing government.[34] Moreover, the elimination of the Hébertists greatly diminished the power of the Paris *sections*, whose insurrectionary interventions had played such a prominent role in the previous course of the Revolution. In consequence, British reports were at first favorable; Robespierre, it seemed, was bringing the radical Revolution to a stable close. To those, like Coleridge, sympathetic already to the Jacobins' stern, tragic politics, news of this first of the regime's internecine purges must have raised considerable hope that the Revolution had, if grimly, reached fair harbor.

Yet, just as the paper's coverage caught up with itself, news arrived of Robespierre's move against the Dantonists, close allies of, and arguably more moderate than, the Robespierrists. Danton had earlier, through his close association with the August 10 Insurrection and the September Massacres, played a considerable role in the radicalization of Revolutionary politics; however, by 1794 he had become the leader of a group determined to institute a Committee of Clemency in order to reverse, or at least mitigate, the Terror. Reports of his arrest, also received in better than average time, made the Jacobin leader's actions seem, if anything, even more ruthless and predatory in London than they had appeared in Paris. "Here is again," the *Times* declared, "another instance of ROBESPIERRE'S growing power! There is every appearance of this man's intention to get himself declared DICTATOR."[35]

The dramatic force generated by such acceleration was reinforced and lent unexpected form just a week later—this time, by the remarkable coincidence and visual juxtaposition of two items in the paper's edition of April 14. The first, leading off the paper's customary presentation of major news under the heading of "The Times," was the announcement of the "Execution of Danton and His Accomplices." Just above, at the head of the column, was another announcement—this one concerning the newly rebuilt Drury Lane Theatre. "The Dramatic Representations at this Theatre," declared the paper, "will commence on MONDAY, April 21, 1794, under the management of Mr. KEMBLE, when his Majesty's Servants will perform Shakespear's Tragedy of MACBETH. "The following day the *Times* played upon the obvious resonances, asserting that in its opinion, "DANTON'S Ghost will be to ROBESPIERRE what *Banquo's* was to *Macbeth*."

There was nothing particularly unusual in the *Times*'s application of drama to politics. The establishment in the early 1770s of the rights of the British press

THE TIMES.

THEATRE ROYAL, DRURY LANE.

MONDAY, APRIL 14, 1794.

The Dramatic Represer.tations at this Theatre will commence
on MONDAY, April 21, 1794, under the Management of Mr.
KEMBLE, when his Majesty's Servants will perform Shakespear's Tragedy of   MACBETH.
    With the original Music and Choruses of Matthew Lock,
    And Accompaniments by Dr. Arne and Mr. Linley;
With entirely new Scenery, Dresses, Decorations and Machinery,
        And an occasional Prologue and Epilogue.
The Characters of the Play, with the Farce, &c. will be expressed
            in a future Advertisement.
    Places to be taken of Mr. Fosbrook, at the Box Book Office,
in Little Russel-street.

LONDON.

Business in the House of Commons this Day.

The House to attend the Trial of Warren Hastings, Esq.—The
Woolcombers, Statute Labour, Election, Consolidated Fund,
Prize Ships, French Property, and Newspaper Stamp Bills to
be read a second time.—Committee on the French Corps Bill,
and of Supply and Ways and Means.—The Slate Duty, National Debt, and Aberdeen Paving Bills to be reported.—Inch
Bonds Bill to be read a third time.

EXECUTION
OF
DANTON AND HIS ACCOMPLICES.

We yesterday received the news from PARIS down
to the 6th inst. and it is extremely important. By
a Gazette of that date we learn, that DANTON,
CAMILLE DESMOULINS, HERAULT SECHELLES,
PHILIPPEAUX, LACROIX, and FABRE D'EGLAN-
TINE, having refused to answer any question proposed to them by the Revolutionary Tribunal, but
in the presence of their accusers, ROBESPIERRE,
ST. JUST, and BARRERE; and having insulted
the President and Members of the Revolutionary
Tribunal, the Convention passed a decree, on the
4th, that in case they should pursue the same conduct, they should be condemned without farther
trial. In pursuanse of this decree, the above Deputies having persisted in the same sentiments and
behaviour, they were all guillotined on the evening
of the 5th, except L'HUILLEIR, who was acquitted.

to report parliamentary debates had accompanied an era of increased theatricality in British political culture as well, and the language of the drama offered the British newspapers a ready set of conventions, gestures, roles, and allusions through which to communicate politics (and to offer safely indirect political commentary) to the emergent reading public. Yet, the characterization of Robespierre as Macbeth signals a rather more complicated interplay of stage and paper than a mere application of fortuitous coincidence or a satirical conceit. In making this connection explicit, the paper had now attached a character and a plot to actual events, not merely foreseeing a tragic end for Robespierre but also drawing particular attention, in its reference to Banquo's ghost, to the Jacobin leader's imagination. Observations of Robespierre's taciturn, inward nature had become commonplace by this time, but in this instance that portrait was undoubtedly lent considerable depth and detail by the character of Kemble's innovative production. As the *Times*'s review of the opening performance at Drury Lane pointed out, "In getting up this Tragedy, great attention has evidently been bestowed to the notes of the several commentators; among the boldest alterations is that of *laying* BANQUO's Ghost, and making the troubled spirit only visible to the "mind's eye" of the guilty and distracted tyrant."[36]

A bold alteration indeed, and one that seems laden with significance when one considers that this is precisely the moment when *Macbeth* begins to resonate with larger cultural anxieties about the murderous power of the imagination. On one level, certainly, Kemble's staging suggests Lamb's 1811 observation that "a ghost by chandelier light, and in good company, deceives no spectators," and it seems reasonable to infer that in 1794 as well the appearance of a ghost on stage might be expected, as Lamb would assert, to excite mirth rather than terror.[37] In fact, the *Times*'s review observed what seems to have been just this sort of response to the spirits that Kemble chose to have dance about the witches' cauldron (a scene the reviewer suspected to have been "suggested by *Fuzeli*").[38] The very fact that Kemble chose to stage the witches' dance and *not* Banquo's ghost, however, reinforces the sense that it is not the absurdity of the supernatural but an emphasis on the imaginary that concerned Kemble here. Such an emphasis, moreover, makes sense when we recall that Kemble's physically undemonstrative acting style and carefully modulated delivery were best suited to such an interiorized portrait of Shakespeare's tortured protagonist. Walter Scott would later argue for the superiority in this regard of Kemble's Macbeth over the more animated and impetuous characterization offered by Garrick, describing Kemble's performance as an "exquisitely and minutely elaborate delineation of guilty ambition."[39] It was thus the "guilty and distracted" mind of the tyrant that Kemble placed at center stage: by laying aside as well the spectacle of a murdered Banquo, the Drury Lane production better allowed its audience to employ its own imagination upon the "thoughts and internal machinery" or, in Macbeth's own terms, the "heated-oppressed brain" of the regicide.[40] And in the spring of 1794, it was as just such a guilty and distracted tyrant that the paper represented Robespierre.

It should come as no surprise, then, that we find Coleridge focusing at just this time upon Robespierre's tragic, guilty imagination, for it is precisely that element of the Jacobin ruler's identity and action that, in the spring of 1794, preoccupied the British public. But such focus—for Coleridge as for the audience of the *Times* and of Kemble's brooding portrait—is a long way from what Roe describes as "self-recognition." That closer sympathy, as we shall see, came later, and was prompted by something rather more curious than merely a conjunction of politics and drama.

The suggestion that Robespierre could be seen as Macbeth would perhaps have quickly faded, except that the very transmission of news from Paris began, in uncanny fashion, to reinforce just such an imaginary drama, and to reinforce rather than set aside just such a focus on Robespierre's mind. On April 15, the very day the *Times* suggested that "DANTON'S Ghost will be to ROBESPIERRE what *Banquo's* was to *Macbeth*," it also informed its readers that "the man who had charge of the Gazettes" had been arrested near Lille.[41] Throughout May, this disruption of the paper's usual courier network combined with heavy military activity along the northern frontier to erode the frequency and the rapidity with which news was transmitted to London, and subsequent events reinforced and deepened the problem. From an average delay during the first four months of the year of just under eight days, the *Times* slipped, in both May and June, to an average delay of just under eleven days. On June 6, as the French advanced toward Brussels, the paper frankly admitted the loss of its primary channels of communication, and on June 10 the passage of the Law of 22 Prairial rendered the very provision of reports significantly more risky.[42] By the time that the British lost control of Oostende at the beginning of July, provision of the Gazettes from Paris had become more erratic than at any point since the outset of the Revolution; through July, the pace slowed to about two reports per week, with an average delay of nearly sixteen days.

In short, news of Paris now took almost twice as long to reach London as the *Times* readers had come to expect over the preceding four years, and this delay was accompanied by both heightened tensions within Paris and Robespierre's noted withdrawal from daily political activity. Paris became, perceptually, more distant, and Robespierre became more isolated. From about June 26, when the *Times* remarked that one might say "of Robert SPIERRE, as Banquo said of Macbeth. 'Thane, Glamis, Caudor, thou hast them all,'" Robespierre had ceased to participate in public politics, continuing only to exercise control over the General Police while carefully gathering evidence and preparing his denunciation of those he suspected of plotting against him.

Throughout July, vague rumors arrived in London of increasing opposition, but the first clear indications of an impending threat to Robespierre's position did not appear until August 2. On the first, an American ship arrived from Havre-de-Grace carrying, remarkably, a *transcript* of Robespierre's speech of July 21 to the Jacobin Club, just twelve days before. The speech, Robespierre's first major address in weeks, contained an outraged but unspecific accusation of a powerful conspiracy; it seemed to suggest that the Jacobin leader's support was threatened or had collapsed, but it was unaccompanied by any commentary by the *Times* correspondents. What was its context? What was its import? The paper's regular Paris coverage extended at the time only to July 13, eight days before the speech. And if the rapid transmission of that transcript reiterated the familiar pattern of acceleration for important news, such acceleration was in this instance followed by an utterly unprecedented phenomenon: after the arrival on the second of regular dispatches of July 14 and 15, which shed no new light on the problem, no further news arrived from the Continent—from *anywhere* on the Continent—for almost a week. By Wednesday, August 6, the paper had exhausted its store of information fit to print.[43] There was nothing but silence from France—and, of course, the speech itself.

In his essay "On the Knocking at the Gate in *Macbeth*," de Quincey asks how it is that Shakespeare managed to "throw the interest on the murderer," to direct our sympathy, despite our natural inclinations, to Macbeth. "Of course," he notes, "I mean a sympathy of comprehension, a sympathy by which we enter into his feelings, and are made to understand them." De Quincey's conclusion is that Shakespeare had to find a way to express and make sensible "the retiring of the human heart and the entrance of the fiendish heart," showing Macbeth's interior transformation with such clarity that we might understand that shift and follow Macbeth through it. Asking then how this shift might effectively "be conveyed and made palpable," de Quincey answers with a description that applies as well to Robespierre's situation in the Paris of the *Times* as it does to Macbeth's own hushed moment of horror. "The murderer and the murder," he suggests, "must be insulated—cut off by an immeasurable gulf from the ordinary tide and succession of human affairs—locked up and sequestered in some deep recess: we must be made sensible that the world of ordinary life is suddenly

arrested—laid asleep—tranced—racked into dread armistice: time must be an-
nihilated; relation to things without abolished; and all must pass self-withdrawn
into a deep syncope and suspension of earthly passion."[44]

This "ordinary tide and succession of human affairs" is precisely what was
cut off in the cessation of news from France. The pressures of time drive the
newspaper press, and here one finds a newspaper "racked into dread armistice":
from August 2 until—as it would turn out—August 11, London was arrested in
the Paris of July twenty-first. Moreover, that arrested date was defined and de-
limited by nothing other than Robespierre's own speech—an address suggestive of nothing so much as the "guilty and distracted mind" of a suspicious, uncertain leader. The result, certainly, was a kind of sympathy of comprehension.
On Friday, August 8, in an extraordinary departure from its usual practice, the
paper offered its readers the following "news":

> There is a kind of infatuation which attends on Ambition; and this has laid strong
> hold of ROBESPIERRE. If such were not the case, he never would have ventured
> to the tip of that very precipice from which he saw his predecessors hurled . . . But
> so glaring is the *ignis fatuus* of power, that the possession of it is the only object
> of his attention, and he looks on the glittering summit above with such earnest-
> ness, that he has not leisure to bestew a single glance on the ruins below. From
> his speech, however, some circumstances may be collected, which plainly point out
> that he dreads the effect of a calm . . . His efforts, therefore, are wholly directed
> to *assist*, not to *appease* the storm. There must be no time for recollection—no mo-
> ment for cool consideration . . . If he was not wicked before he got into power, he
> finds it necessary to become so now; and therefore he gets rid of his conscience,
> that rapine and murder may be pursued without remorse. Thus fortified against all
> the finer feelings of nature, he has nothing to apprehend from reflection; and as he
> has banished from his mind every idea of an hereafter, he riots without a pang
> on the blood of his fellow-creatures.

The *Times* had offered portraits of Revolutionary leaders before, but this one
is extraordinary in its focus not upon public identity or political action but upon
private belief and personal feeling. It explains not who Robespierre is but what
he is thinking and fearing. Most specifically, it takes as its particular aim a portrait of the tyrant's guilty and distracted conscience, examining precisely the troubled relationship between his commanding imagination and his murderous action.

And, crucially, we find here as well an evident source of that image of Robespierre which would dominate Coleridge's mind. In the *ignis fatuus*, the "foolish
light" of power, we can see the "glowing ardor" of the *Conciones* portrait and,

even more clearly, the nightmarish meteor of Barère's soliloquy. Here too appears the image of "impending ruins" that opens *The Fall of Robespierre*. Certainly, the *Times*'s portrait is not without appeal, for it was evidently shaped both by Robespierre's speech and by the *Times*'s self-imagined image of Robespierre as a tragic Macbeth, who likewise banished conscience in the necessity of power. To one convinced, as the youthful radical Coleridge was convinced, that the Incorruptible Robespierre pursued not personal power but the ideals of 1789, this portrait of de Quinceyan sympathy was easily accepted and redeemed—one need only transform the "glittering summit" of tyranny to the "distant prospect" of liberty. Ironically, then, it is in the pages of the *Times*, and not—as Roe suggests—in Coleridge's reflections, that we find the first articulation of romantic imagination, of commanding genius impelled to bring its vision into being even at the risk of destruction. It is here, also, that we might also locate the moment of what Roe describes as "self-recognition," though with de Quincey we should probably call it a "sympathy of comprehension," a more limited effect by which Coleridge was induced to enter into Robespierre's feelings and "made to understand them." In the context of such sympathy, Coleridge's atmospheric opening to *The Fall of Robespierre* takes on additional interest, for we can recognize in its image of a city ruled by the gloomy splendor of Robespierre's soul not merely a reflection of Coleridge's own preoccupations but also a dramatic rendering of the ascendancy of the dictator's figure in the public imagination of Britain during this tense period of silence.

Yet, it is important to realize that this picture is as yet incomplete: no "knocking at the gate" had yet occurred, and the *Times*'s sympathetic participation—and Coleridge's, too—had not yet been dispelled. And before that happened, such sympathy would give rise to yet another dreamt image, this one a collective fantasy that registered, and in its collapse radically threatened, the tragic imagination of British culture.

By the evening of August 8, the very day of the paper's sympathetic portrait of Robespierre, the mood in Printing House Square must have been despairing, for even regular news dispatches should by then have closed the crucial six-day gap between the last news of events in Paris with Robespierre's speech of the twenty-first. Obviously unsettled, the paper's editors lamented in the Saturday edition that "we scarcely recollect such a dearth of news from every part of Europe as during the present week; not a single dispatch or newspaper having been received from the Continent since Sunday last."

The implications of such a dearth were distressing: if no news had arrived since that dispatched on July 21, then some event must have had occurred in Paris of a magnitude sufficient to prevent the departure of news from the French capitol for an unprecedented period of days. In fact, the packets arrived that Saturday evening, carrying news as late as July 22—although no news of any event so decisive as to have brought about that echoed ripple of silence. However, the paper of Monday, August 11, does reflect one important shift: having been forced to pause, to speculate, and to stretch news, the paper now began to hurry, obviously rushing its correspondents' dispatches into print without editorial intervention or emendation. This temporal reversal thus produced an oddly complementary effect, for the paper's attitude of sympathetic participation was now reinforced by a narrative stance of striking immediacy. Monday's paper reprinted what appears to be the Paris correspondent's dispatch of July 22; the tone is terser and more intimate than journalistic, the items arranged in an order less hierarchical than occasional, more like entries jotted into a notebook than news arranged, however capriciously, for publication. Within what seems to be a typeset dispatch—for it is buried, ironically enough, in the middle of an otherwise unremarkable review of executions—is a single, hasty suggestion of the crisis suggested by Robespierre's speech. "Matters of the greatest moment," the correspondent writes, "are on the point of being brought forward. It is a matter of general conversation and belief, that the *Committee of Public Welfare* are about to propose a decree for arresting several Members of the Convention. Their names are even mentioned. Very loud accusations are also made against the heads of the Committee of Public Safety."

With its sense of immediacy as marked as its nearly total lack of hard information, this correspondence could hardly have been better suited to maintaining the paper's sympathetic illusion, and on Wednesday the thirteenth, despite having received no further packets from France, the *Times* published an editorial denouncing Robespierre and offering this remarkable, speculative summary of the situation:

> That there exists at this moment two leading factions in *Paris*, who secretly watch each other, is certain. The *Anti-Robespierrists* are the more numerous in the Convention; and *Robespierre*'s aim is to oppose the Jacobins to them. Nothing decisive has been yet done, but the preparations are in great forwardness.
>
> The explosion which is to determine a new Revolution, cannot be far distant. What will be the issue, or on which side the victory will be, cannot yet be foreseen. Hitherto, in every period of the Revolution, the most infamous party has conquered; and it is difficult to conceive that there can exist one superior to the *Robespierrists* in every species of crime.

FRANCE.

PARIS, July 22.

The anniversary of the taking of July was celebrated in the Convention by several speeches relative to the events of that epocha. *Bourer* said, he was persuaded that the Assembly could not better employ the sitting than in hearing a report upon the means of preparing new elements for victory; and he repeated the eulogium made by Citizen *Stanhope*, in the British Parliament, respecting the *Sans Culottes* who work in the saltpetre manufactories, and added, that Paris alone had furnished 600,600 weight of saltpetre since February. He concluded by announcing, that the new eruption of *Vesuvius* had stopped the fleet of the Neapolitan tyrant, which was ready to join that belonging to GENOA, in the Mediterranean. The eruption, he said, had destroyed half the city of Naples, and all its suburbs.

The executions continue daily as numerous as ever. On the 15th, thirty persons were executed; on the 16th, thirty-one; on the 17th, forty; on the 19th, twenty-four; and on the 20th, fourteen;—in all 139 persons, in the space of 6 days.

Among these are—*Edelman*; the composer, and his brother; the *ci-devant* Count *Fandons*, and his daughter, aged 18; and several persons accused of having endeavoured to throw the French army into confusion in the late action of Fleurus. In the list of those executed on the 19th, are *Magon de la Balue*, aged 81 years, born at St. *Maloes*, and one of the richest men in France, and the whole of his family, sons and daughters. He was accused of having opened an account current with the French Princes. *Legris*, a Clerk of the Revolutionary Tribunal, was guillotined at the same time, as being an accomplice with *Magon*, and having five times emigrated to carry specie out of the country.

Matters of the greatest moment are on the point of being brought forward. It is a matter of general conversation and belief, that the *Committee of Public Welfare* are about to propose a decree for arresting several Members of the Convention. Their names are even mentioned. Very loud accusations are also made against the heads of the Committee of Public Safety.

All the papers belonging to the Emigrants, and those guillotined, are sent hither, and carefully examined by persons appointed for the purpose.

Fouché, of Nantes, has been struck off the list of the Jacobins.

The wife of *La Fayette* has been arrested on her estate near Limoges, and brought to Paris.

Matters of the greatest moment are on the point of being brought forward. It is a matter of general conversation and belief, that the *Committee of Public Welfare* are about to propose a decree for arresting several Members of the Convention. Their names are even mentioned. Very loud accusations are also made against the heads of the Committee of Public Safety.

Times (London), August 11, 1794.

It is difficult but important to keep in mind that the situation this article describes is surmised from nothing more substantive than a single speech and a few suggestive reports that had bent sent from Paris *twenty-two days* before. Yet the paper's tone is immediate and anticipatory: the two leading factions exist "at this

moment," "nothing decisive has yet been done," preparations are "in great for-
wardness," the explosion is "not far distant," and the outcome "cannot yet be
foreseen." But there is more than a very odd temporal disjuncture here: there is
the further irony of the article's public representation of a hidden conflict, of
"secret" oppositions on the verge of open conflict—in short, the *Times* creates
precisely the portentous, brooding atmosphere that characterizes Coleridge's dramatic vision in the opening act of *The Fall of Robespierre.*

Finally, on August 16, a Saturday, the *Times* printed as fact the following report, even though it had been received from Calais rather than through regular
channels, lacked any corroboration, and appeared evidently contradictory to
other, more accurate information. "ROBESPIERRE's greatest enemies," it informed
its readers, "were in the very bosom of the Committee of Public Safety. The first
blows were struck by BARRERE and ST. JUST. On the 27th of July, BARRERE
mounted the Tribune in the Convention, and denounced the DICTATOR, whose
mouth piece and apologist he had been for the last six months. Several Members threw themselves upon ROBESPIERRE, and murdered him with poniards,
crying out, *"Perish the Tyrant!"* The two Factions fought in the Hall, and their
mutual fury reached the city, where the conflict is said to have lasted three days,
in which time from 10 to 14,000 men fell."

One can see why this account made sense. In the spring and summer the *Times*
had carefully cast Robespierre as Macbeth, focusing attention on and investing
significance in his "guilty and distracted" mind. In the "dread armistice" of early
August the paper had turned its attention to his speech, its sympathy directed to
this half-imagined tyrant—"a sympathy of comprehension, a sympathy by
which we are made to enter into his feelings, and made to understand them."
Sympathy with Macbeth, then, but with a Jacobin Macbeth: look through the
eyes of a Jacobin Macbeth and one falls not as a Scot but as a Roman—as Julius
Caesar. Thus we find in the *Times* as well the imaginary source of Coleridge's
brooding Roman city and the inspiration, moreover, for Tallien's act-ending
threat of the "holy poniard, that stabbed Caesar."

Two days later, the *Times* finally received a detailed account of the actual
events of the dictator's fall from its regular Paris correspondent, and reality came
"knocking at the gate." Robespierre had not been stabbed in the convention, the
city had not shaken with mass conflict; instead, Robespierre had been denounced
and arrested, gaining his independence only briefly, and mustering support that
had dissolved overnight. Although the *Times* offered no retraction of its dramatic
report of the sixteenth, the paper's commentary on the eighteenth suggests a
sobriety born of disillusionment and possesses a tone far more in keeping with

the day-to-day rhythms of modernity. "We shall not," the chastened editors caution, "now anticipate the consequences of this new Revolution. The circumstances are not yet sufficiently known to comment on them. We have therefore confined ourselves in giving a very faithful analysis of the proceedings of the Convention, from the 27th of July to the 30th . . . Our extracts have been made with great care; and we trust the history will be found clear and connected. It is taken from the Papers of the *Moniteur* of the 26th, 27th, 28th, 29th, 30th, and 31st of July; and we believe there are not three copies of so late a date in town."

Although there is no way to establish the precise date that Coleridge, Southey, and Lovell sat down to write their historical tragedy, it seems clear, given the character of the collaborators' contributions and revisions, that the project was initiated in response to the *Times*'s report of the assassination fantasy of August 16. In such a scenario it is not difficult at all to see why "poor Lovell's" third act would turn out "not in keeping" and why it would be replaced by Southey's workmanlike rendering into verse of the lengthy reports of the eighteenth.

The result, whatever the circumstances, is more than merely an awkward, failed tragedy, for *The Fall of Robespierre* offers, both in its compositional structure and literally in its action, a stunning record of the failure of tragedy as an appropriate representation of public action. If, on the one hand, the French Revolution had, as Marx observed long ago, adopted Roman tragedy as the "illusion of politics" with which it could reconcile itself to the violence of the Terror, it had also, on the other, catalyzed the formation of an international daily news press, a press that reshaped the nature and the possibilities of political action. If Thermidor marked the end of that tragic illusion, as Marx asserted, it marked as well the establishment of the modern political stage of the news press. *The Fall of Robespierre* captures both facets of that conflict, opening in the imagined world of Jacobinism's tragic vision and closing in chilling political modernity. Appropriately, in Southey's closing act, Thermidor itself is revealed to have been an indirect conflict of news, a political battle waged with competing proclamations and reports. Indeed, in that third act we do not even see Robespierre. Instead, the action is confined to the Convention and consists in the rapid arrival of no fewer than fourteen messengers bearing breathless reports. Southey's acts, in other words, dramatize directly and embody generically the dissolution of tragedy in the regular arrival and dispatch of news.

Scholars of Revolutionary print have in recent years raised the question of whether the newspaper is, in Jeremy Popkin's terms, "the right place to look for what is revolutionary about the Revolution."[45] In terms of the tragic imagination, it may well be, for the newspaper reflects and brings about a radical shift in the texture and the rhythms of historical experience—a shift that, perhaps for the last time in Thermidor, allowed for the kind of dread armistice of ordinary life and the sympathy of comprehension necessary to persuade us of the very possibility, in history, of tragedy.

Epilogue

Post-Thermidorean France, rather than discarding the Revolution's theatricality, institutionalized much of it, particularly during the Directory's brief efforts to consolidate and stabilize its position at the end of the decade. The cycle of Revolutionary festivals and the chronology of the Revolutionary calendar were rigorously if unenthusiastically observed, and the Directory itself implemented, in systematic, material form, the Roman attire and classical form that the Revolutionary assembly had adopted only in its rhetorical imagination. Robespierre had spoken as Brutus and made reference to Catalinean conspiracies, but he did so in the meticulous contemporary garb of a Rousseauist bourgeois advocate; the Directory, in telling contrast, draped itself in Roman togas and discussed finance. Far from discarding the forms and conventions of Revolutionary theatricality, Napoleonic France, in its realization of the Revolution's imperialist capabilities, embraced Revolutionary nationalism's most spectacular idioms and its gaudiest patriotic fashions. Though it employed both with an explicit and even ironic nostalgia, incorporated the exoticism of the reign's Mediterranean focus, and indulged throughout in the cynicism of obvious propaganda, Napoleonic politics—and Napoleonic war—intensified and extended rather than mitigated the Revolution's symbolic pressure on European culture.

British romantic tragedy's long engagement with the Revolution, if it began with Wordsworth' dream reaction to the Terror and Coleridge's imaginative identification with Robespierre at the height of his power, was shaped no less by these post-Revolutionary performances. Similarly, melodrama's rapid evolution in the first years of the nineteenth century—both in form and as the primary constituent of a new, mass theater industry—reflected not only the epistemological shocks of the Revolutionary experience but also the institutional reformations and imperial extensions of the Revolution's dramatic and theatrical imagination in the post-Revolutionary decade, as well as the rapid changes in metropolitan life—in both Paris and London—wrought by what had become almost continuous national warfare. Both of these processes are of obvious significance in the history of the drama, for the afterlife of romanticism would stretch well into the next century, and the longer development of melodrama would constitute a primary force in the emergence of mass culture. However, neither, I believe, belongs properly to the history offered here, for in both the Revolutionary experience serves characteristically as a negative ground, as a memory not to be recovered but buried, an experience not to be clarified but occluded, an influence not to be reconciled but overcome. And while the Revolutionary experience undoubtedly provided the catalyst for these processes, their motion and development, their force and significance, incline away from that moment and find their vitality in relation to other, later events and situations.

CHAPTER FIVE

Reviving the Revolution:
Dantons Tod

Georg Büchner's plays are widely understood to mark the origins of modern drama, and it is to modernism that critics have tended to turn for an interpretive framework in which to situate his work. Many of the most radical and influential figures and movements of the modern age have been enlisted in this process, from Marx, Nietzsche, Brecht, and Camus to dadaism, naturalism, and Artaud's theater of cruelty. To some degree this tendency is a product of the performance history of Büchner's work. *Dantons Tod* (*Danton's Death*) was not staged until 1902, and *Woyzeck* (1837) had to wait another decade, finally reaching the stage seventy-five years after its composition.[1] It was the dramatists of the avant-garde, not scholars of dramatic literature, who first called attention to Büchner, and even today critical perceptions of his plays remain ineluctably filtered through the work of those later theaters.[2]

For the most part, understanding of the avant-garde's indebtedness to Büchner has focused strongly on *Woyzeck*, the last of his plays. Often nominated as the first modern tragedy, *Woyzeck* seems, for any number of reasons—its "open," episodic structure, its unblinking dramatization of a wholly materialist world, its explicit articulation of radical class consciousness, and its representation of sexual violence and criminal insanity among them—to offer an unprecedented, even proleptic expression and example of dramatic modernity. Nothing like it seems to have been written before or for the next fifty years; in fact, the play appears in literary history to be a weirdly anachronistic text, a narrative innovation that is still difficult to place in the literary culture of its moment. And in a material sense it was a kind of outsider text, for *Woyzeck* remained unpublished for decades, entering the vocabulary of the avant-garde through the illicit channels of nineteenth-century Germany's tenuous culture of political and theatrical radicalism.

One result of that anachronistic appropriation has been a critical tendency to foreground those aspects of Büchner's drama which clash most strongly with the

dramatic and theatrical sensibilities of the 1830s. The plays' rapid shifts of scene
would have stymied contemporary production, the radical choices of subject matter would have run afoul of political censors of Büchner's time, and Büchner's
often obscene and pornographic language would in any case have ruled out theatrical performance from the outset.[3] The first two qualities are not unique to
Büchner's drama in his time, but this last characteristic seems to bring his work
a step closer to the modernist avant-garde. It was precisely the striking physical-
ity of Büchner's dramatic worlds—his emphasis on the body and its sensations, as
well as the obscenity and intense sexuality of his characters—that Wedekind and
the Expressionists, for example, found so compelling.[4] *Woyzeck* offers the most
familiar example of such a visceral focus, but in *Dantons Tod*, too, it is evident
from the start. As the play opens, we find Danton sitting at the feet of his wife
Julie, drawing her attention, and ours, to an elaborate scene of sexual play at a
nearby card table: "Look at the pretty lady," he suggests in the opening line, "She
handles her cards so nicely! They say she always plays her heart (*coeur*) to her
husband and her 'diamond' (*carreau*) to the others" (I.I).[5] Danton's obscene pun
sets the tone for the remainder not only of this scene but for the drama as a
whole—and it was that foregrounded obscenity that critics first attacked.[6]

It is of course not only this focus on the sexual body that seems to mark out
Büchner as a modern. An extraordinary sense of individual isolation permeates
his plays—an isolation that finds its most familiar manifestation in Woyzeck's
terror but its most pointed political expression in *Dantons Tod*. Throughout the
play, those characters who are most actively engaged in political speech seem
somehow incapable of dialogue, and self-consciously so: their exchanges pile up
like disconnected, echoing reflections of people who have ceased to be able to
hear each other. As Danton notes in the opening scene, "We're thick-skinned
creatures: we stretch out our hands to each other, but it's futile—hide rubbing
against hide—we're on our own, completely on our own" (I.i).[7] Danton's character is preoccupied with this problem, but all parties seem plagued by it, equally
unable to convey their thoughts without misapprehension, equally isolated as
they are swept along by what seems an irresistible course of events.

In *Dantons Tod*, and more particularly in Danton, such emphatic sensuality
and existential isolation find further expression in yet another characteristic of
Büchner's plays that signals their affinity with much later drama; namely, a sort
of frenetic idleness or earnest lassitude—not the anxious irresolution of Hamlet
but the nihilist disengagement of the modern fatalist.[8] Although well aware of
the dangers that the Jacobins pose to himself, his friends, and the Revolution as
he understands it, Büchner's Danton does little beyond musing and pursuing

apparent distractions, offering nothing but token resistance to the Jacobin purge. As Hérault-Séchelles remarks early on, politics has become merely "a pastime" (*Zeitvertreib*) for the man whose thunderous oratory once rallied *La Patrie* to the defense of France.[9] Rather than actively resisting the erosive collapse of effective speech, Danton seems to accept it as a given and to occupy himself instead with reflection. He is not alone in such seeming disengagement: detached, solipsistic monologues abound, and much of the play is composed of what might be described as idle lyric fugues, polyphonic conversational spirals that rise up into the air until they evaporate or bounce along like slapstick, ending in cynical obscenity or punning deflation. Typically, such linguistic play is read (in Henry Schmidt's representative formulation) as "a means of sublimating alienation and political impotence . . . a form of self-aestheticization," and it is true—Büchner's Revolutionary heroes do not act so much as they talk—and talk, about philosophy, about sex, about politics, about the almost chaotic Revolutionary action that swirls around and about them and that carries them inexorably, wit and all, to the guillotine.[10]

Expressionist sensuality, existentialist isolation, nihilist disengagement: any one of these aspects would mark Büchner's work as proleptic, but taken together the impression that they have produced is one of striking, even unaccountable modernity. Viewed through the lenses of modernism, in particular, Büchner's drama long seemed to stand apart from its time, to mark a radical discontinuity in literary history, and it has often been presented, in consequence, as wholly unprecedented, such a complete departure from context and tradition as to seem inexplicable, uncanny, prophetic.[11] This emphasis on Büchner's anachronistic status conveniently served a larger critical purpose as well. Sprung loose from its historical and cultural context, his drama offered a mythic point of revolutionary origin for the avant-garde's own radical history. Having been fashioned as a playwright whose work was written, in suitably avant-garde fashion, for a theater that did not yet exist, Büchner appeared until recently, to quote Reinhold Grimm's wholly typical formulation, as "our contemporary."[12]

More recent scholarship, however, has made evident the degree to which Büchner's drama was a highly contextual gesture, less a dislocated act of prophetic modernism than the product of immediate political activity and of a bitterly determined critical engagement with—significantly enough—French Revolutionary history. Like Marx, Büchner experienced the farcical collapse of the century's first and most naively imitative efforts to revive the popular politics of the French Revolution. In fact, his direct participation in the failed attempt to catalyze a spontaneous political revolution in Hesse in 1834 and 1835 forced him to go into hiding and then to flee Germany. It was during this period, in the winter of 1835, that Büchner wrote *Dantons Tod,* and these circumstances directly inform the play's focus and concerns. Taking as its scene and setting the rapid purge of the Dantonists by Robespierre and the Jacobins, *Dantons Tod* is by turns a tortured, interiorized drama of the failure of Revolutionary ideals and a darkly materialist, often pornographic farce of the performance of Revolutionary politics at its most radical and violent moment. Both of these elements may be taken as meditations upon Büchner's own revolutionary experience, and in this sense Büchner's work, like that of Pixèrecourt and Coleridge, may be said to locate its originary ground in the disenchantment of Revolutionary history. Yet Büchner, in a manner that would prove significant to subsequent radical drama, turned toward rather than away from that history.

What I would like to suggest is that in this turn Büchner's drama can be recognized as marking not a point of origin but a moment of resumption, and that rather than viewing him as unprecedented, we might find it more useful to see his work as a return to and a confrontation with dramatic precedents—if historical rather than literary—that preceding decades had worked to forget, evade, and elide. Such a perspective helps us to make sense of the apparently fragmented history of the drama during this period, and it allows a better sense of the difficult problem of accounting for modern drama's apparent historical discontinuity with traditional drama. From such a perspective modern drama does not simply break from melodrama and romantic tragedy: instead, it picks up, with Büchner, a formal history that those genres had worked to erase. Such a view implies as well a longer genealogy of modernist theater, for if Büchner's work returned to the Revolution's political drama to take up its problems of dramatic form, it also reappropriated and made available again the radical languages of Revolutionary theatricality.

The Anatomy of Revolution

That this turn toward Revolutionary history occurred when it did is not surprising. By 1835, almost half a century had passed since the fall of the Bastille, and virtually everyone who had participated in the Revolution of 1789–94, like the great majority of those who had watched its progress from afar, were dead. Moreover, institutional historiography had not yet been established, and the Revolution's textual remains consisted, in Carlyle's description of the same year, of a "thousand wagon-loads of . . . Pamphleteering and Newspaper matter rotting slowly in the Public Libraries of our Europe."[13] To a degree that is today difficult to comprehend, the French Revolution was in 1835 a living history, but one that was dying if not already dead, its bodies, both human and textual, rapidly rotting into historical oblivion. It was with pointed emphasis on the corporeality of that history that Hugo had declared, in 1833, that "the physiognomy of this epoch will not be determined until the French Revolution . . . personifies itself in art."[14]

For the most part, both romantic tragedians and melodramatists had applied themselves to quite the opposite project, attempting instead to redeem Robespierre's "sublime drama" of revolution, to salvage its abstract and disembodied ideals while leaving its monstrous violence safely in the depths.[15] Put differently, both melodrama and romantic tragedy had attempted to register the epistemological impact of the Revolution while abstracting, displacing, suppressing, and eliding its specific, concrete, theatrical, and dramatic performance. Turning to Shakespeare and Goethe and in evident kinship with Hugo, Büchner insisted upon creating a drama that would recognize, even personify, that material, grotesque Revolution.[16] Here is a writer who finally, after decades of historically displaced romantic tragedies, claimed that the dramatist's "highest aim is to get as close as possible to history as it actually happened," and "as close as possible" carries here very clearly the connotation of corporeal immediacy.[17] Doing so, Büchner asserted, means offering "characters (*Charaktere*) instead of character portrayals (*Charakteristiken*); full-bodied figures (*Gestalten*) instead of mere descriptions (*Beschreibungen*)."[18] The critical difference, for Büchner, is that the dramatist replaces historical commentary with dramatic dialogue, eschewing the analytical comprehension and distantiation of historical narrative in favor of the immediacy of direct speech. "History," he complained, "was not created by the good Lord to serve as reading material for young ladies, so no one should take it amiss if my drama is just as ill suited for such a purpose. I can't possibly turn Danton and the bandits of the Revolution into heroes of virtue! If I wanted to convey their depravity, then I had to let them be depraved; if I wanted to show their godlessness, then I clearly had to let them speak like atheists."[19]

In short, Büchner as dramatic poet attempted to make the French Revolution speak for itself, and the text of his play evinces this aim throughout. Revolutionary oratory, popular sayings, songs, and all sorts of other verbal fragments from his textual sources are incorporated here, to the extent that almost a fifth of the considerable dramatic text of *Dantons Tod* turns out to have been borrowed directly from Büchner's historical sources.[20] We find lengthy excerpts from Robespierre's speeches, including, for example, his dismissive indictment of the Hébertists' allegorical Festival of Reason as an insolent attempt to "parody the sublime drama of the Revolution" (I.iii).[21] Such sampling is particularly appro-

priate to a dramatic rendering of Robespierre, who appeared, in a way other Revolutionary leaders did not, to live a sternly respectable, entirely public existence,
to exist only—or at least primarily—in his pronouncements.[22] Yet Robespierre is
not the only major character whose lines are patched through with quotation.
Danton is assigned some of that Revolutionary leader's most celebrated aphorisms, including declarations drawn from the thunderous, incendiary oratory of
his trial as well as his wry—if apocryphal—last words.[23] Büchner incorporates,
too, a sample of Camille Desmoulins's satirical editorials in *Le Vieux Cordelier,*
and the play makes reference even to Desmoulins's pseudonymous identity as
"Procurator-General of the Street-lamps" (III.i).[24] Even the character of Saint-
Just, the last (and least prominent and vocal) of the play's four major political figures, is assigned substantial quoted material: he concludes act 2, for example, with
the actual Saint-Just's well-known call for "all the secret enemies of tyranny"
who "bear the dagger of Brutus beneath their cloaks" (II.vii) to join him in the
Revolution's bloody triumph.[25]

Even more striking than this extensive quotation from Revolutionary oratory
and journalism is the play's abundant incorporation of the linguistic detritus of
popular Revolutionary culture. Büchner, we know, spent a considerable amount
of time researching the Revolution, and he was, as is evident in all his plays, a devoted collector of folk songs and stories. In *Dantons Tod* we find a range and multitude of cultural fossils that are still impressive today, when even casual historians of the Revolution have easy access to an abundance of such material. There
are little-known slogans and aphorisms, like a citizen's *sans-culotte* injunction to
"Kill anyone without a hole in his coat" (I.ii), or Lucille Desmoulins's defiant and
suicidal cry—a common phrase, but borrowed by Büchner from accounts of despairing prisoners during the Terror—of "Long live the King!" (IV.ix).[26] There
are obvious references as well to such obscure elements of Revolutionary culture as Sophie Momoro, the Opéra star who was installed in Notre-Dame as the
Goddess of Reason (III.i), and Clichy, the area outside Paris where members of
the Committee of Public Safety were said to have held orgies on seized private
estates (III.vi).[27]

Nor is it merely verbal detail that constitutes the play's historical verisimilitude. Büchner provided as well finely articulated vignettes of political theater,
including glimpses of both the summary justice of lamp-iron executions (I.ii)
and the carnivalesque theatricality of the Place de la Révolution during the
Terror (IV.vii). The latter shows obvious care for close, contemporaneous detail:
the *Carmagnole* is danced at the square's periphery, the crowd taunts the prisoners as they pass in the tumbrils and is treated in turn to parodic scaffold

speeches—defiant, mocking addresses that began to appear at this time, as the Terror accelerated beyond all reason, and aped the tragic last words of earlier and more individually distinct victims.[28]

This turn toward history brought with it obvious formal implications. Rather than giving over the structure of the play to tragedy, and thus reinscribing, as the romantics did, the tortured vision of an idealized, redemptive revolutionary history, Büchner necessarily adopted an "open," episodic form, in which tragedy becomes—as it became within the political culture of Jacobin revolution— merely one among several competing rhetorics of dramatic action and appre- hension. We are shown the tragic rhetoric of the Terror as it is announced by Robespierre and Saint-Just, but Büchner also traced, with careful attention to historical verisimilitude, the impact of competing rhetorics as they are worked out in the politics of marriage and prostitution, the naming of children, the ne- gotiation of social identity, class status, intimacy and trust, the spontaneous vio- lence of hungry crowds, and the ritual of the guillotine at the very height of its theatrical development as a political stage. The rhetoric of comedy, it should be noted, is practically absent from the play, as it was by this time from the political culture of the Revolution.

Büchner's attention to the local, concrete negotiation of Revolutionary politics— his resistance to abstraction and idealization—also extended to his choice of scenes and perspectives. Rather than focusing on exemplary moments of grand politics, we are in *Dantons Tod* most often placed at a slight remove from the public stage, located a bit before or after the moment and scene of the great events of the day. The play's many rapid scenes, rather than focusing our atten- tion upon spectacle and massed public confrontations or culminating at the mo- ment of tragic Revolution's terrible collapse in Thermidor, shift our attention to less-scripted and less-settled moments of the Revolution's theatrical politics, examining the Terror's politics from the margins, from the shadows and pass- ing moments of what remains of everyday life.

Büchner's embrace of Hugo's call for an embodied representation of the Rev- olution was not merely an aesthetic inclination; on the contrary, it seems to have been bound up with his conception of revolutionary politics. Büchner's particu- lar contribution to the Hessian conspiracy had been his collaboration in the com- position of *The Hessian Messenger* (1835), an inflammatory pamphlet intended not only to incite a local revolt but also to spark a popular, pan-German revolution. Mixing radical religious thought with a popular explanation of the first French Revolution, the pamphlet envisions its intended revolution as a kind of *revenance*, prompting the body of a naturally free, revolutionary people to rise, like Lazarus, from the seeming death of post-Revolutionary reaction and repression. The German people, it asserts, are "one body," a single people held under the violent oppression of tyranny. "It is," Büchner argues, "immaterial which part of the seeming corpse begins to twitch. . . . Rise up, and the entire body will rise with you."[29]

To conceive of a revolutionary people in such corporeal terms was not at all uncommon. However, for Büchner such a perspective was more than a conventional trope, for in addition to his activities as a revolutionary pamphleteer he was an exceptionally gifted student of anatomy. Two years later Büchner would be invited to join the faculty of the University of Zurich for his work on cranial anatomy, and for much of the nineteenth century he would be better known for that work than for his plays. Moreover, while in hiding at the house of his unsuspecting parents in Darmstadt, he spent much of his time (under the pretense of pursuing his studies) in the isolation of his father's anatomy laboratory, and *Dantons Tod* was composed, literally, on a dissecting table. Büchner pieced the play together at night, secreting the manuscript between the pages of an anatomical atlas whenever he was disturbed. In this sense his dramatic project might be seen as a continuation of his political efforts: an attempt, by allowing the Revolution to speak for itself—by piecing together and resuscitating the political speech of the Revolution's dying body—to catalyze the political action of a renewed revolutionary drama. As he has Danton remark during his imprisonment, "The flood of the Revolution can dump our corpses wherever it likes: with our fossilized bones they'll still be able to smash in the heads of kings"(IV.v).[30]

But such a reading is naive and romantic; it may suggest something of the ideas that informed the text of the pamphlet, but it is certainly at odds with what we know of Büchner's attitude by the time of the play's composition. His efforts to bring about revolution had failed miserably, and in such a manner as to suggest anything but an idealist's sense of the power of a revolutionary text. Just as the pamphlet was to have been secretly disseminated throughout Hesse the conspiracy was broken, its couriers arrested with masses of the anonymous, incriminating pamphlet sewn into their clothing. Among those was Büchner's closest friend, Carl Minnigerode, who was immediately imprisoned and soon afterward died. In the months following the betrayal the Hessian government eliminated virtually every revolutionary and even progressive movement in the region, although Büchner himself remained, for a short while at least, free. The irony must have been tragic: rather than catalyzing the resuscitation of a great revolutionary body, Büchner's pamphlet—his own revolutionary text—had served only to mark and enable a brutal, unforgiving purge of that body's most vital members. Moreover, his reading of French Revolutionary history had produced anything but a sense of the potential of resuscitated speech. As Büchner had pointed out in a now well-known letter to Minna Jaeglé, his fiancée, the preceding spring, "I've been studying the history of the French Revolution. I felt as though utterly crushed by the hideous fatalism of history. I find in human nature a terrible sameness, in human circumstances an ineluctable violence vouchsafed to all and to none. Individuals but froth on the waves, greatness a mere coincidence, the mastery of geniuses a dance of puppets, a ridiculous struggle against an iron law that can at best be recognized, but never mastered."[31] Yet, if that seemed the case, then why bother to write a revolutionary play at all? Why create history a second time if one is crushed by it, if it is marked only by hideous fatalism, terrible sameness, and ineluctable violence? Even more, why create a second time the very history that has produced such despair?

Part of the answer is suggested by the particular moment of Revolutionary history that he chose to depict. The action of *Dantons Tod* spans a brief and precise period of thirteen days in the spring of 1794, opening just moments after the execution of Jacques-René Hébert and the hard-left *enragés* on March 24 and closing shortly after the execution of Georges Danton and the soft-left *indulgents* on April 5. Both purges were carried out by Robespierre and the Jacobins, who, having thus eliminated all rivals for authority, set the Revolution upon that course of dictatorial Terror which ended a few bloody months later with 9 Thermidor. With a few notable exceptions, Büchner's play manages to present a remarkably full picture of intervening events, including the failed private meeting between Danton and Robespierre, Danton's celebrated trial, and even the alleged conspiracy by Lucille Desmoulins and General Dillon to foster a popular uprising against the Dantonists' arrest.

Although these thirteen days are certainly among the most decisive of the Revolution, they are a curious choice as a dramatic context, for they seem to lack active conflict. Danton, it is generally agreed, did surprisingly little in his own defense, and Büchner, if anything, highlighted that peculiar lack of political action. In fact, with the brief exception of Danton's trial speeches there is not much in the history of these two weeks—or in *Dantons Tod*—to generate real dramatic tension. There is, moreover, nothing exceptional in the way of political spectacle: no riots or *journées*, no gripping moments or defining *tableaux* of grand politics. Büchner carefully avoids even those spectacular moments that define the play's chronological frame: the executions of Hébert and Danton, which stand like bookends to the play's action, remain in Büchner's dramatic treatment oddly peripheral and, quite notably, unstaged. That of Hébert is merely reported in the opening scene, and during the execution of the Dantonists the play's focus is

not the spectacle of the guillotine—the focal point for the crowd of the Place de
la Révolution—but the more intimate conversations taking place among its wait-
ing victims. In a manner that is typical of the play's determined emphasis on
speech rather than spectacle, on the active force of words rather than the fixing
power of images, Büchner cut away from the scaffold even before Danton is executed, refusing us one of the revolution's most memorable and iconic tableaux.
Neither dramatic tension nor grand spectacle, then, were to be served here, and
it was evidently in something other than archetypal scenes and iconic moments of
Revolutionary history that Büchner was interested. But what?

Bouloiseau, reviewing the political history of this period, explains that these
two purges—the first directed against the populist, radical Hébertists to the
Jacobin left, the second at the moderate Dantonists to their right—stunned the
public, for they signaled the Jacobins' determination "no longer to accept re-
straints" and demonstrated their authority to enforce an "exclusive vision of the
State as the embodiment of Jacobin ideals."[32] Mallet du Pan, he notes, "described
this new situation with perspicacity. Previously, 'the aspiring factions had toppled the ruling factions with the aid of popular force'. Now, it was 'the ruling
faction that, in fifteen days, struck down two opposing factions whose intentions
it feared. It struck them down without the people's assistance, without mob agitation, legally, in due form.' Thus did he describe the reality of dictatorship."[33]
With the establishment of that dictatorship, the French Revolution entered its
last, "frozen" phase—that period of intensified terror that ended, as we have seen,
with the debâcle of Thermidor, the collapse of the radical Revolution, and the reassertion of civil society over the illusion of politics.

The moment on which Büchner's play focuses, and which began that phase,
carried a very different meaning. The astonishing ease with which the Jacobins
had arrested, tried, and executed not only Hébert (the writer of *Père Duchêne,*
and thus a highly symbolic voice of popular politics) but also Georges Danton,
the very personification of defiant Revolutionary energy, had suggested even to
contemporaries an unexpectedly deep political *malaise* in the radical *sections* of
Paris. Because of the seemingly "frozen" course of the Jacobin regime over the
next three months, it was (and remained) commonplace to regard the fall of
Danton as marking the demise of the popular Revolution, that surging, impetuous, organic revolution of *Le Peuple* which Michelet would later elevate to the
status of national myth.[34] Thermidor, the fall of Robespierre, appeared by comparison the death rattle of a political corpse, a hollow implosion of cold violence
in a brittle, echoing, already-empty political sphere. The sense that Büchner
pursued an anatomical logic still holds, but the specific gesture is now evident.

It is not a gothic resuscitation that Büchner was pursuing: *Dantons Tod*, as its title suggests, was a dramatic autopsy—a postmortem examination to determine the cause of the Revolution's death.

Rather than concerning itself with the impact of the failure of Revolutionary action, *Dantons Tod* explores its mechanism, dramatizing the process through which the Revolution's collapse was performed and experienced. Like all autopsies, it takes a double view, interrogating death from the perspective of life, explaining it not in terms of its impact but in terms of its advance toward and its movement through the living body. This distinction is analogous to Büchner's well-known comparison between the writer of history and the dramatic poet: the latter is superior, he asserted, because "he creates history a second time for us, and instead of offering us a bare story, he places us into the life of an age."[35] By returning to the Revolution's local, performative contexts and encounters, working back through its theatrical negotiations, Büchner's play interrogates the active links between its imaginary and material dramas. Like the dramatists of pre-Revolutionary France, Büchner thus subjected the drama he reworked to the examination of time, rendering explicit what had become an entrenched but latent structure and revealing, in so doing, the buried relation of drama and history.

The Rhetoric of Revolution

While it is true, and often noted, that Büchner's dramatic representation of Revolutionary Paris lacks the physical particularity of theatrical naturalism, it is equally true that this anatomical reconstruction of the Revolution's political culture reproduces with striking verisimilitude the heterogeneous discursive context and the varied, contestatory theatricality of Revolutionary politics during this period of time. In so doing, *Dantons Tod* manages as well to produce an immediate sense of the political difficulties of the spring of 1794, difficulties that define the conflicts and challenges faced by the play's leading characters. Almost five years had passed since the fall of the Bastille, and the Jacobin dictatorship, with its suppression of political journalism and virtually all voices of dissent, had not yet been established.[36] During these years, political language had proliferated, grown dense with reference and implication, not merely changed but aggregated and mixed. Within the play's action, rhetorical languages, gestures, and signs are overabundant and devalued, misunderstood, misused, and jostling for power from the outset: a "Babel" of political speech fills the play's early scenes. This is the Revolution at its most baroque, at a moment that more than any other appeared to embody Burke's allegations of Revolutionary politics as a "monstrous tragicomic scene."[37] No dramatic genre dominates in this context; instead, it is a moment marked most strongly by the predominance of rhetorics of critique and delegitimation. Clashes of political language, in the paranoid culture of the Terror, with its extreme emphasis on public transparency, seem inevitably to be resolved by denunciation and death. Fear and dearth are here more powerful factors than expectation or sentiment. Starvation, fear, and jealousy, not Revolutionary ideals, compel political violence, and that violence articulates not a cleansing, liberatory justice so much as an insatiable, grotesque mass appetite for mere blood, a desperate hunger for swift revenge.

Danton, perhaps the sine qua non of the power of embodied speech in the Revolution, the lungs that could rouse and unify all of France, becomes in Büchner's drama a haunted private commentator, withdrawn from public politics, steadfastly refusing to engage in political speech, tortured by the thought that Revolutionary rhetoric is merely, and horrifically, murderous—and that his own massive voice is, indeed can be, nothing other than a crude, amplified instrument of blind violence. *Dantons Tod* is not simply a reconstructed textual body: it dramatically revives as well the monstrous body politic of the Revolution, teeming with disorderly and contradictory actions, resistant to rational order.

And here the complex formal demands of Büchner's anatomical perspective begin to merge with the political demands that his characters confront. Stern tragic morality, parodic deflation, exuberant spectacle, disorderly popular justice— how are these local dramatic and theatrical languages to be sorted out? How are they to be formed into a coherent play?[38] Where is authority located in such an environment, and how is it articulated and maintained? In the play's promenade scene (II.ii), which itself recapitulates the period's political heteroglossia in a social montage, Büchner embedded like a gleaming metonymic miniature one brief reference to a (notably fictitious) theatrical drama: "Have you seen the new play?" asks one passing citizen to another. "A Babylonian tower! A confusion of vaults, stairs, passageways, and all thrown so lightly and boldly into the air. One gets dizzy with every step."[39] Formal problems and political problems, issues of dramatic coherence and of political coherence overlap and combine, as the play's characters face within its action questions and issues very like those that the play's author, and its audience, confront from outside. "The world is chaos," observes Danton (IV.v), and in the play's opening scene the problem of locating coherence and establishing stability amid that chaos is flatly foregrounded: "The Revolution has reached the stage where it *must* be re-organized," asserts Hérault-Séchelles to his companions. "The Revolution must end and the Republic begin."[40]

With such reflexive doubling in mind it is possible to reconsider the play's emphasis on, and the characters' preoccupation with, speech—speech that, as Schmidt's assessment reminds us, looks very like a "means to sublimate alienation and political impotence." And it is true, the chaotic, surging play of revolution that is restaged in *Dantons Tod* seems blindly to hustle these babbling rogues across its boards; they converse along the way, amid the hubbub and the pomp and the screams, among the vaults and stairs and passageways of a Piranesian political stage. Yet perhaps such behavior is more consequential, holds more active force, than Schmidt suggests; as I suggested in Chapter 2, speech was anything but politically impotent during the Revolution. To the contrary, as François Furet observed, the Revolution "ushered in a world where mental representations of power governed all actions, and where a network of signs completely dominated political life . . . Since the people alone had the right to govern—or at least, when it could not do so, to reassert public authority continually—power was in the hands of those who spoke for the people . . . Its leaders' 'job' was not to act; they were there to interpret action."[41]

Certainly there seems here to be a strong conjunction between Büchner's au- toptic project and the political role of his protagonists; one might even argue that Danton, Desmoulins, and even Robespierre serve at times as something like Virgilian guides amid the cacophony of the play's world, "there to interpret ac- tion" and to stand apart from the play's action, outside even the Revolution's proscenium arch, pointing inward, *looking* inward, and attempting, like Büchner (and occasionally even in his voice), to decipher, describe, and thus shape the chaotic political violence before their eyes. As Desmoulins asserts in response to Hérault-Séchelles's call for the constitutional establishment of the Republic, the Constitution "must be a transparent veil (*ein durchsichtiges Gewand*) that clings close to the body of the People. Every throb of the arteries, every flexing of the muscles, every twitch of the sinews must be revealed in it. The body can be beau- tiful or ugly; it has the right to be just as it is; we have no right to dress it as we see fit" (I.i.).[42]

Yet it would be a mistake to push this notion of authorial surrogates too far, for there is a crucial difference in perspective between Büchner and his characters. For Büchner, the French Revolution was, like the quiescent Hessian people, "an apparent corpse." For Danton, however, and indeed for all of the play's Revolu- tionary leaders, that Revolutionary body is perhaps *too* alive: "like Saturn," he ob- serves, "it devours its own children" (I.v.).[43] It is the violence of that monstrous body which raises the critical problem of how such action is related to the char- acters' speech—how the interpretation of action affects action *and* how action in turn conditions interpretation. This relation has long been recognized by historians as a crucial element of the Revolution's dynamic; as Furet pointed out, "power was in the hands of those who spoke for the people," and such speech, Hunt reminds us, "did not simply reflect the realities of Revolutionary changes and conflicts" but "was itself transformed into an instrument of political and social change."[44] The difficulties posed by this situation were recognized even by contemporaries. As Saint-Just remarked to the assembled deputies on the Ninth of Thermidor, in what was perhaps the Revolution's most unblinking confrontation with the power and the limits of political speech, "In what language shall I speak to you? How am I to show you errors of which you have no idea; how am I to make sensible to you the evil that a word reveals, that a word rectifies?"[45] For Saint-Just, on 9 Thermidor, language seemed an instrument of unavoidable political violence—a far cry from Schmidt's "means of sublimating alienation and political impotence."

In the "Babylonian" theater of *Dantons Tod*—and this is precisely the dramatic problem that Büchner posed for the play's political figures—we are somewhere in between, at a moment and in an environment in which the very multiplicity of political dialects, both spoken and performed, implies not impotence but confusion, as odd juxtapositions and unlikely diachronic combinations of political rhetoric produce unintended effects and exercise unexpected (if generally diminishing) force. Revolutionary languages in this late moment of Revolutionary struggle are local, limited, and contingent: in the conduct of factional violence, they assert different and competing kinds of authority, suggest different and contradictory modes of action, and imply different narratives of Revolutionary coherence and constitution. If the play's major political figures thus echo Büchner's autoptic investigation in their efforts to locate coherence amid this chaos, they also employ such languages to shape that chaos and to contest for power. To understand the manner in which Büchner reshaped the drama of Revolutionary politics, we must discern the shape of this contest, for Büchner's dramatic form responds not only to the discursive field that this contest defines but also to the dramatic limits that it implies.

Desmoulins's Catachrestic Echo

Scene two of *Dantons Tod,* the play's first glimpse of the public world of Revolutionary Paris, opens on a nearly empty, unspecified street. Onstage are Simon, a *souffleur* (literally, a "blower," occupationally, a theater prompter) and his wife, whom he is beating and verbally abusing: "You pelt-procurer, you wrinkled syphilitic sponge, you worm-eaten apple of sin!"[46] We are given no indication of the cause of the abuse, and at the outset this scene—like such incidents today—declares clearly that it is a private drama, a performance that is inappropriate, vaguely discomfiting, and even intimidating in public. The barrier of privacy is broken, however, by Simon's wife, whose cries for help attract an audience and begin a rhetorical negotiation.

Without hesitation, Simon shifts from obscene abuse to the stern morality of classical tragedy: "Let me be, Romans, that I may tear this carcass limb from limb!"[47] That is, the husband turns prompter, adopting the language of tragedy as the appropriate generic pose for his now public performance of violence.[48] Why tragedy? First, because to the mind of a prompter in the midst of the Terror, tragedy's rhetoric confers legitimacy, power, and distance. Simon appeals to tragedy to hold his unwanted audience at bay—and to keep the particular reason for his violence veiled. For a moment he attempts even to read his victim into his drama: "A real Vestal Virgin you are!" he hisses to his wife.[49] She, however, will have none of the part, and the crowd is equally unwilling to accept the performance. Simon is separated from his wife, his play is interrupted, and the audience demands that he explain "what's going on" (*Was gibt's*). His reply is reminiscent of Saint-Just's Thermidorean balk: "Where is the virgin? Speak! No, I can't say it that way. The maiden! No, not that either. The lady, the woman! Nor that, nor that neither! There's just one name left. Oh, it chokes me! I have no breath for it!"[50] The *souffleur* has "no breath for it" (*keinen Atem dafür*): Simon, or rather, tragedy, cannot speak publicly of "what's going on"—cannot say "prostitute." As his authority disintegrates, the crowd's interrogation shifts to his wife.

FIRST CITIZEN: What's up then?
WIFE: You see, I was sitting there on a stone in the sunshine warming myself you see—as we've no firewood, you see—
SECOND CITIZEN: So use your old man's nose.
WIFE: . . . and my daughter had gone down round the corner—she's an honest girl and takes care of her parents.
SIMON: Ha, she admits it![51]

Admits it, but doesn't name it: a mere suggestion to be taken as the audience thinks fit. Simon, hewing now absurdly to his tragic persona, calls for a knife—"Oh Lucretia! A knife, Romans, give me a knife! Oh Appius Claudius!"[52] His words, now part of a rejected play, are seized upon for a rather different drama: "Yes, a knife," interjects a citizen, "but not for the poor whore, what's she done? It's her hunger that whores and begs. A knife for the people that buy the flesh of our wives and daughters! Woe upon them, they that whore with the daughters of the people!"[53]

What has happened here? At the outset, certainly, the crowd's energies are directed against Simon's closed domestic drama, which is prized open to reveal its internal injustice and its veiled object of desire, the prostituted body of the prompter's daughter—the starving body that "whores and begs." In the same breath, however, the citizen who unveils that commodified body then appropriates it to a larger drama: "A knife for the people that buy the flesh of our wives and daughters!" becomes a diffuse call for revenge against all those who "whore with the daughters of the people!" Having thus claimed the particular for the general, the citizens then reverse the gaze in this broader public economy of desire, calling for "Death to all them with no holes in their coats!"—those men whose appearance suggests that they are not suffering, not a part of the people. A young man is dragged past, and a familiar Revolutionary performance begins as several voices exclaim "He's got a handkerchief! An aristocrat! To the lantern!"[54] On one level, then, Simon's little family drama has just been swallowed up into a larger, though no less violent, political theater, for the citizen's interjection initiates a different performance altogether: within moments, the citizens are chanting "Kill! Kill!" as they seek all who "whore with the daughters of the people."[55]

On another level, however, this episode has been situated in that larger political theater all along, serving as a kind of introductory lesson in the discursive conditions of political playing. Simon's tragedy has been smashed, but it would be a mistake to see the *souffleur* as having had no effect on this performance. Indeed, it is Simon's tragic rhetoric that has "prompted" the crowd's insurrectionary violence, for that rhetoric has provided an immediate and familiar focus for the citizens' frustrations. In his attempts to maintain the privacy of his drama, and particularly in his appeal to tragedy as a means with which to assert his dramatic distance and autonomy, Simon has evoked the closed political theater, hieratic authority, and arbitrary exercise of power that characterized monarchical rule: his loss of breath and his call for a dagger are gestures of exclusion, excision, erasure. Yet it is the audience that will hold power in this context, and it is the audience that insists on exercising such authority over Simon's drama. "What's going on? . . . What's up then?" These are the demands of the politics of publicity, driven by the same anxious mix of desire and suspicion that fueled popular suspicion of authority throughout the Revolution. By 1794, such demands had been heightened by economic distress and internecine political struggles. "The people are like a child," complains Danton early in the play, "they have to break everything to see what's inside" (I.v).[56]

But this scene's rehearsal of the popular insistence upon social transparency and its attendant challenge to authority is less a closed movement than a prelude. As we have seen, lamp-iron executions of the representatives of royal authority had, in July of 1789, marked the People's usurpation of the monarch's surveillant power over civic space—and thus marked as well the assertion of the politics of publicity over the very streets on which Simon's drama is staged. The crowd's attempt to re-enact such insurrectionary executions here thus makes a certain amount of *theatrical* sense, for it responds to an invocation of hieratic authority with an assertion of public authority. In 1794, however—in the late Revolutionary milieu of Büchner's play—the crowd's action is an oddly anachronistic and even contradictory gesture of anarchy, for it is presumably the People that occupies that surveillant position which the crowd here claims. Whose authority then is being usurped in this insurrectionary action, and whose asserted?

The question is—at least for the young man whom the crowd drags toward the lantern rope—a pressing one. "In what language," to echo Saint-Just, might this audience be addressed? "Gentlemen!" he exclaims, but "There are no gentlemen here," reminds a citizen. "Mercy," too, finds no hearers.[57] The young man's third tack, however, elicits a rather different reaction:

> THIRD CITIZEN: String him up on the lamppost!
>
> YOUNG MAN: All right, but you'll see no better for it.
>
> THE OTHERS: Bravo, bravo!
>
> A FEW VOICES: Let him go! (*he escapes*)[58]

Why does this work? In part, because the young man plays specifically on the symbolic appropriation of spectacular authority, and in so doing he echos and acknowledges, rhetorically, the crowd's own belated adoption of 1789's conventions of political theater. However, he does so ironically, catachrestically, playing upon the absurdity of that earlier rhetoric to parody—and not only echo—the People's own farcical act of surveillant usurpation.

A quick one-liner then, delivered by an unnamed character who appears so briefly as to seem merely passing through. But that is in some sense the point: in his fleeting presence, and particularly in the almost negligent ephemerality of his parodic critique, the young man exemplifies the problem of locating some stable language of political authority in this context. Like an endless series of reflections or a volley of echos, political rhetoric in this public theater is—like Simon's tragic call for a knife ("Yes, a knife! But not for the poor whore")—subject to uncontrolled repetition and recycling, to improper reiteration, outright misappropriation, and farcical citation. Just as all *action* is public here, so too is all *language*. In such conditions the rhetoric and the performance of Revolutionary politics split and multiply, proliferating all the more (echoing all the more) with each successive attempt to assert authority and gradually undermining the very possibility of authoritative representation.

Throughout the play, it is Camille Desmoulins, "Procurator-General of the Street Lanterns," in whom such disruptive, proliferating parody is most prominently figured. Desmoulins's oratory had incited the crowds of the Palais-Royal to the riots and executions of the July Days, and his rhetoric was, in history as in Büchner's play, well suited to such disruptive usurpation. As one can see in his self-mocking title, Desmoulins's mimicry of the surveillant language of royal power was less a claim to its authority than a parodic exposé of its pretensions. "Sparkling Camille," as Carlyle described him, illuminated the empty artifice of royal claims to political authority—and thereafter of successive Revolutionary claims to such authority—by adopting with catachrestic irony the guise and the voice of power. Like the young man's ironic invocation of the People's watchful gaze, the historical Desmoulins's rhetoric undermined the façade of political authority through inappropriate, erosive mimicry.[59] "You're a mighty echo!" Danton remarks early on (II.i), and Büchner's Desmoulins pursues throughout the play a consistent practice of such ironic rhetorical citation.[60] By 1794, in a situation already marked by a fundamental lack of authoritative speech, this strategy may seem anachronistic; however, any successful effort to assert authority would offer it renewed force, and as such Desmoulins's language posed a distinct danger to the Jacobin regime.

However, Büchner's character seems never to sense the disorder that his rhetoric implies, exhibiting throughout an almost startling political naiveté as to the implications of his ironic speech. "He's a child; he just laughed at you" is Robespierre's description to Saint-Just of Desmoulins's scathing, sacrilegious parody of the Jacobin leader (I.vi), and, indeed, in its lack of awareness Desmoulins's rhetoric resembles and echos the unthinking, intrusive violence that Danton ascribed to the crowd—a childish desire to hold everything up to scrutiny to see what's inside.[61] His opening scene description of the Constitution as a "transparent veil" that must reveal every structure and movement of the national body invokes the same process of unveiling, repetition, and disruption as that which defined the crowd's behavior on the street. Far from suggesting a basis on which to end the Revolution and initiate the Republic—a basis on which to establish a plausible narrative of the Revolution—Desmoulins's constitutional description exemplifies, ironically enough, that very constellation of rhetoric and political theater (transparency, disorder, vocal multiplicity) that most frustrated such a task. Given its chronological specificity, we might think of Desmoulins's rhetoric as the critical antitype of the Revolution's early comic narrative—as the political language in which the implicit illusions of power are unveiled and made to appear not sympathetic but ridiculous.

Danton's Hyperbolic Body

> FIRST CITIZEN: Our wives and children are screaming for
> bread; we want to feed them on the flesh of the aristocrats.
>
> (I.ii)

At the close of the play's opening scene, after declining to lead the fight in the Convention for Desmoulins's constitution, Danton rises to leave: "I have to get out of here or they'll drive me mad with their politics," he complains, initiating that determined process of disengagement which so strongly marks his action during the play.[62] Yet just as he moves offstage Danton finds himself unable to resist one small political remark. "If I may prophesy in passing," he says, "the statue of freedom is not yet cast: the furnace is roaring, all of us can still burn our fingers."[63] The contrast between Desmoulins's rhetorical dialect and Danton's is striking, particularly as this comment follows so closely on the heels of that constitutional description. If Desmoulins ironically invokes the language of specular authority, Danton's rhetoric is by contrast emphatically tactile: it shapes, forges, and lends coherent form to the molten, inchoate body of liberty.

Once again, Büchner combined quotation with a recognition and invocation of his characters' popular image, playing upon Danton's iconic stature as a massive, black-browed titan—a figure whom Carlyle described with apt license as the dark Atlas, shrouded in smoke, on whose shoulders rested the entire Revolution.[64] That thunderous figure is for the most part absent from this play, but Büchner's Danton does adopt his former persona briefly during his trial (III.iv), when he momentarily invokes his past as a weapon: "They have laid hands on my very existence," he declares, "so let it rise up and do battle: I shall bury the lot of them beneath the weight of my deeds . . . It was I in September," he claims, "who fed the tender brood of the revolution on the shattered bodies of aristocrats. It was my voice that forged weapons for the people from the gold of the rich and the nobility. My voice was the hurricane that buried the lackeys of despotism beneath waves of bayonets."[65]

There is more going on here than Danton's claims to authority. His language combines forging with feeding: bodies and gold are consumed and digested, and the Revolution's tender brood, nourished and grown to the sublime dimensions of nature, is unleashed in an annihilating tide. It is not merely the conflation of metal and flesh that is of interest; rather, it is the manner in which that conflation figures violence in terms of appetite, as a register of the growth and the power of the people. "It was I," announces Danton, "that declared war on the monarchy at the Champ de Mars; I that defeated it on the 10th of August; I that destroyed it on the 21st of January and threw down the head of a king as a gauntlet to challenge the rest of the monarchs."[66] Danton's rhetoric—in Büchner's play as in history—encompasses ever greater acts and confronts ever more generalized enemies, expanding that which is comprehended, contained, and consumed by its language and thus expanding as well the body of that unitary "I" which declares, destroys, consumes—that "I" which will "bury the lot of them beneath the weight of my deeds."[67]

It is in this expansive constitution that Danton's rhetoric, which historically was most dominant (as the events to which he refers imply) from 1791 through 1792, responds to the differentiation and diffusion implied by Desmoulins's catachrestic mimicry. More specifically, it may be understood as a response to the disenchantment of the comic Revolution—as both the antitype and the complement to Marat's antitheatrical critique. In Danton's speech, internal division is contained in hyperbole, and the Revolution's factions make common cause by confronting ever larger enemies. In short, Danton's Revolution, both historically and in Büchner's drama, testifies to its own identity through its continuing consumption of that which it is not and to its greatness through its consumption of increasingly greater foes.

Yet such unifying rhetoric implies as well its own problems—problems that Büchner's Danton confronts in the nightmarish hallucination that he suffers just before his arrest. Recalling those same September massacres that he would later describe as nurturing the tender brood of the Revolution, he imagines that "beneath me the earth was roaring in its flight; I had seized it like a wild horse, clutching its mane and gripping its flanks with giant limbs, with my head bent down, my hair streaming out above the abyss. I was being dragged along. I screamed in fear and awoke (Da schrie ich in der Angst, und ich erwachte)" (II.v).[68] Is this authoritative speech—speech that engenders and originates—or is it a terrified response to action? "I screamed in fear" suggests the latter, and the image as a whole—indeed, the very power and wholeness of the image, of "the earth"—suggests that the appetite and actions of this Revolutionary body, as well as the speech that such actions prompt, are and always were beyond authority's control.

That possibility—that his speech and the violence that it brings are automatic—is precisely what so disturbs Danton about his nightmare:

DANTON: Did I shout?

JULIE: You talked of ugly sins and then you groaned, "September!"

DANTON: Did I? No, I didn't say it. I hardly thought it; those were just quiet, secret thoughts.

JULIE: You're trembling, Danton.

DANTON: And why shouldn't I tremble when the walls begin to talk? . . . I'd like to stop thinking when they speak like that. There are thoughts, Julie, for which there should be no ears. It's not good when they scream like new-born children. It's not good.

. . .

JULIE: There's a child crying somewhere near. (II.v)[69]

Words come to life of their own; Danton's thoughts escape him, bursting violently and hungrily from quiet and secrecy into the public realm.

It is here that Danton's language both recapitulates and extends the problems of Simon's failed drama and Desmoulins's appropriative echo. Like all rhetoric, Danton's is available to all in the public theater of Revolutionary politics; in its hyperbolic appetite, its logic of consumptive unity, that rhetoric not only forges the body of the Revolution but, if turned inward, also echos, and echos as an insatiate, self-consuming violence.[70] As Lacroix observes, noting the Jacobins' awareness of this problem, "the people are a minotaur: if that lot want to avoid being gobbled up themselves, they *have* to keep feeding the beast its diet of corpses" (I.iv); and in Danton's more familiar formulation, "the revolution is like Saturn, it devours its own children" (I.v).[71] Danton's withdrawal from politics is, at least in part, a refusal to participate any longer in that economy: "I would rather be guillotined than guillotine others," he asserts to Desmoulins. "I've had enough" (II.i).[72]

Robespierre's Periphrastic Excision

ROBESPIERRE: Away with them! Quick! Only the dead cannot return.

(I.vi)

As Danton points out in his single meeting (I.vi) with Robespierre, "Where self-defense ends murder begins. I see no reason why we have to go on killing people." For Robespierre, however, the question is not simply one of self-defense,

of eliminating opposition: "The social Revolution is not yet complete," he re-
torts. "The world of the aristocracy is not yet dead."[73] It is not with ironic clarity
or hyperbolic comprehension that Robespierre is concerned here, nor is it to
images of seeing or forging a Revolutionary body that he appeals. For him, the
Revolution is measured in temporal rather than corporeal terms, its conflict one
between the future and the past—between "no longer" and "not yet." It is completion, conclusion for which he aims, and completion conceived as the achievement of an absolute break with the decadent past.[74] Put differently, Robespierre,
unlike Desmoulins or Danton, is attempting to shape a narrative—and specifically,
of course, a tragedy.

Within such a framework the question of violence takes on a rather different valence. A few minutes after his meeting with Danton, pondering the question of his onetime ally's arrest, Robespierre considers to himself whether such
an attack is "so very necessary": "Yes, it is, it is! The Republic! He has to go!
Anyone who stands still in a moving mass offers the same resistance as if he
were opposing it from outside: he gets trampled under foot. We will not permit
the Ship of the Revolution to founder on the shallow notions and mudbanks of
these people; the hand must be hacked away that would hold it back—and if
he grasps it with his teeth! . . . Away with a society that has stolen the clothes of
the dead aristocracy and inherited their sores!" (I.vi).[75] The violence of the
Terror is in such terms both liberating and purifying, both freeing and purgative,
both progressive and redemptive; its goal, as we see in Chapter 2, the punctuating point of rupture when the burden, impediment, and corruption of the past
have been sheared way.[76]

But how is such a rupture to be articulated and achieved given the manner in
which the past echos through this political theater? Desmoulins's catachrestic revolution plays on the languages of the past, and Danton's capacious rhetoric ingests
everything that Robespierre wishes to expunge: the gold of the aristocracy, the
head of a king, "September!" Both strategies reinforce, even rely upon, the synchronic presence of past and present, requiring it in order to create meaning.
Here, as again in Revolutionary history, Robespierre's rhetoric takes a very different course and exhibits a different character than that of either Desmoulins
or Danton; rather than pursuing catachrestic irony or hyperbolic comprehension, it relies on periphrastic negation—innuendo rather than confrontation, abstraction rather than explicitness. Periphrasis, rhetorically, operates as a negative
language of excision. Robespierre attacks "the enemy," refers to "certain persons"
who call for mercy, and to focus his accusations asks the members of the Jacobin
Club to "recall those persons who once lived in attics but now drive about in

carriages" (I.iii). By allowing his audience to fill in possible names, he maintains an inexplicit discursive space that functions as a kind of open challenge and annihilating void.[77] Whoever objects to the condemnatory power of the Committees, he asserts to the members of the National Convention, "is guilty, for innocence never trembles in the face of public vigilance" (II.vii).[78] In Robespierre's revolution there is to be no opportunity for parodic or hyperbolic representation, for his language, as Marie-Hélène Huet observed, sought to define the Revolution "as sublime, as an ideal that would transcend all representation and escape all misrepresentation, as a rhetorical purity that could only be expressed in negative form."[79]

Büchner shows us, in the play's several *parade* scenes, why such a negative strategy held so much appeal at this moment in the Revolution. In the social Babel of a promenade scene (II.ii), a citizen trying to declare the birth of his son gets tangled up in the jargon of new Republican names and proper Republican values; a beggar ties two passing gentlemen in philosophical knots over the value of a smooth coat versus smooth hands; a prostitute engages in a punning, obscene proposition to a strolling soldier; a young man seduces a passing lady's daughter with salacious innuendoes filtered through the poetry of sublime nature. Linguistic play and sexual play merge here—"What fun they're having!" remarks Danton, who here as in many instances plays the role of *flaneur* and of *raisonneur*. "It's in the air, I can smell it, as if the heat of the sun were hatching lechery" (II.ii).[80] Extended to politics, such an atmosphere of polyphonic fecundity gives some sense of why Robespierre, in his meeting with Danton, equates vice and treason.

Similar things happen in the political Babel of a prisoners' *parade*. In a corridor of the Luxembourg (III.iii), Büchner gives us "speeches come to life (*lebendig gewordnen Reden*)" reviewing all of those corrupt dialects of Revolutionary politics that Robespierre's Terror had excised from the stage.[81] Danton, Hérault-Séchelles, and Desmoulins are, on their arrival in the prison (III.i), greeted by mocking echos of their own earlier words: "So, the power of the people and the power of Reason are one?" asks one prisoner of Hérault, and another informs Desmoulins that his "improvement in the street-lighting hasn't made France any brighter."[82] Like Virgil's Hades, Büchner's prisons are a synchronic realm of the past, in which creatures of different moments and mythologies, different narratives and actions, stand side by side, removed now, as if dead, from the temporal world of political action. For Robespierre, they hold all the threat of a lingering, looming past: "Away with of them! Quick! Only the dead cannot return!"

And this perspective must be given some consideration, for, unlike Desmoulins's catachrestic language of disruption or Danton's hyperbolic language of consumption, Robespierre's periphrastic rhetoric of terror holds power here. Robespierre, at this moment, is the voice of the people, the "dogma of the Revolution, something no-one can touch" as Danton phrases it (II.i).[83] Certainly it is not difficult to recognize the appeal of that urge toward tragedy's purging completion: Danton himself, sick with the bloody reverberations of September, complains that "creation has become so full that there is nothing left open, everything is seething" (III.vii).[84] Throughout the play he returns to the idea that peace is "in nothingness" (III.vii), in the annihilation of the grave, asserting even that nothingness is the world's "due messiah"(IV.v).[85] His nightmarish cries, too, are prompted by that teeming polyphonic chaos of creation: "Will it never stop?" he asks himself, "Will the glare never pale and the roar never die? Will it never be dark and still, so we're no longer forced to see and hear our horrible sins?" (II.v).[86] There are echos here of the historical Robespierre's tragic desire for a silent moment of pause and reflection, and Danton is undoubtedly tempted at times by tragedy's ability at least to dignify suffering, to eradicate in its violence the humiliating messiness and base compromise of human failings. The Romans and the Stoics, he muses to his fellow prisoners, managed at least to "a comfortable feeling of self-respect. It's not so bad to drape your toga around you and look around to see how long a shadow you're throwing" (IV.v).[87]

Is *Dantons Tod*, then, to be read as a tragedy, in which the polyphonic bulk of Danton staggers to its punctuated dissolution? Certainly Büchner's very focus on the death of Danton, and in a sense on the death of the popular revolution, appears to share with Robespierre's politics of terror an epistemological privileging of the moment of death, the fatal moment of change. One might even argue that Büchner's drama adopts such an attitude from the outset, aiming everything toward a tragic rendering of the death of Danton and his colleagues and endorsing in that dramatic portrait the same tragic myth of popular revolution that Michelet would later articulate. Such renderings of Danton's death had been produced by his historical contemporaries. Antoine Vincent Arnault, for example, who had composed a number of exemplary republican tragedies for the Revolutionary theaters, offered this eyewitness account of Danton's execution:

> Danton was the last to appear on this stage that was running with the blood of
> his colleagues. Night was drawing on. At the foot of the hideous statue whose
> bulk loomed huge against the sky I saw the form of the tribune stand like some

Dantesque shade; half lit by the dying light, he seemed rather to rise from the tomb than ready himself to enter it. Nothing so bold as the countenance of the athlete of the Revolution; nothing more formidable than the set of that profile which defied the axe, than the expression upon that head, which, doomed to fall so soon, seemed yet to dictate the law. Horrifying dumb show! The memory of it undimmed by time.[88]

Yet, pointedly, no such scene is offered in *Dantons Tod*. Büchner's play traces the pageant procession of the tumbrils from the very door of the Conciergerie to the grotesque fairground of the Place de la Révolution; it stages even the last exchanges and final words of the Dantonists, delivered from the scaffold and at the feet of that seated figure of Liberty that presided over the executions. But it does not show us Arnault's "horrifying dumb show," an image that would remain "undimmed by time." It does not show us, in other words, a tragic, exemplary image of Danton's death.

Instead, Büchner cut away, shifting the scene to an empty side street in which Lucille Desmoulins, standing alone, contemplates the death of her husband and the impossible necessity of just such a tragic cessation.

—Dying—dying—!
—But everything else keeps on living, everything, this little fly here, that bird. Why not him? The stream of life should stop aghast if even a drop is spilt. The earth should show a wound from such a blow.
—Everything keeps going, clocks tick, bells ring, people pass, water flows, and so everything goes on just as before—No! It mustn't happen, no. I'll sit on the ground and scream, that everything stop, shocked still, no more movement.

Lucille "*sits on the ground, covers her eyes and screams*"—but "*After a moment she rises.*"

It doesn't help, everything is just the same: the houses, the streets, the wind blows, the clouds pass by. (IV.viii)[89]

Things have continued; incessant life has marked *no* rupture.

But *have* things continued without interruption? Lucille's meditation is disturbed by several women passing by on their way home from the executions, which have evidently just concluded. Büchner did not simply shift the scene; instead, he jumped well *ahead*—eliding, in the gap between scenes, that tragic moment implied by the very title of the play. In that elision, more pointedly than anywhere else, the play signals a final rejection of tragedy's illusory claim on history, announcing its departure from what Desmoulins—in one of the most strikingly anachronistic turns of phrase in the entire drama—describes as "our guillotine Romanticism" (*unsere Guillotinenromantik*) (I.i).[90]

Soemmerring's Head: The Theater of the Guillotine and the Gestus of Death

DANTON: But there's no hope in death: death is putrefaction
plain and simple; in life we putrefy with more sophistication,
more subtlety, that's the only difference.

(*III.vii*)

The conjunction of the guillotine with the tragic rhetoric of the radical Revolution was strong: the sword of Damocles, the catastrophic reversal, the swift, indeed instantaneous, justice of terror. The effectiveness of the guillotine as an instrument of political and moral suasion derived from just that compression of time, from the immeasurably brief punctuation that marked permanent, irreversible change. In its swiftness the guillotine offered a spectacle of the sublime, a shift from life to death so rapid as to exceed the eye.

Yet, as Daniel Arasse observed, that very attribute gave rise to an extended debate over the question of whether or not death was indeed simultaneous with decapitation.[91] Medical science turned considerable attention to the question, beginning with Samuel Thomas von Soemmerring's essay "Sur le Supplice de la Guillotine," written during or just after the Terror, in which Soemmerring argued that "it seems likely that feeling may persist for a quarter of an hour, given that the head, because it is thick and round, does not lose heat very quickly." The dying, he concluded, "see and hear long after they have ceased to be able to move their limbs."[92]

Soemmerring's argument was supported by the period's exceptional advances in anatomy. During the latter half of the eighteenth century, anatomists had occupied themselves with the dissection, differentiation, and mapping of the body's minute local systems: the arteries, for example, and in particular the nerves (precisely the sort of research in which Büchner was later engaged).[93] In 1800, such research led Xavier Bichat, in his *Recherches physiologiques sur la vie et la mort* to conclude (as Jonathan Crary describes it) "that death was a fragmented process, consisting of the extinction of different organs and processes: the death of locomotion, of respiration, of sense perceptions, of the brain."[94] Such an incremental perspective suggested in turn a disturbing conceptual reversal: if death could be understood as an incremental loss of life through the extinction of one system after another, then life could be understood in turn as the incremental onset of death—as putrefaction "with more sophistication, more subtlety," as Danton puts it (IV.vii), but nonetheless as a sustained and steady rot.[95]

That view informs *Dantons Tod* as the characters wait in the depths of the Conciergerie for the call to execution: "We're all buried alive," remarks Danton, "like kings in three or four layers of coffins . . . We scratch for fifty long years at the coffin lid" (III.vii).[96] Rather than neatly awaiting annihilation with the bloodless atemporality of Virgil's underworld shades, Danton and his fellow representatives of the past begin in the prison cells of Büchner's dramatic Hades to decay and rot: their hair and nails grow without check and their bodies become more corrupted, attracting vermin, beginning to stink.[97] Rather than anticipating execution as a punctuation, they agonize over its potential continuity: "To lie there cold, stiff, alone, in the rank miasma of decay," Desmoulins thinks aloud, "perhaps death only slowly squeezes the life from our being, perhaps we're still conscious while our bodies rot away" (III.vii).[98]

Robespierre senses a similar problem in his attempt to achieve a political punctuation. "Only the dead cannot return" are his words to Saint-Just, but those assertions are countered by his own nightmarish fears, which Büchner composed, appropriately enough, as an echo of *Macbeth*. Just after Danton's departure, Robespierre stands lost in thought:

> Why can't I drive the thought from my mind? With bloody finger it points and points. I swathe it in layer upon layer of rags, but always the blood comes bursting through. [*After a pause*] I don't know which part of me is lying to the rest. [*He goes to the window*] The night snores above the earth, tossing and turning in terrible dreams. Thoughts and wishes, scarcely sensed, confused and formless, that dared not face the light of day, now take shape and substance and steal into the silent house of dreams. They open doors, they stare out windows, they become half flesh, their limbs stretch in sleep, their lips murmur.—And our waking life, isn't it merely a brighter dream? (I.vi)[99]

If death is fragmented, if its demarcation from life is so blurred and incremental that life might extend into the slow decay of the grave, then might not the grave creep forth into life, taking *on* flesh, murmuring and gibbering at the window in the voices of the past? Were it the case that Danton then stalked onto the scaffold, shadowy in the evening light, seeming rather "to rise from the tomb than ready himself to enter it," as Arnault put it, we might assume that the return from the grave which so spooks Robespierre is that last ascent of the

Dantonists from the underworld. Hérault-Séchelles seems to anticipate such a mythic theatrical scene, reassuring Desmoulins as they are taken by the tumbrils that "we'll have a beautiful night for it. The clouds are hanging in the still evening sky—like a burnt-out Olympus, with its fading, dying figures of the gods" (IV.v).[100] That vision corresponds to romanticism's tragic outlook, as the resonance between Robespierre's recapitulation of the nightmare of Macbeth and Coleridge's haunted imagination suggests. But Olympus *has* been burnt out; such tragic scenes, as Büchner had Simon learn at the play's outset, no longer fit in this context. Instead, the play stages the return that Robespierre dreads differently, sweeping the Dantonists into a theater that announces his play's distance from the nightmares and mythic inclinations of romanticism:

SCENE VII—*Place de la Révolution*

The tumbrils are driven on and stop in front of the guillotine. MEN *and* WOMEN
   sing and dance the "Carmagnole," the PRISONERS *strike up the "Marseillaise."*
A WOMAN WITH CHILDREN. Make room here! Let us through! My kids are
   so hungry they're screaming—let 'em watch so they'll shut up! Give us some
   room! (IV.vii)[101]

No horrifying dumb show here. Büchner's Place de la Révolution is raucous, crowded, and emphatically profane; it is also, significantly, a *diversion*—not a high tragic stage so much as street theater, carnival, or fairground. As the mother's remarks imply, the theater of the guillotine here is no punctuating event: the drop of the blade might take a mere instant, but the larger spectacle that surrounded that moment is, like Bichat's representation of death, incrementally fragmented, multiple, and temporally extended. It is, moreover, an ongoing spectacle, staged for popular and *regular* consumption—a way of passing time more than an event marking history. Once again, Büchner stayed close to the historical experience of the Revolution, for during the height of the Terror the guillotine seems to have become just such a daily diversion: seats and even opera glasses could be rented to offer better visibility, and pamphlets relating the lives and crimes of each day's victims were sold at the square's periphery.[102] The very repetition of these executions, their predictability and their eventual ubiquity, generated as well a regular audience of enthusiasts and connoisseurs. In the process, the momentous impact of Arnault's tragic theater ("the memory of it undimmed by time") yielded to the values and the demands of a running show, with passing preferences, fads, and fashions. "Ha!" replies one of Büchner's spectators to Lacroix's defiant scaffold speech, "We've heard that one before! Try again! How boring!" (IV.vii).[103]

During the Terror, especially fine performances were remembered, compared, and even parodied by later victims, and as the demand for novelty became more acute the status of the victims shifted. The one-time nature of each "actor's" performance, held by Robespierre to be a guarantee of the moment's exemplary truth, became integrated into an ongoing repertory.[104] "Good looking man, that Hérault!" remarks one of Büchner's women who pass by Lucille after the executions. "When I saw him standing there by the triumphal arch at the Festival of the Constitution," replies one of her companions, "I said to myself, 'Well *he'll* look good up on the guillotine,' honest I did" (IV.viii).[105] Incorporated for mere moments into the incessant, mechanistic spectacle, the Terror's victims thus become, in the play as, again, in history, increasingly objectified, increasingly mundane, commodified elements in a larger economy of theatrical consumption. As Hérault passes through the crowd to the scaffold another woman cries out "Hérault, that beautiful hair of yours will make me a fine wig!" (IV.vii).[106]

Far from the romantic image of a Danton re-emerging tragically, and whole, from the grave, Büchner's drama offers here the more chilling notion of bodies and phrases being ripped—incrementally, continually, one might even say industrially—into commodified political fragments.[107] "If only it were a real fight, tooth and nail, no holds barred," complains Danton, "but I feel as though I've fallen into a mill, and its cold, physical power is slowly tearing off all my limbs. Such a mechanical way to be killed!" (III.vii).[108] *That* is Danton's death: the realization that modern history is not tragedy but "ineluctable violence," that within it the individual has become "foam on the waves." The Revolutionaries' "fossilized bones" do not appear here as clubs for some passing Samson but as the fragmentary remains of a corpse—as dialectical images of the violence of Revolutionary efforts to impose drama, and tragedy in particular, upon modern historical time.

In the end, Lucille seems to sense something quite similar. In the play's closing moment she sits on the steps of the scaffold, singing a song to the angel of death. When a patrol enters, she cries out "Long live the King!" (IV.ix).[109] Her defiant act of suicide is not simply the retrieval of a fossil from the scaffold's early, aristocratic victims. It is also, in the repressive political context in which Lucille is situated, a starkly demystifying *gestus*, a cry that throws the Terror into dialectical relation to the pre-Revolutionary past, forcing recognition of its tyrannical violence and exposing the Jacobin myth of history as tragedy.[110]

Conclusion

The modernist theatre—understood as a self-consciously revolutionary insurgency—has set itself off from the dramas of the
past. Yet time and again it has been haunted by that which it be-
lieves it has displaced, that "tradition of all the dead generations."
For by defining itself in relation to the past, it betrays a secret
link to history.

David Savran

In the foregoing pages I have argued that the transition from traditional to
modern drama is best understood not as an aggregate of disconnected rup-
tures—of isolated and irreconcilable formal experiments gathered about the
French Revolution's epistemological void—but as a continuous and extended crisis, worked out not only in literature and the theater but also in political and social performance, of the drama's authority as a narrative form. This crisis was not
limited to the Revolutionary decade, though it found there a decisive moment of
realization. Rather, the drama's crisis emerged from, reflected, and contributed
to a more general crisis of representation that was rooted in the late eighteenth
century's awareness of the accelerating pace of time and of historical change.
Within the realm of dramatic practice, this crisis was experienced as a widening gap between the codes and conventions required by the traditional dramatic
genres and the actual conduct and social construction of everyday life. That gap,
which had been understood by neoclassicism as a problem to be rectified by order

and veiled by decorum, came to be seen by enlightenment dramatists as a breach to be exploited and rendered in increasingly explicit terms.

Contemporary consciousness of this crisis in representation was evident in the delegitimation of dramatic form, but it was most thoroughly expressed in the French Revolution itself, a radical revolt in the spheres of political and social life that overturned those codes and conventions of historical representation that had lent stability and authority to the ancien régime. Yet, as others have pointed out, contemporaries understood the Revolution itself in fundamentally theatrical ways, for the articulation and negotiation of political and social crisis in the 1790s were thoroughly inflected by the language of performance, presentation, and the achievement or enforcement of "audience belief." On the evidence of this striking usage, one of my aims in this book has been to argue that the French Revolution marks a moment of convergence in these dual reconceptions of narrative time—a moment, that is, when the temporal authority of both drama and history, their capacities to produce plausible horizons of expectation, became so diminished that they met—and merged—in their mutual reduction to the span of a day.

But this Revolutionary political appropriation of traditional drama, its application of outmoded generic norms to the conduct of contemporary historical action, did not result simply in the mutual delegitimation of both drama and history. Drama became during this period an experimental instrument for self-consciously shaping the perception, the performance, and the course of unfolding events, and history became the primary context in which dramatic form was asserted, tested, and reconceived. The Revolution was not an interruption or an epistemological background to the history of the drama but an integral, constitutive part of that history, every bit as central to its course as any literary work or movement. By appropriating the terms of drama, the French Revolution did not shut drama down but extended and fulfilled its enlightenment critique. It subjected drama, not on the stage or in literary form but in the streets of Paris, to what might be thought of as a radical reality check. By enacting the gap between the representational and the actual, the historical drama of the Revolution exploded the old dramatic forms with a violence that could not have been matched in the arts, not only demonstrating their inadequacy to the pace and structure of modern existence but also revealing in stark terms the limitations of their structures of action and the anachronistic assumptions of their implied social visions. And when this revolutionary moment of convergence had passed, the interpenetration of drama and history remained in the dramatic imagination as a latent formal structure, implicit but no less present for being unacknowledged and unaddressed.

The latency of this formal structure is evident in the way the earliest dramatic responses to the French Revolution avoid it. Romanticism's displacement of Revolutionary history and its efforts to resolve the problem of tragedy (both, it must be noted, reversals of early Romanticism's drive toward historical proximity and generic critique) can be understood as efforts to overcome an evident failure of drama and also a terrifying failure of all efforts to narrate plausible historical action. Melodrama, very differently but in complementary fashion, ritualized the spectacle of that failure, rehearsing the violence of its most extreme moment while containing its threat in the exercise of passion and the reassuring confinement of action to the bounds of the stage. In both cases it is crucial to note that the drama of the Revolution is not confronted but is repressed. Rather than attempting to develop a new poetics of action, new plausible narratives that might be performed, both romantic tragedy and melodrama sought to avoid, suppress, or deny the failure of dramatic action that the Revolution enacted. This historical conservatism marks the politics of both genres in definitive fashion, revealing, beneath whatever claims they may have made to progressive or radical perspectives, a basic desire to return to or to relocate a historical past—and a space of historical action—that no longer existed.

It is in this sense that Büchner's explicit dramatic treatment of the French Revolution—his embrace of the Revolution on the level of content—may be recognized as a reflexively formal gesture of exceptional significance. More than merely constituting a politically radical selection of historical subject, Büchner's investigative, even scholarly return to the documents of the Revolution's historical drama enabled him to recognize and respond to its narrative implications for the generic form of drama itself. The foundation of Büchner's dramatic modernity lay in his realization, at a distance of four decades, that drama and history are inextricably entwined, and with that awareness came the understanding, taken up in earnest by the modernist avant-garde, that the drama must carry within itself a self-conscious formal engagement with the history of its present. With Büchner, then, the drama caught up with revolutionary modernity and thus in a sense with its own formal history, and this belated rapprochement enabled the drama after Büchner to look toward the future, to concern itself not with the accurate recovery or purifying redemption of history as it was but with the reflexive negotiation of history in the making.

It's worth noting in closing that my work on this book has coincided with what might be seen as a critical revolution in the study of modern drama itself, a revolution that has involved not least (as David Savran's remarks in my epigraph suggest) the recognition of modernist drama's enmeshment in modernity's historical past.[1] My book may be understood as an effort to contribute to this critical re-evaluation, as an effort to render explicit, and thus pull into the active present, modern drama's connection—its "secret link"—not only to the drama of the French Revolution but also, and through it, to the dramas of the pre-Revolutionary past.

Introduction

1. Zola: "One can see tragedy, by the start of this century, as a tall, pale, emaciated figure without a drop of blood under its white skin, trailing its robes in tatters across the shadows of stage on which the footlights had gone dark of their own accord" (On croit voir la tragédie, vers le commencement de ce siècle, pareille à une haute figure pâle et maigrie, n'ayant plus sous sa peau blanche une goutte de sang, traînant ses draperies en lambeaux dans les ténèbres d'une scène, dont la rampe s'est éteinte d'elle-même). Émile Zola, "Le Naturalisme au théâtre: Les theories et les exemples" (Paris: G. Charpentier et E. Fasquelle, 1895). Gallica, Bibliothèque nationale de France, May 16, 2005, http://gallica.bnf.fr/. Unless otherwise noted, all translations are my own.

2. This sense of discontinuity, disconnection, and outward inclination, evident enough in any comparative analysis, has been reinforced by the disciplinary separation of the study of the drama of this period into a multitude of periods, traditions, and national literatures.

3. In fact, Goethe's composition of the first part of *Faust* defines much the same space: after the Fragment of 1790, Goethe set the play aside until the summer of 1797 (when he returned to it after being so urged by Schiller).

4. See Benjamin Bennett, *Modern Drama and German Classicism* (Ithaca, NY: Cornell UP, 1979).

5. See Emmett Kennedy et al., *Theatre, Opera, and Audiences in Revolutionary Paris: Analysis and Repertory,* Contributions in Drama and Theatre Studies 62 (Westport, CT: Greenwood, 1996); Graeme Rodmell, *French Drama of the Revolutionary Years* (London: Routledge, 1990); Michèle Root-Bernstein, *Boulevard Theater and Revolution in Eighteenth-Century Paris* (Ann Arbor, MI: UMI Research Press, 1984); André Tessier, *Les Spectacles à Paris pendant la Révolution* (Geneva: Librairie Droz, 1992).

6. What innovation did occur was slow and hesitant. As Emmett Kennedy put it, "analysis of the plays year by year shows that theatre followed the evolution of society rather than the other way around." Kennedy et al., 50. See also Root-Bernstein and Rodmell, both of whom address this issue throughout their work.

7. Hans Ulrich Gumbrecht, *Making Sense of Life and Literature,* trans. Glen Burns, Theory and History of Literature, vol. 79 (Minneapolis: U of Minnesota P, 1992), 177.

8. Victor Hugo, preface to *Odes et ballades* (1824), qtd. in Gumbrecht, 178.

9. Such weakness was particularly evident in the drama, but it extended to other fields as well. As Gumbrecht points out, in France the Revolutionary era was considered to be so devoid

of accomplished writing of any sort that until recently French literary history skipped over it entirely (178).

10. Peter Brooks, *The Melodramatic Imagination: Balzac, Henry James, Melodrama, and the Mode of Excess* (New York: Columbia UP, 1985), 14. Melodrama, Brooks argued, arose directly from this massive institutional and symbolic collapse. Similarly, in *The Death of Tragedy*, George Steiner presented the French Revolution as the decisive political assertion of the Rousseauist and romantic vision of the perfectability of man; this massive shift in consciousness, he argued, closed "the doors of hell" and placed human action firmly within the currents of modern history. In the wake of that shift, Steiner suggested, tragedy could hold no force, and the romantics turned to a "near-tragic" mythology of redemption, closer in its post-traumatic impulse to the reassurances of melodramatic justice than to the cathartic shocks of tragedy. In consigning mankind to secular history, Steiner argued, the Revolution also consigned tragedy to myth. George Steiner, *The Death of Tragedy* (1961; New Haven, CT: Yale UP, 1996). Steiner's more recent work pursued much the same argument. See, e.g., his discussion of Goethe's *Faust* in *Bluebeard's Castle: Some Notes Towards the Redefinition of Culture*, T. S. Eliot Memorial Lectures (New Haven, CT: Yale UP, 1971).

11. See, e.g., Betsy Bolton, *Women, Nationalism, and the Romantic Stage: Theatre and Politics in Britain, 1780–1800* (Cambridge: Cambridge UP, 2001); Catherine Burroughs, *Closet Stages: Joanna Baillie and the Theater Theory of British Romantic Women Writers* (Philadelphia: U Pennsylvania P, 1997); Marc Baer, *Theatre and Disorder in Late Georgian London* (Oxford: Clarendon P, 1992); Julie Carlson, *In the Theatre of Romanticism* (Cambridge: Cambridge UP, 1994); Jeffrey Cox, *In the Shadows of Romance: Romantic Tragic Drama in Germany, England, and France* (Athens: Ohio UP, 1987); Michael Gamer, *Romanticism and the Gothic: Genre, Reception, and Canon Formation* (Cambridge: Cambridge UP, 2000); Jane Moody, *Illegitimate Theatre in London, 1770–1840* (Cambridge: Cambridge UP, 2000); Judith Pascoe, *Romantic Theatricality: Gender, Poetry, and Spectatorship* (Ithaca, NY: Cornell UP, 1997); George Taylor, *The French Revolution and the London Stage, 1789–1805* (Cambridge: Cambridge UP, 2000).

12. In addition to Cox, *In the Shadows of Romance*, and Carlson, see Jeffrey Cox, "Romantic Drama and the French Revolution," in *Revolution and English Romanticism*, ed. K. Hanley and R. Selden (Hertfordshire, UK: Harvester Wheatsheaf, 1990), 241–60; Russell Gillian, *The Theatres of War: Performance, Politics, and Society, 1793–1815* (Oxford: Clarendon P, 1995); Terence Hoagwood, "Prolegomenon for a Theory of Romantic Drama." *Wordsworth Circle* 23, no. 2 (1992): 49–63; David Marshall, "The Eye-Witnesses of *The Borderers*," *Studies in Romanticism* 27, no. 3 (1988): 391–98; Reeve Parker, " 'In some sort seeing with my proper eyes': Wordsworth and the Spectacles of Paris," *Studies in Romanticism* 27, no. 3 (1988): 369–90. On melodrama, see, e.g., Leo Charney and Vanessa Schwartz, eds., *Cinema and the Invention of Modern Life* (Berkeley: U of California P, 1995); Elaine Hadley, *Melodramatic Tactics: Theatricalized Dissent in the English Marketplace, 1800–1885* (Stanford, CA: Stanford UP, 1995); Michael Hays and Anastasia Nikolopoulou, eds., *Melodrama: The Cultural Emergence of a Genre* (New York: St. Martin's P, 1996); Root-Bernstein; Judith Wilt, *Ghosts of the Gothic: Austen, Eliot, and Lawrence* (Princeton, NJ: Princeton UP, 1980).

13. Lynn Hunt, *Politics, Culture, and Class in the French Revolution* (Berkeley: U of California P, 1984), 19–51.

14. Patrick Brasart, *Paroles de la Révolution: Les assemblées parlementaires, 1789–1794* (Paris: Minerve, 1988); Paul Friedland, *Political Actors: Representative Bodies and Theatricality in the Age of the French Revolution* (Ithaca, NY: Cornell UP, 2002); Angelica Goodden, *"Actio" and Persuasion: Dramatic Performance in Eighteenth-Century France* (Oxford: Clarendon P, 1986); Hans Ulrich Gumbrecht, *Funktionen parlementarischer Rhetorik in der franzö-*

sischen Revolution (Munich: W. Fink Verlag, 1978); Paul Metzner, *Crescendo of the Virtuoso: Spectacle, Skill, and Self-Promotion in Paris during the Age of Revolution* (Berkeley: U of California P, 1998).

15. Daniel Arasse, *The Guillotine and the Terror,* trans. Christopher Miller (London: Penguin, 1989); Marie-Hélène Huet, *Rehearsing the Revolution: The Staging of Marat's Death, 1793–1797,* trans. Robert Hurley (Berkeley: U of California P, 1982), and Huet, "The Revolutionary Sublime," *Eighteenth-Century Studies* 28, no. 1 (1994): 51–64.

16. Paul Friedland, *Political Actors: Representative Bodies and Theatricality in the Age of the French Revolution* (Ithaca, NY: Cornell UP, 2002), 2–3.

17. Michael McKeon, *Origins of the English Novel, 1600–1740,* 2d ed. (1987; Baltimore: Johns Hopkins UP, 2002), 269.

One • The Theater of the Revolution

1. Many books have been written on the development of Paris during this period. For two recent works that address the issues and context treated here, see David Garrioch, *The Making of Revolutionary Paris* (Berkeley: U of California P, 2002), and Nicholas Papayanis, *Planning Paris before Haussmann* (Baltimore: Johns Hopkins UP, 2004).

2. Jean-Baptiste Poquelin Molière, *Tartuffe* (1669), V.vii. *Oeuvres complète,* ed. M. Eugène Despois (Paris: Hachette, 1878), 4:524. Gallica,1997, Bibliothèque nationale de France, June 2, 2004, http://gallica.bnf.fr/. Robert Darnton, *The Literary Underground of the Old Regime* (Cambridge, MA: Harvard UP, 1982), 61–62.

3. Frederick Brown, *Theater and Revolution: The Culture of the French Stage* (New York: Viking, 1980), 64–65; Michèle Root-Bernstein, *Boulevard Theater and Revolution in Eighteenth-Century Paris* (Ann Arbor, MI: UMI Research Press, 1984), 41–75.

4. As Wolfgang Schivelbusch puts it, in *Disenchanted Night: The Industrialization of Light in the Nineteenth Century,* trans. Angela Davies (Berkeley: U of California P, 1988), the lanterns "were attached to cables strung across the street so that they hung exactly over the middle of the street, like small suns, representing the Sun King, on whose orders they had been put up. This way of mounting the lanterns was remarked upon by foreign visitors and criticised by residents, who pointed to the fact that they obstructed the traffic. At first glance it seems absurd that the same royal power that had freed the streets from the obstructive medieval shop signs should now hand up equally obstructive lanterns. But at second glance the logic becomes apparent: the lanterns showed who lit the streets and who ruled them" (93–97).

5. Schivelbusch, 86–87.

6. Schivelbusch, 98.

7. Walter Hegemann and Elbert Peets, *The American Vitruvius: An Architect's Handbook of Civic Architecture* (1922; Princeton, NJ: Princeton Architectural P, 1988), 48.

8. Hegemann and Peets, 48, 45.

9. Hegemann and Peets, 48.

10. Schivelbusch, 95. Mercier said that "they make, in Milton's words, darkness itself visible" (709, "Réverbères") Louis-Sébastien Mercier, *Tableau de Paris,* ed. Jean-Claude Bonnet (Paris: Mercure de France, 1994), 2:600.

11. By "social performance" I mean public acts by groups or individuals in which norms of status, class, and often gender are interrogated and at times transgressed.

12. Mercier, *Tableau de Paris,* 1:308 (128, "Banqueroutes"). Similarly, Mercier notes (1:398) that even clerks had begun by this time to adopt velvet coats and lace (168, "Parures").

Richard Sennett, *The Fall of Public Man* (New York: W. W. Norton, 1974), 49–70, discusses this shift at length.

13. One of the most noted elements of this change was a significant increase in the volume and speed of vehicular traffic, which was a source of considerable danger and discontent for pedestrians. Mercier is particularly eloquent on this issue, returning repeatedly to the problem of "the infernal profusion of wheeled traffic" (*le luxe infernal des voitures*). Mercier, *Tableau de Paris*, 1:301 (125, "Prévoyance"). See esp. his chapter "Wiski," 2:694–96 (740, "Wiski") for a sense of the outrage such traffic produced. See the second promenade of Jean-Jacques Rousseau, *Les Rêveries du promeneur solitaire* (1782), for an example of its physical threat.

14. Thus Mercier sets out his desire in the *Tableau* to record "this bizarre mass of mad and sensible, but constantly changing, customs" (Préface, 1:13–21). The idea of constant change informs the *Tableau* throughout, to the degree that it may be taken as a raison d'être of the project. For Mercier, such changeability was closely connected to the sensory intensity of urban life at this time: in Paris, "all the senses are challenged every instant: things are broken, filed down, polished, fashioned". *Tableau de Paris*, 1:25 (1, "Coup d'Oeil général").

15. The rise of fashion was at first driven by the return of the court to the city during the Regency and by the expansion of secondhand clothing sales in the great fairgrounds. By midcentury, fashion culture had been strengthened by the foundation of journals devoted to the up-to-date record of contemporary style, and that serial press helped push fashionable dress toward ever more rapid cycles of change and variation. By the 1770s, such rapidity and transience had themselves become thematized, and the styles of this period in particular moved toward extreme exoticism and ephemerality, seeking novelty wherever it could be found and often emblematizing metamorphosis itself. By the 1780s, although fashion had become simpler, Mercier would suggest that it was no longer possible for a writer to keep pace with its accelerating velocity of transformation. In a discussion of the latest fashionable colors (shades of puce), coiffures, and feathers, he complains: "My book is already obsolete . . . how difficult it is to catch a likeness of anything so fleeting!"(*comment peindre ce qui par son extrême mobilité échappe au pinceau!*). *Tableau de Paris*, 1:398 (168, "Parures").

For relevant histories of fashion and the fashion press, see Daniel Roche, *The Culture of Clothing: Dress and Fashion in the Ancien-Régime*, trans. Jean Birrell (New York: Cambridge UP, 1994), esp. chaps. 3, 5, and 16, and Madeleine Delpierre, *Dress in France in the Eighteenth Century*, trans. Caroline Beamish (New Haven, CT: Yale UP, 1997).

16. These final verses make the whole image appear suddenly quite personal, beginning perhaps as an intensively public work but ending upon a note of exceptional privacy. Indeed, the last of them is signed with the cryptic initials "D.R.S.," a monogram presumably scrutable only by the eponymous Elmonde. It is tempting to see in this scene an equally private image of the author himself: that decidedly unfashionable figure of an unattractive man sitting just behind the old woman, peering out at the spectator in an attitude of Pierrot-like contemplation—the only figure in the tableau not engaged in the activity of changing a head.

17. Both Mercier, *Tableau de Paris*, 2:917–19 (812, "Jockeys") and 935–43 (821, "Suite du Palais-Royal").

18. As Mercier notes, the Palais offers an "indecent parade" that continues at all hours and is distinguished by fashions that last just "a day or two" and by the novelty of renting rooms above the galleries not by the hour but for "so many minutes at a time." *Tableau de Paris*, 2:935–43 (821, "Suite du Palais-Royal").

19. A point made by Robert Darnton in his chapter "Anecdotes" in *The Forbidden Best-Sellers of Pre-Revolutionary France* (New York: W. W. Norton, 1996), 137–68. Du Barry, a

courtesan of illegitimate birth, rose through a series of liaisons with court figures to become the mistress of Louis XV during the last years of his reign.

20. Mercier describes the Palais-Royal in considerable detail. See *Tableau de Paris*, 2:930–35 (820, "Palais-Royal") and 935–43 (821, "Suite du Palais-Royal").

21. Nicolas Edme Rétif de la Bretonne, *Les Nuits de Paris ou le Spectateur-nocturne* (Paris: Hachette, 1960).

22. Rétif de la Bretonne, 59.

23. See, e.g., "Les Bals," "Bal payé," and "Le Garçon en fille," Rétif de la Bretonne, 31–36.

24. "On me parut d'abord assez tranquille. Mais, en écoutant la conversation, je compris qu'un groupe d'ouvriers orfèvres et horlogers de la place Dauphine ne formait un cercle, et ne rassemblait adroitement, au centre, de jeunes personnes assez jolies, que pour les rendre victimes de l'imprudente curiosité qui les aveuglait. 'Attention!' me dit M. du Hameauneuf. J'observai donc le maneouvre, qui se continuait. Je jetai les yeux sur un autre groupe: celui-ci travaillait différemment: il encerclait tous les gens qui paraissent avoir de l'argent et des montres: on les poussait par un petit mouvement ondulatoire, dont ils s'apercevaient à peine; et celui qui les faisait avancer plus brusquement était celui qui se plaignait davantage de la presses. Tout ce monde resta honnête jusqu'aux dernières fusées.

"'Attention! répéta Du Hameauneuf, sans moi, vous étiez entraîné ; mais nous nous sommes soutenus à nous deux.' J'observai que les ondulations redoublaient. Je ne regardais nullement les fusées, et je m'aperçus que les filous en faisaient de même: il me parut qu'ils glissaient la main dans les poches ou les goussets, lorsque la fusée s'élevait, et qu'ils retiraient l'hameçon pendant les cris et les trémoussements qu'excitait chaque baguette tombante. Mais bientôt je quittai cette scène, pour l'autre.

"Les compagnons orfèvres agissaient de leur côté. Les imprudentes renfermées dans les différents cercles qu'ils formaient, me parurent enlevées les unes à deux pieds de terre, les autres couchées horizontalement sur les bras; quelques-unes étaient au milieu d'un double cercle; toutes étaient traitées de la manière la plus indigne, et quelquefois la plus cruelle. Leurs cris n'étaient pas entendus, parce que les polissons choisissaient les instants de la chute des baguettes, et que dans les autres moments, ils poussaient eux-mêmes des cris, qui couvraient ceux de leurs victimes. Du Hameauneuf perçait les différents cercles comme une tarière, et m'y faisaient pénétrer: 'Ne dites pas un mot! m'avait t-il recommandé; nous serions étouffés.' Nous vîmes des choses horribles: entre autres, au milieu d'un triple cercle, une jeune fille avec sa mère, qu'on rendait témoin et participante des infamies faites à sa fille. Cette infortunée se trouva mal . . . Le reste du récit ne peut se faire. Le feu finit heureusement, et ce fut pour la dernière fois. Le prévôt des marchands fut instruit de ce que nous avions vu; et cette cause, réunie à une autre, fit cesser un dangereux enfantillage. Les filous et les polissons s'écoulèrent comme l'eau, et les insultées se trouvèrent entourées de gens tout différents, qui n'imaginaient autre chose, sinon qu'elles avaient été trop pressées." Rétif de la Bretonne, 67–69.

25. Nicolas-Edme Restif de la Bretonne, *Les Nuits de Paris; or, The Nocturnal Spectator*, trans. Linda Asher and Ellen Furtig (New York: Random House, 1964), 360 n 1.

26. Mercier, *Tableau de Paris*, 1:1273 (460, "Émeutes").

27. "En allant au Français, j'avais aperçu à l'un des trottoirs du pont Henri une sorte d'écolier qui se baissait jusqu'à terre, dès qu'une dame approchait. Je ne savais quel était son but. Enfin, j'entendis une jeune personne s'écrier; mais j'imaginai que c'était une polissonnerie, et je ne m'informai pas.

"Le soir, en nous rendant chez Mme de M***, je revis la jeune personne dans une boutique de chapelier . . . Je lui demandai la cause du cri qu'elle avait fait sur le pont Neuf. 'Un polisson m'a coupé, avec un canif, des souliers tout neufs!' . . . Comme c'est la seconde fois depuis un an, je m'en suis aperçue, en me sentant toucher, je me suis écriée, et il s'est enfui.-

C'est un nouveau genre de polissonnerie, dit une jolie voisine; ils coupent avec un canif, et j'ai manqué d'en être estropiée, il y a six mois! Il faut averter de cette manie singulière." Rétif de la Bretonne, 181–82.

28. Although Rétif's episode is not dated, it occurs at the very end of *Les Nuits*, which suggests that it occurred at some point late in 1788.

29. Schivelbusch provides a more substantial analysis of this incident, in particular, at 81ff.

30. Jeremy Popkin, *Revolutionary News: The Press in France, 1789–1799* (Durham, NC: Duke UP, 1990), 32–33. Censorship and all limitations on the right to publish were suspended on August 26.

31. Popkin, 34.

32. Popkin, 32.

33. See Elizabeth Eisenstein's discussion of "publiciste" in "The Tribune of the People: A New Species of Demagogue," in *The Press in the French Revolution*, ed. Harvey Chisick, Studies on Voltaire and the Eighteenth Century 287 (Oxford: Voltaire Foundation, 1991), 150.

34. See, e.g., Madelyn Gutwirth, *The Twilight of the Goddesses: Women and Representation in the French Revolutionary Era* (New Brunswick, NJ: Rutgers UP, 1992), 244.

35. The king's place in Revolutionary events was strongly defined by moments of odd public scrutiny—certainly far more than by any particular action on his part. During the October Days, he famously appeared on the palace balcony with the queen; during the royal family's attempted flight, it was recognition of the king's profile in the carriage window (by the son of a postal clerk) that brought the attempt to a halt at Varennes; and months later, during the August 10, 1792, invasion of the Tuileries, Louis was trapped for several hours in the embrasure of a palace window. During the October Days, on the return from Varennes, and eventually through the streets of Paris in January of 1793, Louis was the spectacular focal point of a procession—and, of course, during his execution he was most famously glimpsed through the fatal eye of the *lunette républicaine*, as the guillotine was known.

36. Bailly, proclamation of August 13, 1789, in Popkin, 3.

37. Priscilla Parkhurst Ferguson, *Paris as Revolution: Writing the Nineteenth-Century City* (Berkeley: U of California P, 1994), 2.

Two • The Drama of the Revolution

1. The Comédie Française possessed exclusive rights to stage all plays by authors no longer living and to stage tragedy and comedy; the Opéra maintained exclusive privileges over dance and song; and the Théâtre des Italiens, rights to Italian theater and comic opera.

2. Michèle Root-Bernstein, *Boulevard Theater and Revolution in Eighteenth-Century Paris* (Ann Arbor, MI: UMI Research Press, 1984), 17–75, offers the definitive account.

3. For an excellent treatment of pantomime in eighteenth-century Paris, see Angelica Goodden, *"Actio" and Persuasion: Dramatic Performance in Eighteenth-Century France* (Oxford: Clarendon P, 1986), 94–111.

4. F. W. J. Hemmings, *Theatre and State in France,1760–1905* (Cambridge: Cambridge UP, 1994), 55.

5. Hemmings, 55–57; Marvin Carlson, *The Theatre of the French Revolution* (Ithaca, NY: Cornell UP, 1966), 1–11.

6. Carlson, 15–16; Hemmings, 55–56.

7. Kennedy et al. (1–3) offers a concise review of this critical assumption. See also Root-Bernstein, 235–41; Graeme Rodmell, *French Drama of the Revolutionary Years* (London: Routledge, 1990), 1–4; André Tessier, *Les Spectacles à Paris pendant la Révolution* (Geneva: Librairie Droz, 1992), 25–49.

8. Marie-Hélène Huet, "Performing Arts and the Terror," *Representing the French Revolution: Literature, Historiography, and Art*, ed. James A. W. Heffernan (Hanover, NH: UP of New England, 1992), 137.

9. My discussion of the formation of the Revolution's political theatre is indebted to Friedland throughout. Paul Friedland, *Political Actors: Representative Bodies and Theatricality in the Age of the French Revolution* (Ithaca, NY: Cornell UP, 2002), 168.

10. Friedland, 168–80; Goodden, "The Dramatising of Politics: Theatricality and the Revolutionary Assemblies," *Forum for Modern Language Studies* 20, no. 3 (1984): 193–212.

11. Hans Ulrich Gumbrecht, *Funktionen parlementarischer Rhetorik in der französischen Revolution* (Munich: W. Fink Verlag, 1978), 193.

12. "Up until the middle of the 18th century," Friedland observes, "the convention that metamorphosis lay at the root of theatrical representation remained largely unchallenged" (20). In 1750, however, with the publication of François Riccoboni's *L'Art du théâtre*, the theory of metamorphosis was challenged—and by the 1770s superseded—by the notion that performance depended rather on *vraisemblance*, the presentation of "passions that seemed real" and that were the product rather of "the bifurcation of the actor's body into believable exteriors and false interiors" (21).

It is probably more accurate to think of this shift as taking place gradually than as a break or rupture. Friedland (22) notes that Diderot's definition of acting in *Paradoxe sur le comédien* (drafts of which, he points out, were "circulated as early as 1769") was "identical to Riccoboni's": The actor's "entire talent consists not in feeling, as you [the spectators] suppose, but in rendering the outward signs of feeling so scrupulously that you [the spectator] mistake them [for real] (que vous vous y trompiez)."

However, as Friedland points out, Diderot understood this goal to be attainable *either* by imitation or, still, by metamorphosis, and he notes as well that "Rousseau's *Letter to d'Alembert on the Theater* is perhaps best understood as a work that stands at the crossroads between these two genres," condemning actors "*both* for denaturing their bodies and for their duplicity and the dangers they presented to society as a whole" (22). A better sense of the complexity of this shift is offered by Joseph Roach, *The Player's Passion: Studies in the Science of Acting* (London: Associated UP, 1985).

13. Friedland, 22.

14. Friedland, 22.

15. Friedland, 175.

16. "Each innovation in the movement to create a more vraisemblable theater," Friedland observes, "seemingly spawned a new idea, as if once a blatantly unrealistic aspect of the stage was removed, other vestiges of the old theater became glaringly apparent" (27).

17. As Tessier notes, similar strategies will continue to inform the theatre and popular spectacle during the Revolutionary period (27, 45–49). Michael McKeon, in *Origins of the English Novel, 1600–1740*, 2d ed. (1987; Baltimore: Johns Hopkins UP, 2002), 21, outlines a similar process of critique in the development of the English novel, where he describes the process as a subjection of "reigning representational codes" to the "empirical epistemology" of "progressive ideology."

18. Friedland suggests that "the fourth wall . . . made possible something greater than the sum of individual illusions produced by each actor's performance. A stage devoid of spectators

suddenly made possible the creation of something that could never have existed before; a new world, purged of mundane reality, and made up entirely of realistic fictions; a universe physically and conceptually set apart from the world inhabited by spectators; a world existing in its own time and place, that took no notice of anyone or anything beyond its borders, and that to the spectators seemed somehow more interesting, more believable, more intoxicating than their own fragmented reality" (27).

19. Scott Bryson, *The Chastised Stage: Bourgeois Drama and the Exercise of Power*, Stanford French and Italian Studies (Saratoga, CA: ANMA Libri, 1991), 4–5, 73–78, 113.

20. Michael Fried, *Absorption and Theatricality: Painting and Beholder in the Age of Diderot* (Chicago: U of Chicago P, 1980), 78, 99.

21. Goodden, *"Actio" and Persuasion*, 398; Fried, 77; Peter Szondi, *"Tableau* and *Coup de théâtre:* On the Social Psychology of Diderot's Bourgeois Tragedy," trans. Harvey Mendelsohn, *New Literary History* 11 (Winter 1980): 323–43. Szondi, it should be noted, conflates courtly aristocracy and autocratic monarchy; Bryson, 68–71 and esp. 97–99 (on the univocality of *tableau*).

22. For Sieyès, the aristocracy is "parasitic precisely in the sense that it no longer fulfills any useful function in the body of the nation." Ferenc Fehér, *The Frozen Revolution: An Essay on Jacobinism*, Studies in Modern Capitalism (Cambridge: Cambridge UP; Paris: Editions de la Maison des Sciences de l'Homme, 1987), 18.

23. Jean Starobinski, *1789: The Emblems of Reason*. trans. Barbara Bray (1973; Cambridge, MA: MIT P, 1988), 17–19. Starobinski provides an excellent, if brief, discussion of the context and the scandalized reaction to the procession.

24. The phrase is taken from the opening of Sieyès, *Qu'est-ce que le Tiers Etat?* (Jan. 1789). "1. What is the Third Estate? Everything. 2. What has it been thus far in the political order? Nothing. 3. What does it demand? To become something."

See Szondi for the most influential account of the political and social implications of Diderot's bourgeois drama. See also Goodden, "The Dramatising of Politics," for a wider survey of the context in which this Diderotian political theater had become so influential. On the fluidity and anonymity of the urban bourgeoisie in *ancien-régime* Paris (an important consideration in understanding the connection between Diderot's aesthetics and Sieyès's rhetoric of constitution), see Richard Sennett, *The Fall of Public Man* (New York: W. W. Norton, 1974), 56–57.

25. Rousseau remarks, "I do not precisely accuse him of being a deceiver, but of cultivating by profession the talent of deceiving men and becoming adept in habits which can be innocent only in the theatre and can serve elsewhere only for doing harm" (Aussi ne l'accusé-je pas d'être précisément un trompeur, mais de cultiver pour tout métier le talent de tromper les homes, et de s'exercer à des habitudes qui, ne pouvant être innocentes qu'au Théâtre, ne servent par-tout ailleurs qu'à mal faire). Lest there be any objection that such habits might be redeemed by their innocence in the theater, Rousseau goes further, asserting that "an actor on stage, displaying other sentiments than his own, saying only what he is made to say, often representing a chimerical being, annihilates himself, as it were, and is lost in his hero. And, in this forgetting of the man, if something remains of him, it is used as the plaything of the spectators" (un Comédien sure la Scène, étalant d'autres sentimens que les siens, ne disant que ce qu'on lui fait dire, représentant souvent un être chimérique, s'anéantit, pour ainsi dire, s'annule avec son héros; et, dans cet oubli de l'homme, s'il en reste quelque chose, c'est pour être le jouet des Spectateurs)." Jean-Jacques Rousseau, *Lettre à M. D'Alembert sur les Spectacles* (Lille: Librairie Giard, 1948), 107, 108. The translation is Jean-Jacques Rousseau, *Politics and the Arts: Letter to M. d'Alembert on the Theatre*, trans. Allan Bloom (1960; Ithaca, NY: Cornell UP, 1991), 80–81.

26. Friedland addresses this issue throughout his book, arguing that this basic theatrical problem crucially informed the development of Revolutionary ideas of political representation.

27. Rousseau, 109.

28. "Donnez les spectateurs en spectacle; rendez-les acteurs eux-mêmes; faites que chacun se voie et s'aime dans les autres, afin que tous en soient mieux unis." Rousseau, 168–69; trans. Bloom, 126.

29. See Mona Ozouf, *Festivals and the French Revolution,* trans. Alan Sheridan (Cambridge, MA: Harvard UP, 1988), 5–6, 197–216.

30. Thomas Crow notes the "presumed menace of the King's troops" outside, while Kennedy notes the lightning bolt's implied judgment upon the religious intolerance of the monarchy. Crow offers a brief, related discussion of the manner in which these problems relate to pictorial (rather than theatrical) aesthetics. Thomas Crow, *Painters and Public Life in Eighteenth-Century Paris* (New Haven, CT: Yale UP, 1985), 255–58; Emmet Kennedy, *A Cultural History of the French Revolution* (New Haven, CT: Yale UP, 1989), 251.

31. Crow, 254.

32. Crow, 258.

33. McKeon, 14.

34. Friedland, 12–13.

35. Claudio Guillén, *The Challenge of Comparative Literature,* trans. Cola Franzen (Cambridge, MA: Harvard UP, 1993), 109.

36. Guillén, 109; René Wellek and Austin Warren, *Theory of Literature* (1942; New York: Harcourt, Brace & World, 1956), 229.

37. Guillén, 112; Wellek and Warren, 261.

38. Wellek and Warren, 261.

39. Guillén, 113.

40. Reinhardt Koselleck, *Futures Past: On the Semantics of Historical Time,* trans. Keith Tribe (Cambridge: MIT P, 1985), 17.

41. Koselleck, 17.

42. Koselleck, 97.

43. Koselleck, 22.

44. Koselleck, 17.

45. Koselleck, 22.

46. Koselleck 35; Diderot, s.v. "Encyclopédie," in *Encyclopédie* (1781), 12:340.

47. "De la trempe de notre esprit, du tour de notre imagination, de la manière enfin don't nous envisagions le trône et la cour, et les révolutions vives et passagères qui en émanoient . . . le tableau de nos moeurs actuelles." Mercier, *Du Théâtre,* 104.

48. Sarah Maza, *Private Lives and Public Affairs: The Causes Célèbres of Pre-Revolutionary France* (Berkeley: U of California P, 1993); and Bryson.

49. "J'ai essayé de donner dans le Fils naturel l'idée d'un drame qui fût entre la comédie et la tragédie. Le Père de famille que je promis alors, et que des distractions continuelles ont retardé, est entre le genre sérieux du Fils naturel, et la comédie. Et si jamais j'en ai le loisir et le courage, je ne déspère pas de composer un drame qui se place entre le genre sérieux et la tragédie. Qu'on reconnaisse à ces ouvrages quelque mérite, ou qu'on ne leur en accorde aucun, ils n'en démontreront pas moins que l'intervalle que j'apercevais entre les deux genres établis, n'était pas chimérique." Denis Diderot, "Discours sur la poésie dramatique," *Oeuvres complètes* (Paris: Le Club français du livre, 1969), 3:412–13.

50. Evaluations of the play's radical rhetoric usually point out, and rightly, that the political sentiments voiced in the play are not exceptional, that Beaumarchais, while certainly a lib-

eral, did not share the Revolution's political vision. Even the notion that the Revolution *began* with *Le Mariage de Figaro*, once understood as a serious statement, has come to be seen as a sort of metaphor, an expression of the play's articulation of a certain spirit of rebelliousness rather than any sort of causal role. Certainly, the phenomenal success of the play continues to be given serious consideration, but even that is now understood more as an epiphenomenon of pre-Revolutionary unrest than as a catalyst of Revolutionary action. Critical literature on *Le Mariage* is extensive: of particular usefulness in relation to the brief reading I offer here are the essays contained in Philip Robinson, ed., *Beaumarchais: Homme de lettres, homme de société*, ed. Philip Robinson (Oxford: Peter Lang, 2000), esp. Gérard Kahn's "Figaro et la Bastille" (91–101).

51. The Bastille was not torn down before the play's premiere, of course, but the interest of Louis's remark has always been its ironic acumen: the link between events is there, but the order is reversed, and Louis's own weakness lies behind both. Danton's observation, usually reported as a flat declaration, becomes more interesting in its original context. Uttered at the premiere of *Charles IX* (Nov. 1789), the tragedy by Chenier that was the first great theatrical controversy of the Revolution, it was not an assertion but an assumption for a hypothesis: "If *Figaro* killed the nobility, *Charles IX* will kill the monarchy" (Si *Figaro* a tué la noblesse, *Charles IX* tuera la royauté). *Charles IX* did nothing of the sort, but Danton's proposition relies implicitly on tacit agreement with his assessment of Beaumarchais's play.

52. See John Dunkley, *Beaumarchais: The Barber of Seville* (London: Grant & Cutler, 1991) for an interesting related discussion of pace in that play.

53. *Dynamicization* refers to the practice of modifying the forms of the narration as the narrative advances. The term is from Franz Stanzel, *A Theory of Narrative*, trans. Charlotte Goedsche (Cambridge: Cambridge UP, 1984), 63–66, and is taken up in more general terms by Guillen, 149, 164–67.

54. Christie McDonald, however, addresses precisely this issue in "The Anxiety of Change: Reconfiguring Family Relations in Beaumarchais' Trilogy," *Modern Language Quarterly* 55, no. 1 (1994): 47–78.

55. "Figaro, jouant la frayeur excessive [acting excessively frightened] . . . 'C'est mon maître!'" (V.x); "qui pourrait m'en exempter, Monseigneur?" (V.xii) Pierre-Augustin Caron de Beaumarchais, *Théâtre [Document électronique]* (1985; Paris: Bibliopolis, 1998–99) Gallica, 1999, Bibliothèque nationale de France, September 15, 2005, http://gallica.bnf.fr/.

56. "On se débat, c'est vous, c'est lui, c'est moi, c'est toi, non, ce n'est pas nous; eh! mais qui donc?" Beaumarchais, *Théâtre*.

57. "Maître ici, valet là, selon qu'il plaît à la fortune." Beaumarchais, *Théâtre*.

58. "Comment cela m'est-il arrivé?" Beaumarchais, *Théâtre*.

59. "Pourquoi ces choses et non pas d'autres?" Beaumarchais, *Théâtre*.

60. "O bizarre suite d'événements!" Beaumarchais, *Théâtre*.

61. Koselleck, 44–45, 257.

62. François Furet, *Interpreting the French Revolution*, trans. Elborg Foster (Cambridge: Cambridge UP, 1981), 47.

63. Hunt Lynn Hunt, *Politics, Culture, and Class in the French Revolution* (Berkeley: U of California P, 1984), 27.

64. Ozouf, *Festivals*, 168.

65. Jeremy Popkin, *Revolutionary News: The Press in France, 1789–1799* (Durham, NC: Duke UP, 1990), 136.

66. Hunt, *Politics, Culture, and Class*, 44.

67. Goodden, "The Dramatising of Politics," 201.

68. Goodden, *"Actio" and Persuasion*, 19.

69. Goodden, *"Actio" and Persuasion*, 20.

70. Louis-Abel Beffroy de Reigny, *Nicodème dans la lune ou la Révolution pacifique, folie en prose et en 3 actes, mêlée d'ariettes et de vaudevilles* (Paris: Froullé, 1791). As Emmet Kennedy pointed out, our impressions of Revolutionary culture, both political and theatrical, tend to privilege the Revolution's most radical voices and images, often at the expense of recognizing broader if more conservative cultural trends. See Emmet Kennedy, "History of the Problem and the Method of Solving It," in Emmett Kennedy et al., *Theatre, Opera, and Audiences in Revolutionary Paris: Analysis and Repertory*, Contributions in Drama and Theatre Studies 62 (Westport, CT: Greenwood, 1996), 1–8.

71. Marie-Laurence Netter, "The Most Performed Genres and Their Evolution," in Kennedy et al., 59–64.

72. Kennedy et al., 32–33.

73. Hunt, *Politics, Culture, and Class*, 34–35.

74. "The movement of comedy, according to Frye, is usually a movement from one society to another . . . In the end, a new society crystallizes around the hero, and its appearance is 'frequently signalized by some kind of party or festive ritual.' Rather than being repudiated altogether, the 'blocking characters,' usually including the arbitrary and conventional father, are most often reconciled with the son or sons." Lynn Hunt, *The Family Romance of the French Revolution* (Berkeley: U California P, 1992), 44.

75. Gumbrecht, 193.

76. Patrice Higonnet provides a valuable analysis of the evolution of this conceptual and political designation in her "'Aristocrate,' 'Aristocratie': Language and Politics in the French Revolution," in *The French Revolution: Two Hundred Years of Rethinking*, A Special Issue of *The Eighteenth Century: Theory and Interpretation*, ed. Sandy Petrey (Lubbock: Texas Tech UP, 1989), 47–65.

77. For a detailed analysis of the Festival of Federation, see Ozouf, *Festivals*, 33–60.

78. Hunt, *Family Romance*, 44.

79. This tension is pointed out by Kennedy, *Cultural History*, 244.

80. Gumbrecht, 97.

81. Qtd. in Ferenc Féher, *The Frozen Revolution: An Essay on Jacobinism*, Studies in Modern Capitalism (Cambridge: Cambridge UP; Paris: Editions de la Maison des Sciences de l'Homme, 1987), 19.

82. For a concise account of the episode, see Mona Ozouf, s.v. "Varennes," in *Critical Dictionary of the French Revolution*, ed. François Furet and Mona Ozouf, trans. Arthur Goldhammer (Cambridge, MA: Belknap P of Harvard UP, 1989), 155–64.

83. Michel Vovelle, *Ideologies and Mentalities*, trans. Eamon O'Flaherty (Chicago: U Chicago P, 1990), 210.

84. Nonetheless, the Assembly's first reaction, and one that would irreparably damage the credibility of the moderates, was to reassert this failed dramatic rhetoric—to restitch the torn veil by asserting, as the government's official view, an entirely imagined comedy, announcing to a plainly unconvinced populace that the king had been rescued at Varennes from an attempted aristocratic abduction. (Georges Lefebvre, *The French Revolution*, vol. 1, trans. Elizabeth Moss Evanson [New York: Columbia UP, 1962], 208–9). Robespierre, giving voice not only to the political doubts of the ascendant left but also to the critical doubts of the Revolution's political audience, wondered aloud "whether nations today are prepared to believe that people abduct kings as they abduct women." Qtd. in Ozouf, s.v. "Varennes," in Furet and Ozouf, 158.

85. Friedland (274–81) offers a detailed look at this turn of opinion in attitudes toward legitimate political theatricality.

86. Hunt, *Politics, Culture, and Class,* 35.

87. On Marat's troubles with the police, see Popkin, 138.

88. Marat, "The Objectives of the Revolution Completely Unattained by the People," *L'Ami du Peuple,* no. 667 (July 7, 1792), in Paul Beik, ed., *The French Revolution* (New York: Harper & Row, 1970), 217.

89. Beik, 217.

90. Beik, 217.

91. The arrest of the Girondins is significant not least in its use of a legal rather than a popular instrument of force, for that instrument is symptomatic of the changes that had taken place in the rhetoric and performance of politics in the Convention.

92. Marc Blanchard, *St. Just et Cie: La Révolution et les mots* (Paris: Librairie A. G Nizet, 1980), 49–50.

93. Blanchard; Gumbrecht, *Funktionen parlementarischer Rhetoric;* and Goodden, "Theatricality and the Revolutionary Assembly."

94. Gumbrecht, 192.

95. According to Gumbrecht, by the "late summer and fall of 1793, all those newspapers that did not serve to propagate and legitimize Robespierre's politics had been forbidden" (196).

96. Couthon, decree of August 2, 1793, qtd. in Marie-Hélène Huet, "Performing Arts: Theatricality and the Terror," in *Representing the French Revolution: Literature, Historiography, and Art,* ed. James A. Heffernan (Hanover, NH: UP of New England, 1992) 92. See also Kennedy et al., 51–58.

97. "A l'avantage de former, dans un état républicain exposé aux plus grands revers, une masse d'hommes préparés à tout et résolus à tout, se joignoit celui de leur faire voir que tous les hommes étoient égaux sous l'empire de la destinée . . . C'est ce qu'il étoit important d'inculquer à des peuples libres." Marmontel, "Tragédie."

98. "Quel est le principe fondamental du gouvernement démocratique ou populaire, c'est-à-dire, le ressort essentiel qui le soutient et qui le fait mouvoir? C'est la vertu; je parle de la vertu publique qui opéra tant de prodiges dans la Grèce et dans Rome." Maximilien Robespierre, "Rapport sur les principes de morale politique qui doivent guider la Convention nationale dans l'administration intérieure de la République," *Oeuvres de Maximilien Robespierre,* vol. 10, *Discours (5ᵉ Partie),* ed. Marc Bouloiseau and Albert Soboul (Paris: Presses universitaires de France, 1967), 353. Throughout the rest of the address, Marx reminds us, Robespierre "continually recalls the ancient community and quotes its heroes as well as its corrupters—Lycurgus, Demosthenes, Miltiades, Aristides, Brutus, and Catalina, Caesar, Clodius and Piso." Marx, *The Holy Family,* in *Marx and the French Revolution,* ed. François Furet, trans. Deborah Kan Furet (Chicago: U Chicago P, 1988), 137. Marx neglects to mention Robespierre's references to Tacitus, Augustus, Tiberius, Vespasian, and Philip.

99. Marx, *The Holy Family,* 138.

100. Blanchard 51 (my translation).

101. "Quand le gouvernement seul en est privé, il reste une resource dans celle du peuple; mais, quand le peuple lui-même est corrumpu, la liberté est déjà perdue . . . Qu'importe que Brutus ait tué le tyran? La tyrannie vit encore dans les cœurs, et Rome n'existe plus que dans Brutus." Robespierre, *Oeuvres de Maximilien Robespierre,* 10:355. This translation is Beik's (282).

102. The newly elected National Convention met for the first time on September 21, the day after the French victory at Valmy; its first act was to abolish the monarchy. The voting

in the trial of Louis occurred between January 14 and 17, and he was executed on January 21, 1794.

103. The corollary to this point is that he challenges his audience to attest to the reality of his vision by realizing it.

104. Marc Bouloiseau, *The Jacobin Republic, 1792–1794,* trans. Jonathan Mandelbaum, The French Revolution 2 (Paris: Maison des Sciences de l'Homme; London: Cambridge UP, 1983), 191–200.

105. "C'est dans la prosperité que les peuples, ainsi que les particuliers, dovient, pour ainsi dire, se recueillir pour écouter, dans la silence des passions, la voix de la sagesse." Robespierre, "Sur les rapports des idées religieuses et morale avec les principes républicains, et sure les fêtes nationales." *Oeuvres de Maximilien Robespierre,* 10:443.

106. "Le monde moral, beaucoup plus encore que le monde physique, semble plein de contrastes et d'énigmes. La nature nous dit que l'homme est né pour la liberté, et l'expérience des siècles nous montre l'homme esclave . . . Le genre-humain respecte Caton, et se courbe sous le joug de César. La postérité honore la vertu de Brutus, mais elle ne la permet que dans l'histoire ancienne. Les siècles et la terre sont le partage du crime et de la tyrannie; la liberté et la vertu se sont à peine reposées un instant sur quelques points du globe. Sparte brille comme un éclair dans des ténèbres immenses . . . Ne dis pas cependant, ô Brutus, que la vertu est un phantôme." Robespierre, "Sur les rapports des idées religieuses," 444.

107. "O peuple sublime! Reçois le sacrifice de tout mon être; heureux celui qui est né au milieu de toi! plus heureux celui qui peut mourir pour ton bonheur!" Robespierre, "Sur les rapports des idées religieuses," 445.

108. "Si le ressort du gouvernement populaire dans la paix est la vertu, le ressort du gouvernement populaire en révolution est à la fois la vertu et la terreur: la vertu, sans laquelle la terreur est funeste; la terreur, sans laquelle la vertu est impuissante. La terreur n'est autre chose que la justice prompte, sévère, inflexible; elle est donc une émanation de la vertu." Robespierre, "Rapport sur les principes de morale politique qui doivent guider la Convention nationale dans l'administration intérieure de la République." *Oeuvres de Maximilien Robespierre,* 10:357.

109. Furet, *Interpreting the French Revolution,* 58.

110. Gumbrecht, 208.

111. Peter Brooks, *The Melodramatic Imagination: Balzac, Henry James, Melodrama, and the Mode of Excess* (New York: Columbia UP, 1985), 14; Gumbrecht, 211.

112. "Le peuple tout entier venait dans les rues et sur les places publiques de jouer le plus grand drame de l'histoire. Tout le monde avait été acteur dans cette pièce sanglante, tout le monde avait été ou soldat, ou révolutionnaire, ou proscrit. A ces spectateurs solennels qui sentaient la poudre et la sang, il fallait des émotions analogues à celles dont le retour de l'ordre les avait sevrés . . . Il fallait leur rappeler dans un thème toujours nouveau de contexture, toujours uniforme de résultats, cette grande leçon dans laquelle se résument toutes les philosophies, appuyées sur toutes les religions: que mêmes ici-bas, la vertu n'est jamais sans récompense, le crime n'est jamais sans châtiment. Et qu'on n'aille pas s'y tromper! Ce n'était pas peu de chose que le mélodrame! C'était la moralité de la révolution." Charles Nodier, introduction to Charles Guilbert de Pixerécourt, *Théâtre Choisi* (Geneva: Slatkin Reprints, 1971), vii–viii.

113. Furet, *Interpreting the French Revolution,* 61.

114. In addition to Brooks's treatment of this question (42–55), see Bruce McConachie's "Pixerécourt's Early Melodramas and the Political Inducements of Neoplatonism," *Melodrama,* ed. James Redmond (Cambridge: Cambridge UP, 1992), 87–103.

115. Frederick Brown, *Theater and Revolution: The Culture of the French Stage* (New York: Viking, 1980), 95.

116. Brown, 95.

117. Ozouf, *Festivals*, 11–12.

118. Friedland notes at the end of the introduction to *Political Actors* that he is "convinced that the revolutions in theatre and politics were themselves manifestations of an underlying revolution in the very categories of perception, in the way that individuals made sense of the world around them" (13). In a sense it is this "underlying revolution" that I am trying to describe.

119. Furet, *Interpreting the French Revolution*, 25, 27. This shift away from a belief in the efficacy of human action in history is evident in the drama as well. As Gumbrecht notes, it "is striking" that the authors of serious drama after Thermidor, while pursuing the goal of inculcating strong feeling in the audience, uniformly avoided any suggestion as to the "intended effect of such feelings on the action of the recipients as had routinely been the case in the Enlightenment" (211). Similarly, Anthony Kubiak notes a shift toward a "more domestic, 'sentimental' drama consonant with the seeming contractions of power from the social sphere and into the family" and a concurrent "'interiorization' of theatrical forms." Anthony Kubiak, *Stages of Terror: Terrorism, Ideology, and Coercion as Theatre History* (Bloomington: Indiana UP, 1991). Both observations fit broadly with Georg Lukács's sense of the drama of this period as evincing a reduction of agency and interiorization of dramatic conflict. Georg Lukács, "The Sociology of Modern Drama," trans. Lee Baxandall, *Tulane Drama Review* 9 (Summer 1965): 149–53.

Three • The Revolution and British Theatrical Politics

1. Miles Ogborn, *Spaces of Modernity: London's Geographies, 1680–1780* (New York: Guilford P, 1998), 34–35.

2. Richard Sennett, *The Fall of Public Man* (New York: W. W. Norton, 1974), 52–56.

3. Wolfgang Schivelbusch, *Disenchanted Night: The Industrialization of Light in the Nineteenth Century*, trans. Angela Davies (Berkeley: U of California P, 1988), 88–89.

4. Marc Baer, *Theatre and Disorder in Late Georgian London* (Oxford: Clarendon P, 1992), 12–13.

5. Sennett (78) notes aptly both the architectural shifts and the changes in the transaction between actors and audience at this time.

6. L. W. Conolly, *The Censorship of English Drama 1737–1824* (San Marino, CA: Huntington Library, 1976), 10; V. J. Liesenfeld, *The Licensing Act of 1737* (Madison: U of Wisconsin P, 1984); Jeremy Black, *The English Press in the Eighteenth Century* (London: Croom Helm, 1987), 165.

7. Jane Moody, *Illegitimate Theatre in London, 1770–1840* (Cambridge: Cambridge UP, 2000), 10–11.

8. Edmund Burke, *Reflections on the Revolution in France*, ed. J. G. A. Pocock (Indianapolis. IN: Hackett, 1987), 9.

9. This strategy has been remarked upon by many scholars, and it serves as the basic topic of inquiry in the most recent substantial contribution to scholarship on the *Reflections*, Elizabeth Samet's "Spectacular History and the Politics of Theater: Sympathetic Arts in the Shadow of the Bastille," *PMLA* 118, no. 5 (2003): 1305–19.

10. Burke, 9.

11. Burke, 60.

12. Burke, 65–66.

13. Burke, 66.

14. Burke, 66.

15. Philip Francis to Burke, in Burke, *Correspondence*, 10 vols. (Cambridge: Cambridge UP, 1958–78), 6:86–87. Qtd. in Steven Blakemore, "Revolution in Representation: Burke's *Reflections on the Revolution in France*," *Eighteenth-Century Life* 15 (Nov. 1991): 8, and in Linda M.G. Zerilli, "Text/Woman as Spectacle: Edmund Burke's 'French Revolution,'" *Eighteenth Century* 33, no. 1 (1992): 47.

16. Thomas Paine, *Rights of Man, Common Sense, and Other Political Writings* (Oxford: Oxford UP, 1995), 110.

17. For notable recent commentary, in addition to Samet, see Blakemore; Zerilli; Tim Gray and Paul Hindson, "Edmund Burke and the French Revolution as Drama," *History of European Ideas* 14, no. 2 (1992): 203–11, of which Blakemore is the most perceptive; among contemporary critics, see Paine and Mary Wollstonecraft, *Vindication of the Rights of Men* (London, 1791), both discussed below.

18. Julie Carlson, "Command Performances: Burke, Coleridge, and Schiller's Dramatic Reflections on the Revolution in France," *Wordsworth Circle* 23, no. 2 (1992): 117.

19. Paine, 102.

20. Not until Blakemore (10) and Samet (1315) does one find clear critical recognition of the manner in which Paine's own tendency to appeal to dramatic effect contradicts this stance.

21. Elaine Hadley, *Melodramatic Tactics: Theatricalized Dissent in the English Marketplace, 1800–1885* (Stanford, CA: Stanford UP, 1995), 20: "Burke, in many respects the quintessential eighteenth-century aristocrat, continues to use theatrical metaphor in his description of the French Revolution because, for him, history is a social stage and the people shaping it are public actors. Paine, however, interprets Burke's rhetorical theatricality as intentional evasion. Holding Burke to Paine's own rationalist standard, a revisionist denigration of the theatrical exchange that considers a costume a disguise and scenic prose a facade, Paine accuses Burke of seeking refuge in theatricality from some alternative 'reality' of sympathetic exchange." Hadley argues that in so doing Paine's critique "reflects a larger cultural shift in the dominant, populist forms of cultural transmission from oral, public communication to written, private dissemination."

22. See, e.g., Baer; Betsy Bolton, *Women, Nationalism, and the Romantic Stage: Theatre and Politics in Britain, 1780–1800* (Cambridge: Cambridge UP, 2001); Russell Gillian, *The Theatres of War: Performance, Politics, and Society, 1793–1815* (Oxford: Clarendon P, 1995); Moody; and George Taylor, *The French Revolution and the London Stage, 1789–1805* (Cambridge: Cambridge UP, 2000).

23. *Le Moniteur* is the most notable example, having attempted at the outset of its publication to pursue a format modeled explicitly upon that of the British daily press. See Jeremy Popkin, *Revolutionary News: The Press in France, 1789–1799* (Durham, NC: Duke UP, 1990), 109.

24. On coffeehouses and the commercial press, see Sennett, 80–81; on the origins of particular London papers of this period, see Lucyle Werkmeister, *A Newspaper History of England, 1792–93* (Lincoln: U of Nebraska P, 1967), 19–42; and esp. Black, 1–24.

25. Some historians attribute to the Junius letters the inauguration of the role of the press as a source of independent political commentary, but Black has clearly indicated that this explanation is an oversimplification. Black, 135–96.

26. Not the least of these other factors was economics. Most of newspapers received subsidies from the government or the opposition, in return for which they accepted contributions by party writers and generally supported their patrons' policies. As Black points out, the

influence of political subsidies should not be overestimated, as they did not in most cases amount to much (149–50). Werkmeister provides an excellent and more detailed review of all of the London newspapers during the 1780s and 1790s, including their ownership, party affiliation, specializations, and writers (Werkmeister, *A Newspaper History*, 19–41).

27. A notorious example of this inclination is the fate of John Walter, the proprietor of the *Times*, during the Regency crisis. Walter was prosecuted and jailed for a libelous paragraph against the Duke of York—a paragraph that Walter had been instructed to publish by Thomas Steele, Joint Secretary of the Treasury and the paymaster for the *Times's* £300 annual subsidy by Pitt's administration. Walter was imprisoned for sixteen months before the Treasury obtained his release.

28. Black, 165.

29. The *Times*, which is featured in the next chapter, offers a good example of the formal layout of British papers of the time. Like all fourteen London dailies of the early 1790s, the *Times* was printed on a conventional single sheet, which, folded once, produced a four-page paper. Each page was laid out into four columns, and the first (cover) page was devoted wholly to advertising. The second page, which offered the most important news, normally consisted of three sections. The first, appearing in the upper left corner, contained brief, large-type theater and opera announcements. Following those was what might now be called the feature news article, a long piece that in the 1790s typically offered a report of parliamentary debates or of some important event in France. This second section was followed by the "intelligence," a long series of brief items ranging over the whole spectrum of news events and including factual reports, editorial comments, theater reviews, letters from readers, social gossip (including regular news of the royal family), and even poetry and songs. It was in this section, which bore the heading "The Times," that the paper carried out its sly political commentary—frequently offering a pastiche of opaque or seemingly innocuous items that took on pointed significance when read in conjunction with other news. See Werkmeister, *A Newspaper History*, 19, for a more general description of the London daily papers. The third and fourth pages of the paper offered transcriptions of speeches, reprints from foreign gazettes, shipping news, and various items of commercial and municipal news.

30. *Times*, April 30, May 2, 1794. Pitt's Tory Ministry became the Théâtre de la Nation, while Fox and the Whig Opposition appeared as the Théâtre République. Interestingly, the paper's primary criticism, even though it was a ministry paper, was that "the Public is quite tired with a piece, which has had a most unaccountable run; and that after being represented for seven years successively, the Manager [Pitt] may very safely lay aside the *Battle of Hastings*" (Apr. 30). The Trial of Warren Hastings had occasioned the era's two most memorable parliamentary performances, Sheridan's sensational "Begums of Oude" speech and Burke's outrageous "Daggers" speech.

31. *Times*, July 1, 1789.

32. Burke, 60.

33. Philip Yorke in 1784: "The publication of the debates and opposition speeches have lost America, and the fewer there are to be published, the better the business will be done, if in good hands." Qtd. in Black, 139–40.

34. Werkmeister, *A Newspaper History*, 19–42.

35. William Cobbett, *The Political Proteus, A View of the Public Character and Conduct of R. B. Sheridan Esquire* (London 1804). Qtd. in Werkmeister, *The History of the "Times,"* vol. 1, *"The Thunderer" in the Making: 1785–1841* (New York: Macmillan, 1935), 48.

36. Cobbett, qtd. in Werkmeister, *The History of the "Times,"* 48.

37. Peter Davison, ed., Sheridan, *Comedies*, Casebook Series (London: Macmillan, 1986) 9.

38. Davison, 9.

39. Sheridan's "calm dignity" and comparatively lax private speech were noted by his sister Elizabeth in William Lefanu, ed., *Betsy Sheridan's Journal* (London, 1960); and his "good sense, ingenuity, and temper" by Thomas Moore, *Memoirs of . . . Sheridan* (London, 1825). These sources are quoted in excerpts by Davison, 30 and 26, respectively.

40. Thomas Sheridan, *A Course of Lectures on Elocution* (London, 1762), 30, qtd. in Thomas M. Conley, *Rhetoric in the European Tradition* (Chicago: U of Chicago P, 1990), 215.

41. Thomas Sheridan, 30, qtd. in Conley, 215.

42. Conley, 215.

43. Conley, 193.

44. W. Benzie, *The Dublin Orator: Thomas Sheridan's Influence on Eighteenth-Century Rhetoric and Belles Lettres* (Leeds: U of Leeds P, 1972), 65–66, qtd. in Davison, 23–24.

45. Benzie, in Davison, 24.

46. Burke, 29.

47. Burke, 30.

48. Burke, 68.

49. Burke, 30.

50. Burke, 67.

51. Burke, 67.

52. Burke, 66.

53. Burke, 65, 67.

54. Paine, 102.

55. David Bromwich, "Wollstonecraft as a Critic of Burke," *Political Theory* 23, no. 4 (1995): 620, 624.

56. Mary Wollstonecraft, *Vindication of the Rights of Men*, vol. 3 of *The Works of Mary Wollstonecraft*, 7 vols., ed. Janet Todd and Marilyn Butler (New York: New York UP, 1989), 3:72.

57. Wollstonecraft, 48.

58. Wollstonecraft, 70–71.

59. Paine, 102.

60. Wollstonecraft, 75, 70.

61. Paine, 102.

62. Wollstonecraft, 75, 76.

63. *Times,* July 30, 1789.

64. The spectacular presentation of historical events was not new to the stage. In 1779, as Cecil Price notes, Sadler's Well's "drew 'immense audiences' with its performances of 'A New Musical Piece consisting of Airs, serious and comic, Recitatives, Choruses, etc. called THE PROPHECY; or, QUEEN ELIZABETH AT TILBURY. In the course of which will be displayed a Transparency, representing the destruction of the Spanish Armada, and a Moving Perspective View representing the present GRAND FLEET.' " What *was* novel was the presentation of *current* events in such a manner.

Richard Brinsley Sheridan, *The Dramatic Works of Richard Brinsley Sheridan*, ed. Cecil Price, 2 vols. (Oxford: Clarendon P, 1973), 2:466. Price quotes from the *Morning Chronicle,* September 29, 1779.

65. *Times,* August 5, 1789.

66. Noted on the title page of the printed version of the play. John Dent, *The Bastille: including the celebrated speech delivered the 29th of July to the French troops, by Mons. Moreau de St. Merry, on the destruction of the above fortress* (London, 1789).

67. *Prelude*, book 11, though Wordsworth there incorporates the body of a poem he had previously written (and published in "The Friend" in 1810): "The French Revolution, as it appeared to enthusiasts at its inception." William Wordsworth, *The Complete Poetical Works* (London: Macmillan, 1905), 234, 315–16.

68. Dent, 16.

69. Jeffrey Cox, "Romantic Drama and the French Revolution," in *Revolution and English Romanticism*, ed. K. Hanley and R. Selden (Hertfordshire, UK: Harvester Wheatsheaf, 1990), 244.

70. Cox, "Romantic Drama," 245.

71. Terence Hoagwood and Cox both emphasize the severity of such censorship, and Hoagwood provides as illustration the comments of Elizabeth Inchbald on the ban against certain tragedies, including *Julius Caesar:* "When the circumstances of certain periods make certain incidents of history most interesting, those are the very seasons to interdict their exhibition . . . The lovers of the drama will, probably, be compelled to accept of real conspiracies, assassinations, and the slaughter of war, in lieu of such spectacles, ably counterfeited." It is worth noting that Inchbald's comments were markedly inaccurate concerning counterfeit spectacles of war. Cox, "Romantic Drama," 245; Hoagwood, 50.

72. Paine, 108.

73. Jack D. Durant, "Sheridan, Burke, and Revolution," *Eighteenth-Century Life* 6, nos. 2–3 (1981): 104.

74. *Times,* July 2, 1793.

75. And at the height of the Kotzebue craze. See Sheridan, 2:636–37, for contemporary accounts of Kotzebue mania.

76. Davison, 12.

77. Sheridan, 699.

78. Price, in Sheridan, 631.

79. Sheridan, 699.

80. Joseph Donohue, *Theatre in the Age of Kean* (Totowa, NJ: Rowman & Littlefield, 1975), 1.

81. See especially Elaine Hadley's *Melodramatic Tactics: Theatricalized Dissent in the English Marketplace, 1800–1885* (Stanford, CA: Stanford UP, 1995).

Four • The Fall of Robespierre *and the Tragic Imagination*

1. George Steiner, *The Death of Tragedy* (New Haven, CT: Yale UP, 1966. rpt. 1996); Ronald Paulson, *Representations of Revolution* (New Haven, CT: Yale, 1983); Mary Jacobus, *Romanticism, Writing, and Sexual Difference* (Oxford: Oxford UP, 1989); Jeffrey Cox, *In the Shadows of Romance: Romantic Tragic Drama in Germany, England, and France* (Athens: Ohio UP, 1987), "The French Revolution and Romantic Drama," in *Revolution and English Romanticism*, ed. Keith Hanley and Raman Selden (Hertfordshire, UK: Harvester Wheatsheaf, 1990), 241–60, and "Ideology and Genre in the British Antirevolutionary Drama in the 1790s," *ELH* 58 (1992): 579–610 (rpt. in *British Romantic Drama: Historical and Critical Essays*, ed. Terence Allan Hoagwood and Daniel P. Watkins); Julie Carlson, *In the Theatre of Romanticism* (Cambridge: Cambridge UP, 1994); Terence Hoagwood, "Prolegomenon for a Theory of Romantic Drama," *Wordsworth Circle* 23, no. 2 (1992), rpt. as "Romantic Drama and Historical Hermeneutics," in Hoagwood and Watkins, 22–55; Reeve Parker, "Reading Wordsworth's Power: Narrative and Usurpation in *The Borderers*," *ELH* 54, no. 2 (1987): 299–331, and " 'In some sort seeing with my proper eyes': Wordsworth and the Spectacles of Paris," *Studies in Romanticism* 27, no. 3

(1988): 369–90, and "Osorio's Dark Employments: Tricking Out Coleridgean Tragedy," *Studies in Romanticism* 33, no. 1 (1994): 119–60; Marjean Purinton, *Romantic Ideology Unmasked: The Mentally Constructed Tyrannies in Dramas of William Wordsworth, Lord Byron, Percy Shelley, and Joanna Baillie* (Newark: U of Delaware P, 1994); and William Jewett, *Fatal Autonomy: Romantic Drama and the Rhetoric of Agency* (Ithaca, NY: Cornell UP, 1997).

2. Hoagwood cites as examples of romantic drama's historical displacement of revolution Wordsworth's *The Borderers* (set in the period of the Crusades); Byron's *Werner* (central Europe during the Thirty Years' War); Lamb's *John Woodvil*, Shelley's *Charles the First*, and Godwin's *Faulkener* (all set in seventeenth-century England); Coleridge's *Osorio* (sixteenth-century Spain); and Shelley's *The Cenci* (Rome, 1599). Terence Hoagwood "Prolegomenon for a Theory of Romantic Drama," *Wordsworth Circle* 23, no. 2 (1992): 51.

3. For Paulson, Jordan observes, "style . . . inhabits a world apart, related but vaguely to the history of the artist's time and place." David P. Jordan, "Paulson's Representations of Revolution" (review), *Eighteenth Century* 27, no. 2 (1986): 206–8.

4. There are important exceptions to this tendency, as I noted in the introduction. Reeve Parker and David Wallace, especially, have interrogated precisely this problem of the romantics' spectatorial relations to the specific events of the Revolution. See Reeve Parker, " 'In some sort seeing with my proper eyes': Wordsworth and the Spectacles of Paris," *Studies in Romanticism* 27, no. 3 (1988): 369–90, and David Marshall, "The Eye-Witnesses of *The Borderers*," *Studies in Romanticism* 27, no. 3 (1988): 391–98.

5. Jeremy Black, *The English Press in the Eighteenth Century* (London: Croom Helm, 1987); Jeremy Popkin, *Revolutionary News: The Press in France, 1789–1799* (Durham, NC: Duke UP, 1990); Pierre Retat, "The Revolutionary Word in the Newspaper in 1789," in Jeremy Popkin, ed., *Media and Revolution: Comparative Perspectives* (Lexington: UP of Kentucky, 1995); Hannah Barker, *Newspapers, Politics, and Public Opinion in Late Eighteenth-Century England* (Oxford: Clarendon P, 1998); Stuart Andrews,. *The British Periodical Press and the French Revolution, 1789–99* (New York: Palgrave, 2000).

6. George Steiner, *The Death of Tragedy* (1961; New Haven, CT: Yale UP, 1996),The Death of Tragedy 116.

7. Immanuel Kant, *The Conflict of the Faculties*, trans. Mary J. Gregor (Lincoln: U of Nebraska P, 1979), 153.

8. William Wordsworth, *The Complete Poetical Works* (London: Macmillan, 1905), 316. As I noted in the preceding chapter, there is good reason to believe that Wordsworth's initial reaction to the July Days as an act of liberatory romance was influenced, as many Britons' reaction must have been influenced, by John Dent's hugely popular romantic rendering of the event at the Royal Circus in August 1789.

9. Jacobus, 34–35.

10. Nicholas Roe makes this observation, noting that Wordsworth's "effort to damn Robespierre momentarily relaxes at one point [in *The Prelude*] where he admits that even during the "rage and dog-day heat" of the Terror he had found

> Something to glory in, as just and fit,
> And in the order of sublimiest laws.
> And even if that were not, amid the awe
> Of unintelligible chastisement
> [He] felt a kind of sympathy with power—
> (x.412–16)

Nicholas Roe, *Wordsworth and Coleridge: The Radical Years* (Oxford, Clarendon P, 1988), 221.

11. see Jacobus, 39: "The *Macbeth* allusion is the nearest we come to a sense of Wordsworth's complicity—if only the complicity of sympathy—in that regicide."

12. Carlson, *Theatre of Romanticism*, 24.

13. Steiner, *Death of Tragedy*, 130–33. Of course, not all "guilt" (Carlson) produces a "thematic concern with remorse" (Steiner). However, the viability of such a link in the instance will become evident below. In Steiner's view, such evasion takes form as "near-tragedy," plays in which "four acts of tragic violence and guilt are followed by a fifth act of redemption and innocence regained." The compromise of such redemption, he contends, registers not only a loss of belief in the finality of evil but also the arrival of melodrama.

14. Carlson, *Theatre of Romanticism*, 22–23.

15. Jonathan Wordsworth supports this continuity, as (of course) does Roe. Jonathan Wordsworth, "The Infinite I AM," *Coleridge's Imagination: Essays in Memory of Pete Laver*, ed. Richard Gravil, Lucy Newlyn, and Nicholas Roe (Cambridge: Cambridge UP, 1985), 28–29.

16. Samuel Taylor Coleridge, *Biographia Literaria*, ed. James Engell and Walter Jackson Bate, vol. 7 of *The Collected Works of Samuel Taylor Coleridge*, Bollingen Series 75 (Princeton, NJ: Princeton UP, 1983), bk.1:32, qtd. in Carlson, *Theatre of Romanticism*, 22.

17. Carlson, *Theatre of Romanticism*, 1–29.

18. In other words, until Bonaparte's youthful heroism had been superseded by his bid for power on 18 Brumaire (Nov. 9, 1799).

19. It is rather curious that Carlson would suggest otherwise, for the result of such oversimplification is that she misses entirely the significance for her own argument of *The Fall of Robespierre*.

20. Roe, 210. Roe's discussion of Coleridge's self-recognition in Robespierre forms the central portion of his chapter "Imagining Robespierre," which offers an invaluable discussion of how the figure of the Jacobin leader offered Wordsworth and John Thelwall, as well as Coleridge, a powerful foil to set against the rationalism of William Godwin's *Political Justice*.

21. Coleridge, *Lectures 1795 on Politics and Religion*, ed. L. Patton and P. Mann. Vol. 1 of *The Collected Works of Samuel Taylor Coleridge*, Bollingen Series 75 (Princeton, NJ: Princeton UP, 1971), 35, qtd. in Roe, 208.

22. All references to the play are from Samuel Taylor Coleridge and Robert Southey, *The Fall of Robespierre: 1794*, facsimile edition (Oxford: Woodstock, 1991).

23. Roe (207) offers in support Milton's portrait of Satan:

> above the rest
> In shape and gesture proudly eminent
> Stood like a tower; his form had not yet lost
> All her original brightness, nor appeared
> Less than archangel ruined, and the excess
> Of glory obscured . . .
> (i.589–94)

24. See I..iii, Casca's midnight meetings with Cicero and with Cassius and Cinna. As is well known, a comet did in fact appear in 44 BC. and was thereafter associated with Caesar's assassination.

25. A similar observation is made by William Jewett in his excellent discussion of the play; see Jewett, 36–39.

26. Speaking in reference to the "ends" and "means" of the 1795 *Conciones* portrait, he suggests that Coleridge's "idea of Robespierre was probably influenced by [his] reading of [Robespierre's] speeches to the National Convention," and Roe cites in particular Robespierre's

February 5 "Address on Political Morality." Indeed, although Roe is concerned with a source for Robespierre's doctrinal statements rather than his rhetorical stance, the February 5 address does offer (as I discuss in Chap. 2) an unusual glimpse into Robespierre's sternly Roman interior world.

27. For a brief but informative account of the *Times'* coverage of the Revolution, see Neal Ascherson's introduction to his *"The Times" Reports the French Revolution: Extracts from "The Times," 1789–1794* (London: Times Books, 1975).

28. *Times,* July 15, 1789.

29. *Times,* July 15, 1789.

30. The identity of this correspondent remains unknown, although it is evident that he was well placed within the Revolution's political system (and such placement argues strongly that he *was* a man). Jeremy Popkin recently mentioned to me that it is likely that such a correspondent would have been a French journalist.

31. During the same period, military news from Holland arrived with comparable frequency, but with an average delay of only four to six days. As the express post service from Paris to the northern frontier could only with great effort be made in two days, regular (and therefore unobtrusive) conveyance of news across that frontier in four clearly required considerable skill.

The proceedings of the National Convention constituted the lengthiest portion of the regular Paris news, and the necessity for translation meant that transcripts and summaries of the Convention's proceedings appeared in the *Times* more than two or three days after arrival. One of the advantages of this situation, incidentally, was that the impact of continuing French military successes in Belgium was offset by the ability of the British government and military to establish their version of events at least two weeks before the Convention's version was offered.

32. Thus in the paper of Friday, January 25, Londoners received a full account, received "by an express which arrived yesterday morning from Messrs. *Fector* and Co. at Dover," of the execution of Louis at "about a quarter past ten o'clock" on "Monday morning."

33. Both more militant and more popular that the Jacobins, this group received its name from Jacques-René Hébert, better known in his pseudonymous role as the editorial voice of the most popular of Revolutionary papers, *Père Duchesne.* As Albert Soboul observed, *Père Duchesne* "was, as much and perhaps even more than Marat's *Ami du peuple,* both the voice and the guide of the popular masses." Originally, Père Duchesne was an archetypal character of the fairground theater, possessed of a vocabulary of scandalous vulgarity. As Hébert's journalistic persona, Père Duchesne devoted his acid-tongued commentary to a Revolutionary politics that became increasingly militant. In the autumn of 1793 the paper began openly to oppose the Montagnards. Although a direct attack on the Hébertists had been expected at least since Robespierre's denunciation of de-Christianization in November, the rapidity of this first strike in the Jacobin seizure of power shocked contemporary observers. The Hébertists' scandalous Festival of Reason, staged in Notre Dame in November of 1793, had provided Robespierre with a suitable pretense for the condemnation of de-Christianization which inaugurated his attack on the Hébertists' exuberantly secular radicalism. "We will not," Robespierre insisted in his "Address on Political Morality, "permit these grotesque parodies to disfigure the sublime drama of the Revolution."

34. Bouloiseau, *Jacobin Republic,* 118. "Mallet du Pan described this new situation with perspicacity. Previously, 'the aspiring factions had toppled the ruling factions with the aid of popular force.' Now, it was 'the ruling faction that [struck down its opposition. It did so] without the people's assistance, without mob agitation, legally, in due form.'"

35. *Times,* April 8, 1794.

36. *Times,* April 22, 1794.

37. Charles Lamb, "On the Tragedies of Shakespeare," in *Shakespearean Tragedy,* ed. D. F. Bratchell (London: Routledge, 1990), 46. Mary Jacobus, too, reads Lamb in light of the textual drama of the Revolution, although her focus is on Wordsworth's nocturnal hallucinations during his visit to Paris after the September Massacres. Accordingly, she emphasizes Lamb's assertion in regard to Shakespeare's supernatural phenomena that it is "the solitary taper and the book that generates faith in these terrors" (34).

38. "The black spirits," he remarked, "passed muster tolerably well, but the white ones wore greatly the resemblance of the dancing dogs of old.—Those barren spectators who regarded not the text, indulged in a hearty laugh at their expence!" There is more of interest here than the amusement generated by inept stage spirits: we should note as well that the hearty laugh was engaged in by those who "*regarded not the text.*" Here it seems possible to read Lamb against the grain, not as an antitheatrical critic but as a chronicler of the increasingly literary dramatic imagination of his era, an imagination to which Kemble's stagecraft was addressed. As Lamb notes, "the reading of a tragedy . . . presents to the fancy just so much of external appearances as to make us feel that we are among flesh and blood, while by far the greater and better part of our imagination is employed upon the thoughts and internal machinery of the character." Lamb, in Bratchell, 46.

39. Sir Walter Scott, review of Boaden's *Kemble,* "Article 10," *Quarterly Review* 34 (1826): 218f, qtd. in Bertram Joseph, *The Tragic Actor* (London: Routledge & Kegan Paul, 1959), 202–3.

40. It was not only in its staging of a reading that Kemble's *Macbeth* suited its dramatic moment; as the audience at Drury Lane would undoubtedly have recognized, Kemble's cool, formidably monomaniacal Macbeth evoked admirably the famously taciturn, single-minded character of Robespierre. As Bertram Joseph notes, "Kemble was a classic, not [only] in the sense that he concentrated on the outward appearance of calm grandeur, formal dignity and comparative stiffness, but because he worked from within outwards, from a classical tragic conception to the details of the acting in which it was embodied. And for him the tragic conception was essentially one of consistent intensity: the character must be developed undeviatingly in one straight line of progressive intensity: everything must point to the same end. This was the aim with which he studied, conceived and embodied a part."

Sarah Siddons, also characteristically, offered a Lady Macbeth of "terrifying grandeur"; Campbell considered "her peculiar element" to be "the sublime and energetic." For Hazlitt, she was, as Lady Macbeth, "tragedy personified": "Power was seated on her brow, passion emananted from her breast as from a shrine." The differing manner in which these two actors are constructed in the press is a question well worth asking; unfortunately, it is a question that lies outside the scope of this chapter.

William Hazlitt, *The Complete Works of William Hazlitt,* ed. P. P. Howe, 21 vols. (London, 1930–34), 4:189–90, qtd. in Jacobus, 63n77; Joseph, 187, 236–37.

41. *Times,* April 15, 1794.

42. On June 6, the paper reported that "all communication with France being for the moment intercepted," primarily because French troops had "cut off the channel between *Bouillon, Liege,* and *Brussells,* through which the Paris Gazettes have lately passed."

43. On Monday the fourth, the paper devoted its entire Paris coverage to the translated transcript of Robespierre's speech. The following day it printed the remaining Convention proceedings and provided a tentative analysis of the opposition to Robespierre. On Wednesday a previously received transcript of a report by Barrère on the capture of Ostend was printed, and on Thursday there was no mention of news from France whatsoever.

44. Thomas De Quincey, *De Quincey as Critic,* ed. John E. Jordan, The Routledge Critics Series (London: Routledge & Kegan Paul, 1973), 243.

45. Jeremy Popkin, keynote address, "Revolutions in Print," Thirteenth Annual DeBartolo Conference on Eighteenth-Century Studies, University of South Florida, Tampa, February 1999.

Five • Reviving the Revolution: Dantons Tod

1. *Dantons Tod* (1835) was first performed in 1902 in a production by Max Reinhardt at the Freie Volksbühne in Berlin; *Woyzeck* (1837) did not receive its first production for another decade, when it was staged at the Munich Residenztheater. *Leonce et Lena* (1836) received its premiere in 1885 in an outdoor performance by Munich's Intimes Theater.

2. It was German Naturalists (Hauptmann, Rudolf Gottschall, Robert Griepenkerl) who first brought Büchner's work out of the obscurity in which it had languished since his death; Wedekind followed, and after him the Expressionists (Georg Heym, Kasimir Edschmid, Hans Henny Jahnn, Ernst Toller, Georg Kaiser) claimed Büchner as something approaching a patron saint. Büchner's plays received their first widespread attention during this period, and it was through the Expressionists that Brecht was introduced to Büchner's plays.

Scholarly work on Büchner came in the wake of such theatrical attention, and for much of its history such work was been dominated by attempts to claim Büchner's heritage for one or another competing political and aesthetic position (with the left emphasizing Büchner's radical political stance in readings that align him with early socialism, and the right emphasizing instead the modernity of his alleged fatalism). In the last three decades, and with the end of the cold war, such polarities have yielded to more complex readings of Büchner's work, although the political debate over his work remains recognizably continuous with that construction of the field.

The most influential scholar in this re-evaluation of Büchner's work has been Thomas Michael Mayer, who insisted upon a clear recognition of Büchner's political radicalism even as he helped move the terms of debate to much more complex ground. Perhaps Mayer's greatest contribution was his establishment of a larger body of known source texts and his concomitant demonstration of the complexity of Büchner's literary-historical context. For a useful articulation of this critical history, see both Helmut Fuhrmann, "Die Dialektik der Revolution—Georg Büchners 'Dantons Tod,'" *Jahrbuch der Deutschen Schillergesellschaft* (1991) as well as Mayer's response ("Gegendarstellung," *Jahrbuch der Deutschen Schillergesellschaft* (1991).

Büchner scholarship now constitutes a substantial field of study, and while my work engages with recent scholarship, it does not represent a specialist's contribution to that field. For a representative review and condensed selection of major critical work on Büchner from its origins through 2002, see Dietmar Goldschnigg, ed., *Georg Büchner und die Moderne: Texte, Analysen, Kommentar,* 3 vols. (Berlin: Erich Schmidt Verlag, 2004).

The best monograph in English on Büchner is John Reddick's *Georg Büchner: The Shattered Whole* (Oxford: Clarendon P, 1994). For a concise if limited review in English of Büchner scholarship in the postwar period through the mid-eighties, see Reinhold Grimm, "Culmination, Conclusions, and a New Beginning: The Present State of Büchner Reception and Research," in *Love, Lust, and Rebellion: New Approaches to Georg Büchner* (Madison: U of Wisconsin P, 1985), 115–38.

Valuable source document resources include Thomas Michael Mayer, ed., *Gesammelte Werke. Erstdrucke und Erstausgaben in Faksimiles,* 10 vols. (Frankfurt, 1987); Heinz Ludwig

Arnold, ed., *Georg Büchner I/II,* A Special Issue of *Text + Kritik.* (Munich, 1979) and *Georg Büchner III,* A Special Issue of *Text + Kritik* (Munich, 1981); Richard Thieberger, *La Mort de Danton de Georg Büchner et ses sources* (Paris: Presses Universitaires de France, 1953).

3. The last of these characteristics is perhaps the most obvious reminder that *Dantons Tod* was composed not for the theatrical stage of the day but as (in Büchner's terms) a "dramatic poem," a "book" (letter to his parents, July 28, 1835, in Büchner, *Complete Plays,* 201–2). That this was so should not be taken to suggest that *Dantons Tod* is not a script for theatrical performance; to the contrary, it merely suggests the degree to which Büchner considered the theater of his time to be inadequate to the theatrical demands of his drama.

4. See Frederich Rothe, "Georg Büchner's 'Spätrezeption': Hauptmann, Wedekind, und das Drama der Jahrhundertwende," *Georg Büchner Jahrbuch* 3 (Frankfort, 1983).

5. Georg Büchner, *Complete Plays, Lenz, and Other Writings,* trans. John Reddick (London: Penguin, 1993), 5. Georg Büchner, *Sämtliche Werke, Briefe, und Dokumente,* ed. Henri Poschmann, 2 vols. (Frankfort: Deutscher Klassiker Verlag, 1992–99), 1:13.

As I believe that a significant portion of my audience will not be familiar with German, I have chosen to present all quotation in English, with reference to the original where, as here, it seems useful. In several instances I have chosen to include the German text in full in the accompanying note. In all cases, I have provided citational reference to it. Most quotations in English are taken for convenience from John Reddick's English translation, which is generally quite accurate. Where necessary, I have modified his text or offered my own translation. For the sake of convenience, Büchner, *Complete Plays* is abbreviated *CP* and Büchner, *Sämtliche Werke, SW.*

6. Büchner testifies to the nature of such reception in his letter of July 28, in which he defends the play against the critical attacks on its "obscenities" (*Gemeinheiten*) and "so-called immorality" (*sogenannte Unsittlichkeit*). *CP* 201, 202; *SW,* 2:409, 410.

7. *CP* 5. *SW,* 1:13.

8. Well-known interpretations of Büchner in such terms include Karl Vietor's foundational *Georg Büchner: Politik.Dichtung.Wissenschaft* (Bern, 1949); Hans Mayer, *Georg Büchner und sein Zeit* (1946; Frankfort, 1972); and Maurice Benn, *The Drama of Revolt. A Critical Study of Georg Büchner* (Cambridge, 1976). See also Robert Mühlher, "Georg Büchner und die Mythologie des Nihilismus," in *Georg Büchner,* ed. W. Martens (Darmstadt, 1965).

9. My translation; *SW,* 1:17. Danton is best known in Revolutionary history for his inspirational oratory in September 1792, when the Duke of Brunswick's invading army captured Verdun and threatened Paris. Confronting a panicked Legislative Assembly, he declared "Il nous faut de l'audace, et encore de l'audace, et toujours de l'audace!" After the subsequent victory at Valmy, the speech was widely credited as having galvanized French resistance.

10. Henry J. Schmidt, *How Dramas End: Essays on the German Sturm und Drang, Büchner, Hauptmann, and Fleisser* (Ann Arbor, MI: U of Michigan P, 1992), 98.

11. The perception of Büchner's distantiation from the dramatic culture of his time is, in certain ways, accurate; he seems not to have been a regular theatregoer, and his antipathy to the predominant idealist drama of German romanticism is notorious. Yet, it would be a mistake to say that Büchner was unfamiliar with the drama or that his work is either unprecedented or unrelated to contemporary dramatic issues and concerns. His range of references to dramatic literature, particularly to Shakespeare and to Goethe, is substantial; moreover, he prepared translations of Hugo's *Lucretia Borgia* and *Maria Tudor,* work that his publisher Karl Gutzkow thought indicative of a "genuine poetic kinship" (Grimm, 210 n 85).

12. Grimm, 28. As Katharina Mommsen has noted, "Something very striking keeps occurring decade after decade: Büchner is constantly viewed as being absolutely up-to-date.

'Spricht dieser Büchner nicht wie ein Heutiger?' queried Max Frisch in 1958. In 1978 Volker Braun wrote: 'Büchners Briefe lesend, muß man sich mitunter mit Gewalt erinnern, daß es nicht die eines Zeitgenossen sind.' In 1980 Christa Wolf said: 'Aus Sätzen Büchners wollte ich eine Rede halten, die klingen sollte, als wäre sie heute geschrieben.' " Katharina Mommsen, "Georg Büchner and Posterity," *Momentum Dramaticum: Festschrift for Eckehard Catholy*, ed. Linda Dietrich and David G. John (Waterloo, ON: U of Waterloo P, 1990), 414.

13. Thomas Carlyle, *The French Revolution*, ed. K. J. Fielding and David Sorenson (Oxford: Oxford UP, 1989), 247. I am not suggesting here that histories of the Revolution were not being written; however, in France Louis XVIII and Charles X had certainly done everything in their power to erase national memory of the Revolution. François Guizot and Augustin Thierry, like the more liberal Adolphe Thiers and Auguste Mignet, wrote historical treatments of the Revolution during the 1820s, but all were writing to defend the reforms of 1789, and little else, from the *ultras'* attacks on the legitimacy of the entire Revolution. Buchez's *Histoire parlementaire de la Révolution française* was the first work to publish source materials from the Revolutionary period, and it was not until Michelet (in the mid-1840s) that anyone undertook the task of a sustained and systematic investigation into the enormous archival compost of Revolutionary materials. For an introduction to early historiography of the Revolution, see s.v. "Historians and Commentators," in *Critical Dictionary of the French Revolution*, ed. François Furet and Mona Ozouf, trans. Arthur Goldhammer (Cambridge, MA: Belknap P of Harvard UP, 1989), 881–1034.

14. Victor Hugo, "Ymbert Galloix" (1833), *Philosophie*, vol. 1 of *Oeuvres complètes*, ed. Paul Meurice et al. (Paris: Albin Michel, 1904–52), 184; qtd. in Jeffrey Cox, "Romantic Drama and the French Revolution," *Revolution and English Romanticism*, ed. Keith Hanley and Raman Selden (Hertfordshire, UK: Harvester Wheatsheaf, 1990), 241.

15. Robespierre, "Rapport sur les principes de morale politique qui doivent guider la Convention nationale dans l'administration intérieure de la République," in *Oeuvres de Maximilien Robespierre*, vol. 10, *Discours (5ᵉ Partie)*, ed. Marc Bouloiseau and Albert Soboul (Paris: Presses universitaires de France, 1967), 355.

16. Büchner had in 1834 translated Hugo's *Lucretia Borgia* and *Maria Tudor*.

17. Letter of July 28, 1835, to his parents. *CP*, 202. *Seine höchste Aufgabe ist, der Geschichte, wie sie sich wirklich begeben, so nahe als möglich zu kommen. SW*, 2:410.

18. Letter of July 28, 1835. *CP*, 202. *SW*, 2:410.

19. Büchner is here concerned with refuting, to his parents, charges of the play's immorality. Letter of July 28, 1835, *CP*, 202. *SW*, 2:410.

20. My reference to Büchner's use of source materials is based on Thieberger's comprehensive guide.

21. My translation (*"parodierte das erhabne Drama der Revolution"*). *SW*, 1:23. Büchner took the phrase from Robespierre, *Rapport sur les principes de morale politique, Oeuvres de Maximilien Robespierre*, 10:355.

22. As Büchner's Danton observes (with undeniable accuracy) in the play's single direct confrontation between its opposing protagonists, "You've taken no bribes, made no debts, slept with no women, kept your nose quite clean and never got drunk. Robespierre, you are disgustingly decent." (I.vi). *CP*, 23. *SW*, 1:33.

23. The most prominent examples include his response to the Tribunal's request for his name ("The Revolution declares my name. My place of abode will soon be in nothingness and my name in the Pantheon of History" (III.iv). My translation. *SW*, 1:62) and his immediately celebrated (though probably apocryphal) response to a soldier's attempt to prevent him from embracing a compatriot at the foot of the guillotine: "Can you prevent our heads from kissing down there in the basket?" (IV.vii). My translation. *SW*, 1:88.

24. *CP,* 47. *SW,* 1:60. At I.vi, Robespierre reads from *Le Vieux Cordelier,* Desmoulins's satirical characterization of Saint-Just as St. John to Robespierre's Messiah. The editorial's remark that Saint-Just "carries his head like the holy sacrament" is followed as well by the response attributed to Saint-Just: "I'll make him carry it like Saint-Denis" *CP,* 26; *SW,* 1:36.

25. *CP,* 43. *SW,* 1:55.

26. *CP,* 10, 73. *SW,* 1:19, 90. "J'ai vu plus de dix femmes qui, n'osant prendre du poison, avaient crié "*Vive le Roi,*" et chargeaient par ce moyen cet abominable tribunal du soin de terminer leurs jours." Riouffe, *Mémoires d'un Détenu, pour servir à l'Histoire de la Tyrannie de Robespierre,* 2nd ed.(Paris, l'an III de la République Française [1795]). Qtd. in Thieberger, 27.

27. *CP,* 235 n 102.

28. For an account of the theatre of the guillotine, see Daniel Arasse, *The Guillotine and the Terror,* trans. Christopher Miller (London: Penguin, 1989), 87–133.

29. *CP,* 178. *Es ist einerlei, wo die Scheinleiche zu zucken anfängt ... erhebt euch und der ganze Leib wird mit euch aufstehen.* Georg Büchner, *Sämtliche Werke und Briefe,* vol. 2, *Vermischte Schriften und Briefe* (Hamburg: Christian Wegner Verlag, 1971), 59.

30. My translation. *SW,* 1:83.

31. Büchner, letter to Minna Jaeglé, middle/end of January,1834. *CP,* 195–96. "Ich studierte die Geschichte der Revolution. Ich fühlte mich wie zernichtet unter dem gräßlichen Fatalismus der Geschichte. Ich finde in der Menschennatur eine entsetzliche Gleichheit, in den menschlichen Verhältnissen eine unabwendbare Gewalt, Allen und Keinem verliehen. Die Einzelne nur Schaum auf der Welle, die Größe ein bloßer Zufall, die Herrschaft des Genies ein Puppenspiel, ein lächerliches Ringen gegen ein ehernes Gesetz, es zu erkennen das Höchste, es zu beherrschen unmöglich." *SW,* 2:377.

32. Bouloiseau, *Jacobin Republic,* 118.

33. Bouloiseau, *Jacobin Republic,* 118.

34. On Michelet and the popular Revolution, see Lionel Gossman, "Michelet and the French Revolution," in *Representing the French Revolution; Revolution: Literature, Historiography, and Art,* ed. James A. Heffernan (Hanover, NH: UP of New England, 1992), 81–105, and Roland Barthes, *Michelet,* trans. Richard Howard (1952; Berkeley: U of California P, 1992).

35. Büchner, letter to his parents, July 28, 1835. My translation. "Er uns die Geschichte zum zweiten Mal erschafft und uns gleich unmittelbar, statt eine trockne Erzählung zu geben, in das Leben einer Zeit hinein versetzt." *SW,* 2:410.

36. That dictatorship is precisely what the death of Danton inaugurates. With the fall of Danton and the successful imposition of Jacobin rule, the remarkable discursive heterogeneity that had characterized popular political culture since 1789 was stifled. Censorship of the press, successful repression of the power of the Paris *sections,* and the exceptional danger (in the wake of the Law of 22 Prairial) of voicing any sort of dissent all contributed to a sudden, even eerie, homogenization of political rhetoric.

37. Edmund Burke, *Reflections on the Revolution in France,* ed. J. G. A. Pocock (Indianapolis, IN: Hackett, 1987), 9.

38. Maria Porrmann focuses upon this generic heteroglossia as a marker of Büchner's modernity in her "Die Französische Revolution als Schauspiel," *Grabbe und die Dramatiker seiner Zeit: Beitrage zum II. Internationalen Grabbe-Symposium 1989,* ed. Detlev Kopp and Michael Vogt (Tubingen: Niemeyer, 1990), 149–68.

39. *CP,* 33. *SW,* 1:44.

40. *CP,* 7, 69. *SW,* 1:15, 86.

41. François Furet, *Interpreting the French Revolution,* trans. Elborg Foster (Cambridge: Cambridge UP, 1981), 46–50.

42. *CP*, 7. *SW*, 1:15.

43. *CP*, 21. *SW*, 1:31.

44. Hunt, *Politics, Culture, and Class*, 24.

45. "Que langage vais-je vous parler? Comment vous peindre des erreurs dont vous n'avez aucune idée, et comment rendred sensible le mal qu'on mot décèle, qu'un mot corrige?" Qtd. by Carol Blum in "Representing the Body Politic: Fictions of the State," in *Representing the French Revolution*, ed. Heffernan, 123.

46. My translation. *SW*, 1:17.

47. *CP*, 8. *SW*, 1:17.

48. For an extended examination of Simon's character, see Theo Buck's "Der 'gefahrliche Gemutsmensch': Zu Büchners Simon-Figur in 'Dantons Tod,' " in *Les Songes de la raison: Mélanges offerts à Dominique Iehl*, ed. David Claude (Bern: Peter Lang, 1995), 53–63.

49. *CP*, 8. *SW*, 1:17.

50. *CP*, 8. "Wo ist die Jungfrau? Sprich! Nein, so kann ich nicht sagen. Das Mädchen! Nein auch das nicht; die Frau, das Weib! Auch das, auch das nicht! Nur noch ein Name! Oh der erstickt mich! Ich habe keinen Atem dafür." *SW*, 1:17.

51. My translation. *SW*, 1:18.

52. My translation. *SW*, 1:18.

53. *CP*, 10. "Ja ein Messer, aber nicht für die arme Hure, was tat sie? Nichts! Ihr Hunger hurt un bettelt. Ein Messer für die Leute, die das Fleisch unserer Weiber und Töchter kaufen! Weh über die, so mit den Töchtern des Volkes huren!" *SW*, 1:18.

54. My translation. *SW*, 1:18.

55. My translation. *SW*, 1:19.

56. My translation. "Das Volk ist wie ein Kind, es muß Alles zerbrechen, um zu sehen was darin steckt." *SW*, 1:31.

57. *CP*, 11. *"Ach meine Herren!; Es gibt hier keine herren!; Erbarmen!" SW*, 1:20.

58. *CP*, 11.

DRITTE BÜRGER: An die Laterne!

JUNGER MENSCH: Meinetwegen, ihr werdet deswegen nicht heller sehen!

DIE UNSTEHENDEN: Bravo, bravo!

EINIGE STIMMEN: Laßt ihn laufen! (Er entwischt) (*SW*, 1:20)

59. "Camille Desmoulins has appointed himself *Procureur-Général de la Lanterne*, Attorney-General of the Lamp-iron; and pleads, *not* with atrocity, under an atrocious title; editing weekly his brilliant *Revolutions of Paris and Brabant*. Brilliant, we say; for if, in that murk of Journalism, with its dull blustering, with its mixed or loose fury, any ray of genius greet thee, be sure it is Camille's. The thing that Camille touches, he with his light finger adorns: brightness plays, gentle, unexpected, amid horrible confusions; often is the word of Camille worth reading, when no other's is. Questionable Camille, how thou glitterest with a fallen, rebellious, yet still semi-celestial light; as is the starlight on the brow of Lucifer! Son of Morning, into what times and what lands art thou fallen!" Carlyle, 1:247.

60. *CP*, 29. *SW*, 1:40.

61. My translation. *SW*, 1:36.

62. *CP*, 8. *SW*, 1:16.

63. *CP*, 8. "Zwischen Tür und Angel will ich euch prophezeien, die Statue der Freiheit ist noch nicht gegossen, der Ofen glüht, wir Alle können uns noch die Finger dabei verbrennen." *SW*, 1:16.

64. Carlyle, 1:90, 102.

65. *CP,* 50–51. "Sie haben die Hände an mein ganzes Leben gelegt, so mag es sich denn aufrichten und ihnen eentgegentreten, unter dem Gewichte jeder meiner Handlungen werde ich sie begraben . . . Ich habe im September die junge Brut der Revolution mit den zerstücken Leibern der Aristokraten geatzt. Meine Stimme hat aus dem Golde der Aristokraten und Reichen dem Volke Waffen geschmiedet. Meine Stimme war der Orkan, welcher die Satelliten des Despotismus unter Wogen von Bajonetten begrub." *SW,* 1:63–64.

Danton refers here to the events of September 1792. His oratory in early September (*De l'audace. Encore de l'audace. Toujours de l'audace*) had inspired the French to rally a volunteer army that would on the twentieth halt the advance of the Duke of Brunswick at Valmy. However, popular fears that crisis would serve as an opportunity for a counter-revolution in Paris led to the most notorious outbreak of violence of the Revolution. Between September 2 and 6, impromptu tribunals set up at the prisons around Paris summarily executed between eleven hundred and fourteen hundred prisoners, under the apparent impression that there were among these many counter-Revolutionaries. In fact, no more than a quarter were political prisoners, the rest being common criminals. Danton was Minister of Justice at the time but chose not to intervene.

66. July 17, 1791. After Varennes, the Cordeliers (Danton's club) petitioned for the removal of the king and held a rally for that cause on the Champ-de-Mars on July 17. Bailly and Lafayette declared martial law and sent the National Guard to disperse the crowd. However, the guard fired upon the demonstrators, an act that split the Patriot party into the moderate Feuillants and the group that would become known as the Jacobins. On August 10, 1792, a popular attack on the Tuileries led to the suspension of the monarchy. On January 21, 1793, Louis was executed. *CP,* 51. "Ich habe auf dem Marsfelde dem Königtume den Krieg erklärt, ich habe es am 10. August geschlagen, ich habe es am 21. Januar getötet und den Königen einen Königskopf als Fehdehandschuh hingeworfen." *SW,* 1:64.

67. As Furet and Richet have pointed out, Danton's oratory "was aimed not at provoking the internal conflicts and schisms, which Robespierre considered beneficial to the currents of the revolution, but at the necessity of unity against the common enemy. His strategy—the key to all the apparent contradictions in his political attitudes—was to present as broad a front as possible to the enemy and to avoid any divisions within the Revolutionary movement." François Furet and Denis Richet, *The French Revolution,* trans. Stephen Hardman (New York: Macmillan, 1970), 192. Carlyle, again, offers a good sense of the impression: "Great and greater waxes President Danton in his Cordeliers Section; his rhetorical tropes are all 'gigantic': energy flashes from his great brows, menaces his athletic figure, rolls in the sound of his voice 'reverberating from the domes.'" Carlyle, 1:321.

68. *CP,* 38. *SW,* 1:49.

69. *CP,* 37.

DANTON: Rief ich?
JULIE: Du sprachst von garstigen Sünden und dann stöhntest du: September!
DANTON: Ich, ich? Nein, ich sprach nicht, das dacht ich kaum, das waren nur ganz leise heimliche Gedanken.
JULIE: Du zitterst Danton.
DANTON: Und soll ich nicht zittern, wenn so die Wände plaudern? . . . Ich möchte nicht mehr denken, wennn das gleich so Spricht. Es gibt Gedanken Julie, für die es keine Ohren geben sollte. Das ist nicht gut, daß sie bei der Geburt gleich scheien, wie Kinder. Das ist nicht gut . . .
JULIE: Ein Kind scheit in der Nähe. (*SW,* 1:48)

70. Unlike all of the other events to which Danton refers, the massacres of September 1792 were carried out against internal elements that were by no means clear enemies and inaugurated that Manichaean cycle of internecine violence, the negative logic of the conspiracy, which by late 1793 had come to seem fundamental to Revolutionary politics

In a similar fashion, John B. Lyon has argued that Büchner describes, in the rhetorical violence of *Dantons Tod*, "a relation of self to society strikingly similar to that of the Lacanian subject to the symbolic order." See his "The Inevitability of Rhetorical Violence: Büchner's *Dantons Tod*," *Modern Language Studies* 26, nos. 2 and 3 (1996): 99–109.

71. *CP*, 17, 21. *SW*, 1:26, 31.

72. *CP*, 29. *SW*, 1:39.

73. *CP*, 23.

DANTON: Wo die Notwehr aufhört fängt der Mord an, ich sehhe keinen Grun, der uns länger zum Töten zwänge.

ROBESPIERRE: Die soziale Revolution ist noche nicht fertig . . . Die gute Gesellschaft ist noch nicht tot. (*SW*, 1:32)

74. To illustrate this idea, Hunt offers a quotation from Marat-Mauger: "All the revolutions which history has conserved for memory as well as those that have been attempted in our time have failed because people wanted to square new laws with old customs and rule new institutions with old men . . . REVOLUTIONARY means outside of all forms and all rules; REVOLUTIONARY means that which affirms, consolidates the revolution, that which removes all the obstacles which impede its progress." *Politics, Culture, and Class*, 27.

75. *CP*, 24–25. "Ist's denn so notwendig? Ja, ja! Die Republik! Er muß weg . . . Wer in einer Masse, die vorwärts drängt, stehen bleibt, leistet so gut Widerstand als trät' er ihr entgegen; er wird zertreten. Wir werden das Schiff der Revolution nicht auf den seichten Berechnungen und den Schlammbänken dieser Leute stranden lassen, wir müssen die Hand abhauen, die es zu halten wagt und wenn er es mit den Zähnen packet! Weg mit einer Gesellschaft, die der toten Aristokratie die Kleider ausgezogen und ihren Aussatz geerbt hat." *SW*, 34.

76. Hunt, *Politics, Culture, and Class*, 27–28.

77. *CP*, 14–15. "den Feind," "gewisse Leute," "an Leute denkt, welche sonst in Dachstuben lebten und jetzt in Karossen fahren." *SW*, 1:24–25.

78. *CP* 41. "Ist schuldig, denn nie zitter die Unschuld vor der öffentlichen Wachsamkeit." *SW*, 53.

79. Huet, "Performing Arts and the Terror," 141.

80. *CP*, 32. *SW*, 1:43.

81. "*Mercier:* Just follow your slogans through to the point where they turn into flesh and blood. Look around you: what you see is what you've said—a precise translation of your words. These miserable wretches, their executioners. The guillotine: they are your speeches come to life." *CP*, 49. *SW*, 1:62.

82. My translation. *SW*, 1:60.

83. *CP*, 29. *SW*, 1:39.

84. My translation. *SW*, 1:72.

85. *CP*, 58, 69. *SW*, 1:72, 86.

86. *CP*, 37. *SW*, 1:47–48.

87. My translation. *SW*, 1:85.

88. Qtd. in Arasse, 88.

89. My translation. *SW*, 1:88–89.

90. *CP*, 6. *SW*, 1:14.

91. Arasse, 39ff.

92. Qtd. in Arasse, 40. Soemmerring's statement raised obvious questions, of course, including most pointedly the question of just where consciousness was located in the body. In keeping with the politics of the Revolution, many anatomists held that consciousness "had no specific or exclusive seat," being rather spread throughout the sensory system; thus decapitation, by breaking the unity of the body, eliminated at the same time any sense of self.

93. K. B. Roberts and J. D. W. Tomlinson, *The Fabric of the Body: European Traditions of Anatomical Illustration* (Oxford: Clarendon P, 1992), 356–59, 364–67.

94. Jonathan Crary, *Techniques of the Observer: On Vision and Modernity in the Nineteenth Century.* An October Book (Cambridge, MA: MIT P, 1990), 78. Crary links Bichat to Schopenhauer, quoting the latter to clarify the relation:

> "His reflections and mine mutually support each other, since his are the physiological commentary on mine, and mine are the philosophical commentary on his; and we shall best be understood by being read together side by side." Although by the 1840s Bichat's work was generally considered scientifically obsolete and part of an increasingly discredited vitalism, he nonetheless provided Schopenhauer with a crucial physical model of the human subject. Bichat's physiological conclusions grew primarily out of his study of death, in which he identified death as a fragmented process, consisting of the extinction of different organs and processes: the death of locomotion, of respiration, of sense perceptions, of the brain. If death was thus a multiple, dispersed event, then so was organic life.

95. Crary 78 (see preceding note); see also Michel Foucault, *Birth of the Clinic*, trans. Alan Sheridan (New York: Vintage, 1975), 146.

96. My translation. *SW*, 1:72–73.

97. LACROIX: One's hair and nails grow so much—I feel quite ashamed.

HERAULT: Hey, a bit more careful when you sneeze, I got a face full of sand!

LA CROIX: And don't you tread on my toes like that, I've got corns.

HERAULT: You've got lice as well.

LACROIX: Bugger the lice, it's the worms that bother me.

HERAULT: . . . Keep your nails to yourself while you sleep! There! Stop tugging at our shroud, it's cold down there. (IV.iii. *CP*, 63. *SW*, 1:78.)

98. *CP*, 58. *SW*, 1:72.

99. *CP*, 25. *SW*, 1:35.

> Macbeth . . . Now o'er the one half world
> Nature seems dead, and wicked dreams abuse
> The curtained sleep. Witchcraft celebrates
> Pale Hecate's offerings, and withered Murder,
> Alarumed by his sentinel, the wolf,
> Whose howl's his watch, thus with stealthy pace,
> With Tarquin's ravishing strides, towards his design
> Moves like a ghost. (*Macbeth* II.ii.50–57)

100. My translation. *SW*, 1:86.

101. *CP*, 71. *SW*, 1:87

102. Arasse, 112.

103. *CP*, 71. *SW*, 1:88.

104. Arasse, 112.

105. *CP*, 72. *SW*, 1:89.

106. My translation. *SW*, 1:87.

107. The irony of such appropriative fragmentation runs through the play, but perhaps the most pointed instance of it occurs at III.vi: "Dare!" exclaims Saint-Just when urging the tribunal to cut short Danton's trial, "Danton taught us the word—let's show him we learnt it!" *CP*, 54. *SW*, 1:68.

108. My translation. *SW*, 1:72.

109. *CP*, 73.

110. A number of recent critics have focused on the play's competing, contradictory models of history, finding in their unresolvable multiplicity one of the strongest markers of Büchner's literary modernity. See Harro Müller, "Poetische Entparadoxierung: Anmerkungen zu Büchners Dantons Tod und zu Grabbes Napoleon oder Die hundert Tage," *Grabbe un die Dramatiker seiner Zeit*, ed. Detlev Kopp and Michael Vogt (Tubingen: Niemeyer, 1990), 187–201. Müller broadens the same argument in "Identity, Paradox, Difference: Conceptions of Time in the Literature of Modernity," *MLN* 111, no. 3 (1996): 523–32. See also Gerard Raulet's similar argument in "Die 'Moderne' als Kategorie der Literaturgeschichtsschreibung: Georg Büchners 'Dantons Tod,'" *Kontroversen, alte und neue*, vol.11 of *Historische und aktuelle Konzepte der Literaturgeschichtsschreibung; Zwei Konigskinder? Zum Verhaltnis von Literatur und Literaturwissenschaft*, ed. Albrecht Schone, Wilhelm Vosskamp, and Eberhard Lammert (Tubingen: Niemeyer, 1986), 93–104.

Perhaps more relevant here, certainly closer to what I am suggesting, is Kubiak's discussion of the play's "double vision," the way it shows us that "the revolution is *in every sense* theatre: it is theatre operating as 'the site of violence' . . . , and it is also Buechner's play text itself, the shadowy emanation of an actual historical pain." While Büchner's play, Kubiak notes, "may be seen as the mere reformulation of the events of 1789 and after, in a more important sense the play . . . is an extension and prolepsis of the terror of 'guillotine logic' into the modern period" (118).

On the specific relevance of Brecht's notion of *gestus* to this kind of political act, see Elin Diamond, *Unmaking Mimesis: Essays on Feminism and Theater* (London: Routledge, 1997), 146–47. Büchner's incorporation of such a gesture is also a quotation from the Terror, when prisoners languishing hopelessly in prison would cry out thus in order to force the tribunal to order their execution.

Conclusion

1. For a review and evaluation of that critical transformation, see Ric Knowles's introduction to the volume in which Savran's essay appears.